THE NEW FOLGER LIBRARY SHAKESPEARE

Designed to make Shakespeare's great plays available to all readers, the New Folger Library edition of Shakespeare's plays provides accurate texts in modern spelling and punctuation, as well as scene-by-scene action summaries, full explanatory notes, many pictures clarifying Shakespeare's language, and notes recording all significant departures from the early printed versions. Each play is prefaced by a brief introduction, by a guide to reading Shakespeare's language, and by accounts of his life and theater. Each play is followed by an annotated list of further readings and by a "Modern Perspective" written by an expert on that particular play.

Barbara A. Mowat was Director of Research *emerita* at the Folger Shakespeare Library, Consulting Editor of *Shakespeare Quarterly*, and author of *The Dramaturgy of Shakespeare's Romances* and of essays on Shakespeare's plays and their editing.

Paul Werstine is Professor of English at the Graduate School and at King's University College at Western University. He is a general editor of the New Variorum Shakespeare and author of *Early Modern Playhouse Manuscripts and the Editing of Shakespeare* and of many papers and articles on the printing and editing of Shakespeare's plays.

The Folger Shakespeare Library

The Folger Shakespeare Library in Washington, D.C., a privately funded research library dedicated to Shakespeare and the civilization of early modern Europe, was founded in 1932 by Henry Clay and Emily Jordan Folger, and incorporated as part of Amherst College in Amherst, Massachusetts, one of the nation's oldest liberal arts colleges, from which Henry Folger had graduated in 1879. In addition to its role as the world's preeminent Shakespeare collection and its emergence as a leading center for Renaissance studies, the Folger Shakespeare Library offers a wide array of cultural and educational programs and services for the general public.

EDITORS

BARBARA A. MOWAT
Former Director of Research emerita
Folger Shakespeare Library

PAUL WERSTINE
Professor of English
King's University College
at Western University, Canada

Folger SHAKESPEARE LIBRARY

Henry IV

Part 2

By
WILLIAM SHAKESPEARE

EDITED BY BARBARA A. MOWAT
AND PAUL WERSTINE

Simon & Schuster Paperbacks
NEW YORK LONDON TORONTO SYDNEY NEW DELHI

Simon & Schuster
1230 Avenue of the Americas
New York, NY 10020

This Simon & Schuster trade paperback edition July 2020

SIMON & SCHUSTER and colophon are registered trademarks of Simon & Schuster, Inc.

For information about special discounts for bulk purchases, please contact Simon & Schuster Special Sales at 1-866-506-1949 or business@simonandschuster.com.

The Simon & Schuster Speakers Bureau can bring authors to your live event. For more information or to book an event, contact the Simon & Schuster Speakers Bureau at 1-866-248-3049 or visit our website at www.simonspeakers.com.

Manufactured in the United States of America

10 9 8 7 6 5 4 3

ISBN 978-1-9821-5740-1
ISBN 978-1-5011-4994-8 (ebook)

From the Director of the Folger Shakespeare Library

It is hard to imagine a world without Shakespeare. Since their composition more than four hundred years ago, Shakespeare's plays and poems have traveled the globe, inviting those who see and read his works to make them their own.

Readers of the New Folger Editions are part of this ongoing process of "taking up Shakespeare," finding our own thoughts and feelings in language that strikes us as old or unusual and, for that very reason, new. We still struggle to keep up with a writer who could think a mile a minute, whose words paint pictures that shift like clouds. These expertly edited texts, presented here with accompanying explanatory notes and up-to-date critical essays, are distinctive because of what they do: they allow readers not simply to keep up, but to engage deeply with a writer whose works invite us to think, and think again.

These New Folger Editions of Shakespeare's plays and poems are also special because of where they come from. The Folger Shakespeare Library in Washington, D.C., where the Editions are produced, is the single greatest documentary source of Shakespeare's works. An unparalleled collection of early modern books, manuscripts, and artwork connected to Shakespeare, the Folger's holdings have been consulted extensively in the preparation of these texts. The Editions also reflect the expertise gained through the regular performance of Shakespeare's works in the Folger's Elizabethan Theatre.

I want to express my deep thanks to editors Barbara Mowat and Paul Werstine for creating these indispensable editions of Shakespeare's works, which incorporate the best of textual scholarship with a richness of commentary that is both inspired and engaging. Readers who want to know more about Shakespeare and his plays can follow the paths these distinguished scholars have trod by visiting the Folger itself, where a range of physical and digital resources (available online) exists to supplement the material in these texts. I commend to you these words, and hope that they inspire.

Michael Witmore
Director, Folger Shakespeare Library

Contents

Editors' Preface

In recent years, ways of dealing with Shakespeare's texts and with the interpretation of his plays have been undergoing significant change. This edition, while retaining many of the features that have always made the Folger Shakespeare so attractive to the general reader, at the same time reflects these current ways of thinking about Shakespeare. For example, modern readers, actors, and teachers have become interested in the differences between, on the one hand, the early forms in which Shakespeare's plays were first published and, on the other hand, the forms in which editors through the centuries have presented them. In response to this interest, we have based our edition on what we consider the best early printed version of a particular play (explaining our rationale in a section called "An Introduction to This Text") and have marked our changes in the text—unobtrusively, we hope, but in such a way that the curious reader can be aware that a change has been made and can consult the "Textual Notes" to discover what appeared in the early printed version.

Current ways of looking at the plays are reflected in our brief prefaces, in many of the commentary notes, in the annotated lists of "Further Reading," and especially in each play's "Modern Perspective," an essay written by an outstanding scholar who brings to the reader his or her fresh assessment of the play in the light of today's interests and concerns.

As in the Folger Library General Reader's Shakespeare, which this edition replaces, we include explanatory notes designed to help make Shakespeare's language clearer to a modern reader, and we place the notes on the page facing the text that they explain. We also follow the earlier edition in including illustrations—of objects, of clothing, of mythological figures—from books and manuscripts in the Folger Library collection. We provide fresh accounts of the life of Shakespeare, of the publishing of his plays, and of the theaters in which his plays were performed, as well as an introduction to the text itself. We also include a section called "Reading Shakespeare's Language," in which we try to help readers learn to "break the code" of Elizabethan poetic language.

For each section of each volume, we are indebted to a host of generous experts and fellow scholars. The "Reading Shakespeare's Language" sections, for example, could not have been written had not Arthur King, of Brigham Young University, and Randall Robinson, author of *Unlocking Shakespeare's Language,* led the way in untangling Shakespearean language puzzles and shared their insights and methodologies generously with us. "Shakespeare's Life" profited by the careful reading given it by the late S. Schoenbaum, "Shakespeare's Theater" was read and strengthened by Andrew Gurr and John Astington, and "The Publication of Shakespeare's Plays" is indebted to the comments of Peter W. M. Blayney. Among the texts we consulted, we found Thomas L. Berger's Malone Society Reprint *The Second Part of King Henry the Fourth 1600* especially helpful. We, as editors, take sole responsibility for any errors in our editions.

We are grateful to the authors of the "Modern Perspectives"; to Leeds Barroll and David Bevington for their generous encouragement; to the Huntington and Newberry Libraries for fellowship support; to King's College for the grants it has provided to Paul Werstine; to the Social Sciences and Humanities Research Council of Canada, which provided him with a Research Time

Stipend for 1990–91; to R. J. Shroyer of the University of Western Ontario for essential computer support; to the Folger Institute's Center for Shakespeare Studies for its fortuitous sponsorship of a workshop on "Shakespeare's Texts for Students and Teachers" (funded by the National Endowment for the Humanities and led by Richard Knowles of the University of Wisconsin), a workshop from which we learned an enormous amount about what is wanted by college and high-school teachers of Shakespeare today; and especially to Steve Llano, our production editor at Pocket Books, whose expertise and attention to detail are essential to this project.

Our biggest debt is to the Folger Shakespeare Library—to Werner Gundersheimer, Director of the Library, who made possible our edition; to Deborah Curren-Aquino, who provides extensive editorial and production support; to Jean Miller, the Library's Art Curator, who combs the Library holdings for illustrations, and to Julie Ainsworth, Head of the Photography Department, who carefully photographs them; to Peggy O'Brien, former Director of Education at the Folger and now Director of Education Programs at the Corporation for Public Broadcasting, who gave us expert advice about the needs being expressed by Shakespeare teachers and students (and to Martha Christian and other "master teachers" who used our texts in manuscript in their classrooms); to Allan Shnerson and Kevin Madden for their expert computer support; to the staff of the Academic Programs Division, especially Amy Adler, Mary Tonkinson, Kathleen Lynch, Keira Roberts, Carol Brobeck, Kelleen Zubick, Toni Krieger, and Martha Fay; and, finally, to the generously supportive staff of the Library's Reading Room.

Barbara A. Mowat and Paul Werstine

King Henry IV.
From John Speed, *The Theatre of the empire of*
Great Britaine . . . (1627 [i.e. 1631]).

Shakespeare's *Henry IV, Part 2*

Shakespeare is credited with writing about three dozen surviving plays, and *Henry IV, Part 2* is unique among them in being a sequel to an earlier play of his, *Henry IV, Part 1*. Like many of the movie sequels that are so familiar to us today, *Henry IV, Part 2* reproduces the plot structure of its popular antecedent with considerable fidelity. Like *Part 1*, *Part 2* puts on stage Prince Hal, son of King Henry IV and heir to the throne, who remains committed to the plan he disclosed early in *Part 1* of distancing himself from his father's court and of concealing his potential greatness as a future ruler by consorting with tavern dwellers. Among Prince Hal's companions again appears Sir John Falstaff, whose delightfully witty set speeches have perhaps even greater prominence in this sequel than they did in *Part 1*. Falstaff's part was apparently a strong attraction when the play was first printed, as strong as the fat old knight continues to be for many today, for the title page of the play's first printing included reference to "the humours of sir Iohn Falstaffe." And the title page went on to name his lieutenant, the "swaggering Pistoll," a loud, quarrelsome brawler whose speeches are often a fascinating combination of bits from classical mythology and, occasionally, also from plays written by Shakespeare's predecessors. As in *Part 1*, Prince Hal's relationship with his tavern companions is complex: he and Falstaff seek to best each other in conversation, while Falstaff tries to ingratiate himself with Hal and Hal disdains him.

But *Part 2* adds to Falstaff's companions some fresh characters, the rural justices Shallow and Silence and Shallow's household. In years past Shallow and Falstaff

were young men together in London. Now the rich, old
Shallow is helping the impoverished and unscrupulous
Captain Falstaff recruit troops to crush yet another of
the rebellions against the rule of Henry IV. In Shallow
and Silence, Falstaff thinks he detects opportunities to
be exploited in filling his purse, and he tries to ingratiate
himself with them just as he does with Prince Hal, while
also attempting to maintain a sense of his superiority
over them. *Part 2* then joins to the verbal competition
between Prince Hal and Falstaff a struggle between
Falstaff's talents as a parasite and Justice Shallow's
wiliness in his own self-promotion.

Political rebellion, while certainly a major feature of
Part 2's plot, does not loom as large as it did in *Part 1*,
which climaxed in an apparently decisive combat between the rebel champion Harry Hotspur and the
victorious Prince Hal defending his father's claim to the
throne. In *Part 2* there are no glorious champions on
either side of the conflict, and combat is supplanted by
deception, cunning, and treachery. *Part 2* is, in many
ways, much darker and more grim than *Part 1*. As the
title page to *Part 2* candidly reports, this play is "continuing" the story of Henry IV "to his death." But however
much *Part 2* is just a sequel, it is nonetheless a powerfully moving work of dramatic art. Its fascination for
many lies in its unblinking representation of much in
life from which we ordinarily shield ourselves: exhaus-
tion, disappointment, betrayal, hypocrisy, old age, and
death.

After you have read the play, we invite you to turn to
the essay printed after it, *"Henry IV, Part 2:* A Modern
Perspective," written by Professor A. R. Braunmuller of
the University of California at Los Angeles.

Reading Shakespeare's Language: *Henry IV, Part 2*

For many people today, reading Shakespeare's language can be a problem—but it is a problem that can be solved. Those who have studied Latin (or even French or German or Spanish), and those who are used to reading poetry, will have little difficulty understanding the language of Shakespeare's poetic drama. Others, though, need to develop the skills of untangling unusual sentence structures and of recognizing and understanding poetic compressions, omissions, and wordplay. And even those skilled in reading unusual sentence structures may have occasional trouble with Shakespeare's words. Four hundred years of "static" intervene between his speaking and our hearing. Most of his immense vocabulary is still in use, but a few of his words are not, and, worse, some of his words now have meanings quite different from those they had in the sixteenth century. In the theater, most of these difficulties are solved for us by actors who study the language and articulate it for us so that the essential meaning is heard—or, when combined with stage action, is at least *felt*. When reading on one's own, one must do what each actor does: go over the lines (often with a dictionary close at hand) until the puzzles are solved and the lines yield up their poetry and the characters speak in words and phrases that are, suddenly, rewarding and wonderfully memorable.

Eastcheap.

MARKET

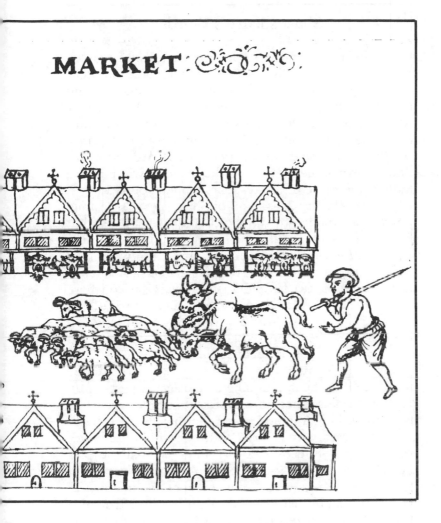

From Hugh Alley, *A caveat for the city of London* . . . (1598).

Shakespeare's Words

As you begin to read the opening scenes of a play by Shakespeare, you may notice occasional unfamiliar words. Some are unfamiliar simply because we no longer use them. In the opening scenes of this play, for example, you will find the words *forspent* (worn out), *hilding* (good-for-nothing), *outbreathed* (out of breath), *gan* (began to), and *vaward* (vanguard). Words of this kind are explained in notes to the text and will become familiar the more of Shakespeare's plays you read.

In *Henry IV, Part 2*, as in all of Shakespeare's writing, more problematic are the words that we still use but that we use with a different meaning. In the opening scenes of *Henry IV, Part 2*, for example, the word *grief* has the meaning of "grievance," *jealousies* is used where we would say "suspicions," *orchard* is used where we would say "garden," and *flood* where we would say "ocean." Such words will be explained in the notes to the text, but they, too, will become familiar as you continue to read Shakespeare's language.

Some words are strange not because of the "static" introduced by changes in language over the past centuries but because these are words that Shakespeare is using to build a dramatic world that has its own space, time, and history. In *Henry IV, Part 2*, within the larger world of early-fifteenth-century England that the play creates, Shakespeare uses one set of words to construct the worlds of King Henry's court and of the meetings at which his mighty rivals plot to unseat him from his throne. He uses a second set of words to construct the world of commoners—the hostess of the tavern, the sheriff's officers, the butcher, the "bona roba," the "pantler," the "vitlars," the rural justices of the peace, the corporal, the "ancient," and the captains. The world of

King Henry and his noble allies and opponents is luxurious, with its "silken points," "perfumed chambers," and "canopies of costly state." The exclusive privilege of enjoying such luxury is maintained through success in combat, which is idealized as "stiff-borne action" and "dole of blows," in which "best-tempered courage" faces with "forehead bold and big" the "hideous god of war." Commoners enjoy lesser pleasures: "small beer," "sack" in a "parcel gilt goblet" by a "sea-coal fire," or a "mess of vinegar" with a "good dish of prawns." And those commoners who must "fill up the muster book" do not idealize war, nor are they idealized. According to Falstaff, Simon Shadow is "like to be a cold [rather than zealous] soldier," and Francis Feeble will "be as valiant as the wrathful dove or most magnanimous mouse." The exalted martial language of the play's highborn characters is reproduced with a difference in the ranting of Falstaff's officer Pistol during a tavern brawl: "What, shall we have incision? Shall we imbrue? Then death rock me asleep, abridge my doleful days. Why then, let grievous, ghastly, gaping wounds untwind the Sisters Three."

Shakespeare's Sentences

In an English sentence, meaning is quite dependent on the place given each word. "The dog bit the boy" and "The boy bit the dog" mean very different things, even though the individual words are the same. Because English places such importance on the positions of words in sentences, on the way words are arranged, unusual arrangements can puzzle a reader. Shakespeare frequently shifts his sentences away from "normal" English arrangements—often to create the rhythm he seeks, sometimes to use a line's poetic rhythm to emphasize a particular word, sometimes to give a character his or her own speech patterns or to allow the character to speak in a special way. When we attend a good performance of the play, the actors will have worked out the sentence structures and will articulate the sentences so that the meaning is clear. In reading for yourself, do as the actor does. That is, when you become puzzled by a character's speech, check to see if words are being presented in an unusual sequence.

Shakespeare often, for example, rearranges subjects and verbs (i.e., instead of "He goes" we find "Goes he"). In *Henry IV, Part 2*, when Northumberland says "There am I till time and vantage crave my company" (2.3.70–71), he is using such a construction. Shakespeare also frequently places the object before the subject and verb (i.e., instead of "I hit him," we might find "Him I hit"). Northumberland's "This thou wouldst say" (1.1.87) is an example of such an inversion, as is Gower's "The rest the paper tells" (2.1.141). The "normal" order would be "Thou wouldst say this" and "The paper tells the rest." Sometimes Shakespeare inverts the entire normal order of subject-verb-adjective-object to confront us with object-adjective-verb-subject; an example is the Archbishop's statement "An habitation giddy and unsure hath he" (1.3.93–94).

Inversions are not the only unusual sentence structures in Shakespeare's language. Often in his sentences words that would normally appear together are separated from each other. Again, this is often done to create a particular rhythm or to stress a particular word. Take, for example, Rumor's self-introduction in the play's first lines: "*I*, from the orient to the drooping west, making the wind my post-horse, still *unfold the acts* commencèd on this ball of earth." Here, the phrase "from the orient to the drooping west" and the phrase "making the wind my post-horse" and the adverb "still" all separate subject ("I") from verb and object ("unfold the acts"). Or take Northumberland's lines "Contention, like a horse full of high feeding, madly hath broke loose" (1.1.12–13). Here, the subject and verb "Contention hath broke loose" are separated by the phrase "like a horse full of high feeding" and by the adverb "madly." In order to create for yourself sentences that seem more like the English of everyday speech, you may wish to rearrange the words, putting together the word clusters ("I unfold the acts . . ." or "Contention hath broke loose . . ."). You will usually find that the sentence will gain in clarity but will lose its rhythm or shift its emphasis.

Often in *Henry IV, Part 2,* rather than separating basic sentence elements, Shakespeare simply holds them back, delaying them until other material to which he wants to give greater emphasis has been presented. Prominent examples appear in Westmoreland's formal address to the rebels led by the Archbishop:

> If that rebellion
> Came like itself, in base and abject routs,
> Led on by bloody youth, guarded with rage,
> And countenanced by boys and beggary—
> I say, if damned commotion so appeared
> In his true, native, and most proper shape,
> *You,* reverend father, and these noble lords
> *Had not been here* to dress the ugly form
> Of base and bloody insurrection
> With your fair honors. You, Lord Archbishop,
> Whose see is by a civil peace maintained,
> Whose beard the silver hand of peace hath touched,
> Whose learning and good letters peace hath tutored,
> Whose white investments figure innocence,
> The dove and very blessèd spirit of peace,
> *Wherefore do you so ill translate yourself*
> Out of the speech of peace, that bears such grace,

Into the harsh and boist'rous tongue of war,
Turning your books to graves, your ink to blood,
Your pens to lances, and your tongue divine
To a loud trumpet and a point of war?

(4.1.35–55)

Westmoreland's speech begins with five and a half lines
of conditional clauses. The lengthy conditionals delay
the appearance of the sentence's subject and verb for so
long that Westmoreland is made to reassert the "if" at
the beginning of the sentence's fifth line ("I say if") so
that the audience can keep track of the sentence's
structure until he gets to the subject and verb ("You . . .
had not been here"). By not addressing the Archbishop
directly in this sentence until after characterizing the
nature of the Archbishop's act of "rebellion" in the
harshest terms, Westmoreland can insult the act without also insulting the Archbishop personally, thereby
leaving some room for negotiation. Westmoreland's
next sentence is a question, but its structure does not
become clear until again he has delivered five and a half
lines of it. Only in his sixth line does he provide the
subject ("you") and verb ("do translate") that make up
the question "Wherefore [i.e., why] do you so ill translate yourself?" By delaying the question's formation,
Shakespeare can have Westmoreland first detail all the
ways in which the Archbishop is a figure of peace, who
can then be contrasted in the question itself to the
warlike figure he has now become.

Finally, in many of Shakespeare's plays, sentences are
sometimes complicated not because of unusual structures or interruptions but because Shakespeare omits
words and parts of words that English sentences normally require. (In conversation, we, too, often omit
words. We say, "Heard from him yet?" and our hearer
supplies the missing "Have you.") Often Shakespeare
too omits words in order to give dialogue a conversa-

tional flavor, as, for example, in the following informal exchange between Justice Shallow and Justice Silence, in which we have inserted in square brackets the words Shakespeare has omitted:

SHALLOW   And how doth my cousin your bedfellow? And [how doth] your fairest daughter and mine, my goddaughter Ellen?
SILENCE   Alas, [she is] a black ousel, cousin Shallow.
(3.2.5–8)

However, on other occasions in *Henry IV, Part 2* Shakespeare's omissions of words seem to increase the formality of expression in verse. In the following example, Northumberland, upon guessing that his son Hotspur has died in battle, presents himself in the most grandiose terms as suffering a loss equal to that of the mythological King Priam, whose subjects were destroyed when Greek enemies burned his city, Troy; and Northumberland compares the messenger bringing news of Hotspur's death to the messenger who came to tell Priam of the fire (but was unable to speak). Again we add in square brackets the words that may be imagined to have been omitted:

Even such a man, so faint, so spiritless,
So dull, so dead in look, so woebegone,
Drew Priam's curtain in the dead of night
And would have told him half his Troy was burnt;
But Priam found the fire ere he [found] his tongue,
And I [have correctly guessed at] my Percy's death
  ere thou report'st it.
(1.1.81–86)

Through the omission of words from Northumberland's speech, Shakespeare can bring the comparison between

Northumberland's plight and Priam's to a powerfully compact close. By filling in the words that may be missing, we have not only indicated approximately what was omitted but also spoiled the rhythm of the verse and lessened its power.

Shakespearean Wordplay

Shakespeare plays with language so often and so variously that entire books are written on the topic. Here we will mention only two kinds of wordplay, puns and metaphors. Puns play on the multiple meanings of a single word or on the similarity of sound between words with different meanings. While puns can convey a speaker's delight in wordplay, they can also have quite different tones. When, for example, a dying Henry IV predicts that after his death his successor will fill the kingdom with dissolutes attracted from the rest of Europe, the king's bitter tone is in part conveyed in the pun that concludes the following lines:

> Now, neighbor confines, purge you [i.e., yourselves]
>   of your scum.
> Have you a ruffian that will swear, drink, dance,
> Revel the night, rob, murder, and commit
> The oldest sins the newest kind of ways?
> Be happy, he will trouble you no more.
> England shall double gild his treble guilt.
> England shall give him office, honor, might.
>   (4.3.278–84)

The king's pun plays on the identical sounds of the words *guilt* and *gilt* (a thin layer of gold applied to the surface of an object), as the term *gilt* is called up by the verb "gild," which means to apply *gilt*.

When Falstaff puns, his tone, in contrast to Henry IV's, is delight in his own power over his recruits, on whose surnames he plays. In Falstaff's puns, the recruits' names refer to the men themselves and at the same time mean something else. For example, when Falstaff announces to Rafe Mouldy "Mouldy, it is time you were spent" (3.2.121–22), Falstaff speaks to Mouldy as if he were food that should be used up because it is already covered with mould, but the joke has a dark undertone in that Falstaff expects Mouldy to be used up by being killed in battle. Falstaff also puns extravagantly on Simon Shadow's name:

Thy mother's son! Like enough, and thy father's shadow. So the son of the female is the shadow of the male. It is often so, indeed, but much of the father's substance.

(3.2.133–36)

These lines contain multiple wordplay on "shadow" as, for example, "portrait, image," "a delusive semblance" (contrasted with "substance"), "a remnant" or "a form from which the substance has departed," and "a small insignificant portion."

A metaphor is a play on words in which one object or idea is expressed as if it were something else, something with which it shares common features. The first speech in *Henry IV, Part 2*, Rumor's Induction to the play, is thick with metaphors, as the following brief excerpt indicates:

I, from the orient to the drooping west,
Making the wind my post-horse, still unfold
The acts commencèd on this ball of earth.
Upon my tongues continual slanders ride.

(3–6)

Rumor's first metaphor makes the "wind" his "post-horse" (a fast horse kept at an inn for the use of travelers); the common feature of the wind and the horse is swiftness, with the wind being incomparably faster. He then moves to another metaphor, which shrinks the round "earth" into a "ball," indicating how the speed of Rumor reduces the size of the planet to insignificance, while showing how the world is Rumor's plaything. Finally, in the words "Upon my tongues continual slanders ride," Rumor speaks in a metaphor that equates the slanderous tongues of Rumor with horses whose riders are "slanders." The cumulative effect of these metaphors is to present the destructive power of Rumor as myriad false reports spread at the speed of the wind.

King Henry also uses metaphor at a critical moment in the play to instruct his son Thomas in the power the young man has to protect his relatives ("friends") from Prince Hal and thereby to secure family unity:

> Learn this, Thomas,
> And thou shalt prove a shelter to thy friends,
> A hoop of gold to bind thy brothers in,
> That the united vessel of their blood,
> Mingled with venom of suggestion,
> (As, force perforce, the age will pour it in),
> Shall never leak, though it do work as strong
> As aconitum or rash gunpowder.
>   (4.3.45–53)

First Henry briefly compares Thomas to a "shelter" but then fashions a second more complex metaphor in which Thomas becomes a gold ring that encircles and secures the integrity of a chalice containing the blood of the royal family. Henry imagines this ring (and Thomas's influence over Prince Hal) to be so strong that it can prevent the royal blood from spilling no matter how violently that blood may be stirred by the operation of virulent poison ("aconitum") or even of gunpowder.

Implied Stage Action

Finally, in reading Shakespeare's plays we should always remember that what we are reading is a performance script. The dialogue is written to be spoken by actors who, at the same time, are moving, gesturing, picking up objects, weeping, shaking their fists. Some stage action is described in what are called "stage directions"; some is suggested within the dialogue itself. We must learn to be alert to such signals as we stage the play in imagination. Often the stage action is unambiguous. When, in *Henry IV, Part 2*, 1.1.159–60, Northumberland says "Hence therefore, thou nice crutch," it seems clear that he accompanies the statement by throwing away his crutch. And when he says "And hence, thou sickly coif" (162–63), it again seems clear that he takes from his head the kerchief in which the sick wrapped their heads in Shakespeare's time.

Occasionally in *Henry IV, Part 2*, signals about stage action are not quite so clear. The scene in which Falstaff makes a selection of recruits offers both a challenge and an opportunity to reader and director alike. At some point in the scene, five potential recruits (Mouldy, Shadow, Wart, Feeble, and Bullcalf) enter and then one by one are called forward for Falstaff to inspect them. The earliest printed text of the play, the 1600 Quarto, offers no stage directions at all for the entrance of the recruits. In the 1623 Folio text of the play, stage directions call for the recruits to enter at the beginning of the scene, even though they take no part in the dialogue or action for over a hundred lines. In a production of the play, the danger of following the Folio in this case is that the comic look of most of the recruits may be largely wasted because an audience will have grown accustomed to their appearances before they become the object of the dialogue's jokes. Because the Quarto provides no stage directions, if the reader or director chooses to depart from the Folio, then she or he will have to devise a staging from the clues provided in the dialogue. The major clue is Justice Shallow's order "Let them appear as I call." Perhaps, that order may signal the entrance of all the recruits to the rear of the stage as the action turns to the process of their selection; from there each can readily come forward as his name is called. Or perhaps, after Shallow's general order, each recruit enters only when his name is called. We have in this case as elsewhere inserted stage directions at what seemed to us the most probable places, but these are ultimately matters that directors and actors—and readers in their imaginations—must decide.

It is immensely rewarding to work carefully with Shakespeare's language so that the words, the sentences, the wordplay, and the implied stage action all become clear—as readers for the past four centuries have discovered. It may be more pleasurable to attend a good performance of a play—though not everyone has thought so. But the joy of being able to stage one of Shakespeare's plays in one's imagination, to return to passages that continue to yield further meanings (or further questions) the more one reads them—these are pleasures that, for many, rival (or at least augment) those of the performed text, and certainly make it worth considerable effort to "break the code" of Elizabethan poetic drama and let free the remarkable language that makes up a Shakespeare text.

Shakespeare's Life

Surviving documents that give us glimpses into the life of William Shakespeare show us a playwright, poet, and actor who grew up in the market town of Stratford-upon-Avon, spent his professional life in London, and returned to Stratford a wealthy landowner. He was born in April 1564, died in April 1616, and is buried inside the chancel of Holy Trinity Church in Stratford.

We wish we could know more about the life of the world's greatest dramatist. His plays and poems are testaments to his wide reading—especially to his knowledge of Virgil, Ovid, Plutarch, Holinshed's *Chronicles*, and the Bible—and to his mastery of the English language, but we can only speculate about his education. We know that the King's New School in Stratford-upon-Avon was considered excellent. The school was one of the English "grammar schools" established to educate young men, primarily in Latin grammar and literature. As in other schools of the time, students began their studies at the age of four or five in the attached "petty school," and there learned to read and write in English, studying primarily the catechism from the Book of Common Prayer. After two years in the petty school, students entered the lower form (grade) of the grammar school, where they began the serious study of Latin grammar and Latin texts that would occupy most of the remainder of their school days. (Several Latin texts that Shakespeare used repeatedly in writing his plays and poems were texts that schoolboys memorized and recited.) Latin comedies were introduced early in the lower form; in the upper form, which the boys entered at age ten or eleven, students wrote their own Latin orations and declamations, studied Latin historians and rhetoricians, and began the study of Greek using the Greek New Testament.

Since the records of the Stratford "grammar school" do not survive, we cannot prove that William Shakespeare attended the school; however, every indication (his father's position as an alderman and bailiff of Stratford, the playwright's own knowledge of the Latin classics, scenes in the plays that recall grammar-school experiences—for example, *The Merry Wives of Windsor,* 4.1) suggests that he did. We also lack generally accepted documentation about Shakespeare's life after his schooling ended and his professional life in London began. His marriage in 1582 (at age eighteen) to Anne Hathaway and the subsequent births of his daughter Susanna (1583) and the twins Judith and Hamnet (1585) are recorded, but how he supported himself and where he lived are not known. Nor do we know when and why he left Stratford for the London theatrical world, nor how he rose to be the important figure in that world that he had become by the early 1590s.

We do know that by 1592 he had achieved some prominence in London as both an actor and a playwright. In that year was published a book by the playwright Robert Greene attacking an actor who had the audacity to write blank-verse drama and who was "in his own conceit [i.e., opinion] the only Shake-scene in a country." Since Greene's attack includes a parody of a line from one of Shakespeare's early plays, there is

CATECHISMVS

paruus pueris primùm Latinè
qui ediscatur, proponendus
in Scholis.

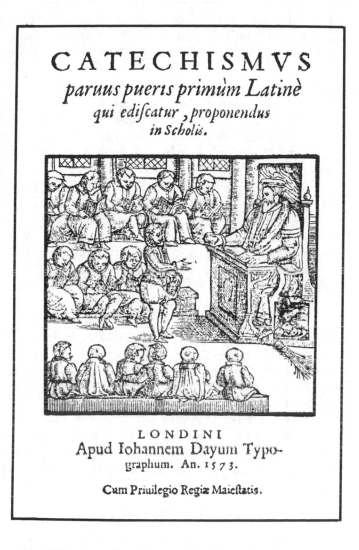

LONDINI
Apud Iohannem Dayum Typo-
graphum. An. 1573.

Cum Priuilegio Regiæ Maieſtatis.

Title page of a 1573 Latin and Greek catechism
for children.

little doubt that it is Shakespeare to whom he refers, a "Shake-scene" who had aroused Greene's fury by successfully competing with university-educated dramatists like Greene himself. It was in 1593 that Shakespeare became a published poet. In that year he published his long narrative poem *Venus and Adonis;* in 1594, he followed it with *The Rape of Lucrece.* Both poems were dedicated to the young earl of Southampton (Henry Wriothesley), who may have become Shakespeare's patron.

It seems no coincidence that Shakespeare wrote these narrative poems at a time when the theaters were closed because of the plague, a contagious epidemic disease that devastated the population of London. When the theaters reopened in 1594, Shakespeare apparently resumed his double career of actor and playwright and began his long (and seemingly profitable) service as an acting-company shareholder. Records for December of 1594 show him to be a leading member of the Lord Chamberlain's Men. It was this company of actors, later named the King's Men, for whom he would be a principal actor, dramatist, and shareholder for the rest of his career.

So far as we can tell, that career spanned about twenty years. In the 1590s, he wrote his plays on English history as well as several comedies and at least two tragedies (*Titus Andronicus* and *Romeo and Juliet*). These histories, comedies, and tragedies are the plays credited to him in 1598 in a work, *Palladis Tamia,* that in one chapter compares English writers with "Greek, Latin, and Italian Poets." There the author, Francis Meres, claims that Shakespeare is comparable to the Latin dramatists Seneca for tragedy and Plautus for comedy, and calls him "the most excellent in both kinds for the stage." He also names him "Mellifluous and honey-tongued Shakespeare": "I say," writes Meres, "that the Muses would speak with Shakespeare's fine filed phrase, if they would speak English." Since Meres also mentions Shakespeare's "sugared sonnets among his private friends," it is assumed that many of Shakespeare's sonnets (not published until 1609) were also written in the 1590s.

In 1599, Shakespeare's company built a theater for themselves across the river from London, naming it the Globe. The plays that are considered by many to be Shakespeare's major tragedies (*Hamlet, Othello, King Lear,* and *Macbeth*) were written while the company was resident in this theater, as were such comedies as *Twelfth Night* and *Measure for Measure*. Many of Shakespeare's plays were performed at court (both for Queen Elizabeth I and, after her death in 1603, for King James I), some were presented at the Inns of Court (the residences of London's legal societies), and some were doubtless performed in other towns, at the universities, and at great houses when the King's Men went on tour; otherwise, his plays from 1599 to 1608 were, so far as we know, performed only at the Globe. Between 1608 and 1612, Shakespeare wrote several plays—among them *The Winter's Tale* and *The Tempest*—presumably for the company's new indoor Blackfriars theater, though the plays seem to have been performed also at the Globe and at court. Surviving documents describe a performance of *The Winter's Tale* in 1611 at the Globe, for example, and performances of *The Tempest* in 1611 and 1613 at the royal palace of Whitehall.

Shakespeare wrote very little after 1612, the year in which he probably wrote *King Henry VIII*. (It was at a performance of *Henry VIII* in 1613 that the Globe caught fire and burned to the ground.) Sometime between 1610 and 1613 he seems to have returned to live in Stratford-upon-Avon, where he owned a large house and consider-

A stylized representation of the Globe theater.
From Claes Jansz Visscher, *Londinum florentissima
Britanniae urbs* . . . [c. 1625].

able property, and where his wife and his two daughters and their husbands lived. (His son Hamnet had died in 1596.) During his professional years in London, Shakespeare had presumably derived income from the acting company's profits as well as from his own career as an actor, from the sale of his play manuscripts to the acting company, and, after 1599, from his shares as an owner of the Globe. It was presumably that income, carefully invested in land and other property, which made him the wealthy man that surviving documents show him to have become. It is also assumed that William Shakespeare's growing wealth and reputation played some part in inclining the crown, in 1596, to grant John Shakespeare, William's father, the coat of arms that he had so long sought. William Shakespeare died in Stratford on April 23, 1616 (according to the epitaph carved under his bust in Holy Trinity Church) and was buried on April 25. Seven years after his death, his collected plays were published as *Mr. William Shakespeares Comedies, Histories, & Tragedies* (the work now known as the First Folio).

The years in which Shakespeare wrote were among the most exciting in English history. Intellectually, the discovery, translation, and printing of Greek and Roman classics were making available a set of works and worldviews that interacted complexly with Christian texts and beliefs. The result was a questioning, a vital intellectual ferment, that provided energy for the period's amazing dramatic and literary output and that fed directly into Shakespeare's plays. The Ghost in *Hamlet,* for example, is wonderfully complicated in part because he is a figure from Roman tragedy—the spirit of the dead returning to seek revenge—who at the same time inhabits a Christian hell (or purgatory); Hamlet's description of humankind reflects at one moment the

A tilt-yard.

Der Quintain

From Theodor Graminaeus, *Beschreibung derer fürstlicher güligscher* . . . (1587).

Neoplatonic wonderment at mankind ("What a piece of work is a man!") and, at the next, the Christian disparagement of human sinners ("And yet, to me, what is this quintessence of dust?").

As intellectual horizons expanded, so also did geographical and cosmological horizons. New worlds—both North and South America—were explored, and in them were found human beings who lived and worshiped in ways radically different from those of Renaissance Europeans and Englishmen. The universe during these years also seemed to shift and expand. Copernicus had earlier theorized that the earth was not the center of the cosmos but revolved as a planet around the sun. Galileo's telescope, created in 1609, allowed scientists to see that Copernicus had been correct; the universe was not organized with the earth at the center, nor was it so nicely circumscribed as people had, until that time, thought. In terms of expanding horizons, the impact of these discoveries on people's beliefs—religious, scientific, and philosophical—cannot be overstated.

London, too, rapidly expanded and changed during the years (from the early 1590s to around 1610) that Shakespeare lived there. London—the center of England's government, its economy, its royal court, its overseas trade—was, during these years, becoming an exciting metropolis, drawing to it thousands of new citizens every year. Troubled by overcrowding, by poverty, by recurring epidemics of the plague, London was also a mecca for the wealthy and the aristocratic, and for those who sought advancement at court, or power in government or finance or trade. One hears in Shakespeare's plays the voices of London—the struggles for power, the fear of venereal disease, the language of buying and selling. One hears as well the voices of Stratford-upon-Avon—

references to the nearby Forest of Arden, to sheep herding, to small-town gossip, to village fairs and markets. Part of the richness of Shakespeare's work is the influence felt there of the various worlds in which he lived: the world of metropolitan London, the world of small-town and rural England, the world of the theater, and the worlds of craftsmen and shepherds.

That Shakespeare inhabited such worlds we know from surviving London and Stratford documents, as well as from the evidence of the plays and poems themselves. From such records we can sketch the dramatist's life. We know from his works that he was a voracious reader. We know from legal and business documents that he was a multifaceted theater man who became a wealthy landowner. We know a bit about his family life and a fair amount about his legal and financial dealings. Most scholars today depend upon such evidence as they draw their picture of the world's greatest playwright. Such, however, has not always been the case. Until the late eighteenth century, the William Shakespeare who lived in most biographies was the creation of legend and tradition. This was the Shakespeare who was supposedly caught poaching deer at Charlecote, the estate of Sir Thomas Lucy close by Stratford; this was the Shakespeare who fled from Sir Thomas's vengeance and made his way in London by taking care of horses outside a playhouse; this was the Shakespeare who reportedly could barely read but whose natural gifts were extraordinary, whose father was a butcher who allowed his gifted son sometimes to help in the butcher shop, where William supposedly killed calves "in a high style," making a speech for the occasion. It was this legendary William Shakespeare whose Falstaff (in *1* and *2 Henry IV*) so pleased Queen

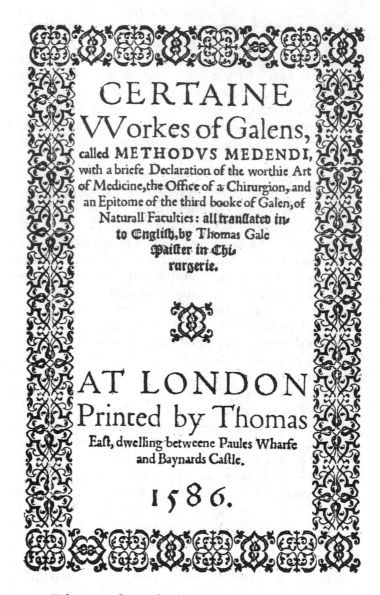

CERTAINE
VVorkes of Galens,
called METHODVS MEDENDI,
with a briefe Declaration of the worthie Art
of Medicine, the Office of a Chirurgion, and
an Epitome of the third booke of Galen, of
Naturall Faculties: all translated into English, by Thomas Gale
Maister in Chi-
rurgerie.

AT LONDON
Printed by Thomas
East, dwelling betweene Paules Wharfe
and Baynards Castle.

1586.

Title page of a medical treatise by Galen. (1.2.120)
From Galen, *Certaine workes of Galens . . .* (1586).

Elizabeth that she demanded a play about Falstaff in love, and demanded that it be written in fourteen days (hence the existence of *The Merry Wives of Windsor*). It was this legendary Shakespeare who reached the top of his acting career in the roles of the Ghost in *Hamlet* and old Adam in *As You Like It*—and who died of a fever contracted by drinking too hard at "a merry meeting" with the poets Michael Drayton and Ben Jonson. This legendary Shakespeare is a rambunctious, undisciplined man, as attractively "wild" as his plays were seen by earlier generations to be. Unfortunately, there is no trace of evidence to support these wonderful stories.

Perhaps in response to the disreputable Shakespeare of legend—or perhaps in response to the fragmentary and, for some, all-too-ordinary Shakespeare documented by surviving records—some people since the mid–nineteenth century have argued that William Shakespeare could not have written the plays that bear his name. These persons have put forward some dozen names as more likely authors, among them Queen Elizabeth, Sir Francis Bacon, Edward de Vere (earl of Oxford), and Christopher Marlowe. Such attempts to find what for these people is a more believable author of the plays is a tribute to the regard in which the plays are held. Unfortunately for their claims, the documents that exist that provide evidence for the facts of Shakespeare's life tie him inextricably to the body of plays and poems that bear his name. Unlikely as it seems to those who want the works to have been written by an aristocrat, a university graduate, or an "important" person, the plays and poems seem clearly to have been produced by a man from Stratford-upon-Avon with a very good "grammar-school" education and a life of experience in London and in the world of the London theater. How this particular man produced the works that dominate the cultures of much of the world almost four hundred years after his death is one of life's mysteries—and one that will continue to tease our imaginations as we continue to delight in his plays and poems.

Shakespeare's Theater

The actors of Shakespeare's time are known to have performed plays in a great variety of locations. They played at court (that is, in the great halls of such royal residences as Whitehall, Hampton Court, and Greenwich); they played in halls at the universities of Oxford and Cambridge, and at the Inns of Court (the residences in London of the legal societies); and they also played in the private houses of great lords and civic officials. Sometimes acting companies went on tour from London into the provinces, often (but not only) when outbreaks of bubonic plague in the capital forced the closing of theaters to reduce the possibility of contagion in crowded audiences. In the provinces the actors usually staged their plays in churches (until around 1600) or in guildhalls. While surviving records show only a handful of occasions when actors played at inns while on tour, London inns were important playing places up until the 1590s.

The building of theaters in London had begun only shortly before Shakespeare wrote his first plays in the 1590s. These theaters were of two kinds: outdoor or public playhouses that could accommodate large numbers of playgoers, and indoor or private theaters for much smaller audiences. What is usually regarded as the first London outdoor public playhouse was called simply the Theatre. James Burbage—the father of Richard Burbage, who was perhaps the most famous actor in Shakespeare's company—built it in 1576 in an area north of the city of London called Shoreditch. Among the more famous of the other public playhouses that capitalized on the new fashion were the Curtain and the Fortune (both also built north of the city), the Rose, the Swan, the Globe, and the Hope (all located on the Bankside, a region just across the Thames south of the city of London). All these playhouses had to be built outside the jurisdiction of the city of London because many civic officials were hostile to the performance of drama and repeatedly petitioned the royal council to abolish it.

The theaters erected on the Bankside (a region under the authority of the Church of England, whose head was the monarch) shared the neighborhood with houses of prostitution and with the Paris Garden, where the blood sports of bearbaiting and bullbaiting were carried on. There may have been no clear distinction between playhouses and buildings for such sports, for we know that the Hope was used for both plays and baiting and that Philip Henslowe, owner of the Rose and, later, partner in the ownership of the Fortune, was also a partner in a monopoly on baiting. All these forms of entertainment were easily accessible to Londoners by boat across the Thames or over London Bridge.

Evidently Shakespeare's company prospered on the Bankside. They moved there in 1599. Threatened by difficulties in renewing the lease on the land where their first theater (the Theatre) had been built, Shakespeare's company took advantage of the Christmas holiday in 1598 to dismantle the Theatre and transport its timbers across the Thames to the Bankside, where, in 1599, these timbers were used in the building of the Globe.

The weather in late December 1598 is recorded as having been especially harsh. It was so cold that the Thames was "nigh [nearly] frozen," and there was heavy snow. Perhaps the weather aided Shakespeare's company in eluding their landlord, the snow hiding their activity and the freezing of the Thames allowing them to slide the timbers across to the Bankside without paying tolls for repeated trips over London Bridge. Attractive as this narrative is, it remains just as likely that the heavy snow hampered transport of the timbers in wagons through the London streets to the river. It also must be remembered that the Thames was, according to report, only "nigh frozen" and therefore as impassable as it ever was. Whatever the precise circumstances of this fascinating event in English theater history, Shakespeare's company was able to begin playing at their new Globe theater on the Bankside in 1599. After the first Globe burned down in 1613 during the staging of Shakespeare's *Henry VIII* (its thatch roof was set alight by cannon fire called for by the performance), Shakespeare's company immediately rebuilt on the same location. The second Globe seems to have been a grander structure than its predecessor. It remained in use until the beginning of the English Civil War in 1642, when Parliament officially closed the theaters. Soon thereafter it was pulled down.

The public theaters of Shakespeare's time were very different buildings from our theaters today. First of all, they were open-air playhouses. As recent excavations of the Rose and the Globe confirm, some were polygonal or roughly circular in shape; the Fortune, however, was square. The most recent estimates of their size put the diameter of these buildings at 72 feet (the Rose) to 100 feet (the Globe), but we know that they held vast audiences of two or three thousand, who must have been squeezed together quite tightly. Some of these

A stage play.
From [William Alabaster,] *Roxana tragœdia* . . . (1632).

spectators paid extra to sit or stand in the two or three
levels of roofed galleries that extended, on the upper
levels, all the way around the theater and surrounded an
open space. In this space were the stage and, perhaps,
the tiring house (what we would call dressing rooms), as
well as the so-called yard. In the yard stood the spectators who chose to pay less, the ones whom Hamlet
contemptuously called "groundlings." For a roof they
had only the sky, and so they were exposed to all kinds
of weather. They stood on a floor that was sometimes
made of mortar and sometimes of ash mixed with the
shells of hazelnuts. The latter provided a porous and
therefore dry footing for the crowd, and the shells may
have been more comfortable to stand on because they
were not as hard as mortar. Availability of shells may not
have been a problem if hazelnuts were a favorite food for
Shakespeare's audiences to munch on as they watched
his plays. Archaeologists who are today unearthing the
remains of theaters from this period have discovered
quantities of these nutshells on theater sites.

Unlike the yard, the stage itself was covered by a roof.
Its ceiling, called "the heavens," is thought to have been
elaborately painted to depict the sun, moon, stars, and
planets. Just how big the stage was remains hard to
determine. We have a single sketch of part of the interior
of the Swan. A Dutchman named Johannes de Witt
visited this theater around 1596 and sent a sketch of it
back to his friend, Arend van Buchel. Because van
Buchel found de Witt's letter and sketch of interest, he
copied both into a book. It is van Buchel's copy,
adapted, it seems, to the shape and size of the page in his
book, that survives. In this sketch, the stage appears to
be a large rectangular platform that thrusts far out into
the yard, perhaps even as far as the center of the circle
formed by the surrounding galleries. This drawing,

combined with the specifications for the size of the stage in the building contract for the Fortune, has led scholars to conjecture that the stage on which Shakespeare's plays were performed must have measured approximately 43 feet in width and 27 feet in depth, a vast acting area. But the digging up of a large part of the Rose by archaeologists has provided evidence of a quite different stage design. The Rose stage was a platform tapered at the corners and much shallower than what seems to be depicted in the van Buchel sketch. Indeed, its measurements seem to be about 37.5 feet across at its widest point and only 15.5 feet deep. Because the surviving indications of stage size and design differ from each other so much, it is possible that the stages in other theaters, like the Theatre, the Curtain, and the Globe (the outdoor playhouses where we know that Shakespeare's plays were performed), were different from those at both the Swan and the Rose.

After about 1608 Shakespeare's plays were staged not only at the Globe but also at an indoor or private playhouse in Blackfriars. This theater had been constructed in 1596 by James Burbage in an upper hall of a former Dominican priory or monastic house. Although Henry VIII had dissolved all English monasteries in the 1530s (shortly after he had founded the Church of England), the area remained under church, rather than hostile civic, control. The hall that Burbage had purchased and renovated was a large one in which Parliament had once met. In the private theater that he constructed, the stage, lit by candles, was built across the narrow end of the hall, with boxes flanking it. The rest of the hall offered seating room only. Because there was no provision for standing room, the largest audience it could hold was less than a thousand, or about a quarter of what the Globe could accommodate. Admission to Blackfriars was correspondingly more expensive. Instead of a penny to stand in the yard at the Globe, it cost a minimum of sixpence to get into Blackfriars. The best seats at the Globe (in the Lords' Room in the gallery above and behind the stage) cost sixpence; but the boxes flanking the stage at Blackfriars were half a crown, or five times sixpence. Some spectators who were particularly interested in displaying themselves paid even more to sit on stools on the Blackfriars stage.

Whether in the outdoor or indoor playhouses, the stages of Shakespeare's time were different from ours. They were not separated from the audience by the dropping of a curtain between acts and scenes. Therefore the playwrights of the time had to find other ways of signaling to the audience that one scene (to be imagined as occurring in one location at a given time) had ended and the next (to be imagined at perhaps a different location at a later time) had begun. The customary way used by Shakespeare and many of his contemporaries was to have everyone onstage exit at the end of one scene and have one or more different characters enter to begin the next. In a few cases, where characters remain onstage from one scene to another, the dialogue or stage action makes the change of location clear, and the characters are generally to be imagined as having moved from one place to another. For example, in *Romeo and Juliet,* Romeo and his friends remain onstage in Act 1 from scene 4 to scene 5, but they are represented as having moved between scenes from the street that leads to Capulet's house into Capulet's house itself. The new location is signaled in part by the appearance onstage of Capulet's servingmen carrying napkins, something they would not take into the streets. Playwrights had to be quite resourceful in the use of hand properties, like the napkin, or in the use of dialogue to specify where the action was taking place in their plays because, in contrast to most of today's theaters, the playhouses of Shakespeare's time did not use movable scenery to dress the stage and make the setting precise. As another consequence of this difference, however, the playwrights of Shakespeare's time did not have to specify exactly where the action of their plays was set when they did not choose to do so, and much of the action of their plays is tied to no specific place.

Usually Shakespeare's stage is referred to as a "bare stage," to distinguish it from the stages of the last two or three centuries with their elaborate sets. But the stage in Shakespeare's time was not completely bare. Philip Henslowe, owner of the Rose, lists in his inventory of stage properties a rock, three tombs, and two mossy banks. Stage directions in plays of the time also call for such things as thrones (or "states"), banquets (presumably tables with plaster replicas of food on them), and beds and tombs to be pushed onto the stage. Thus the stage often held more than the actors.

The actors did not limit their performing to the stage alone. Occasionally they went beneath the stage, as the Ghost appears to do in the first act of *Hamlet*. From there they could emerge onto the stage through a trapdoor. They could retire behind the hangings across the back of the stage (or the front of the tiring house), as, for example, the actor playing Polonius does when he hides behind the arras. Sometimes the hangings could be drawn back during a performance to "discover" one or more actors behind them. When performance required that an actor appear "above," as when Juliet is imagined to stand at the window of her chamber in the famous and misnamed "balcony scene," then the actor probably climbed the stairs to the gallery over the back of the stage and temporarily shared it with some of the spectators. The stage was also provided with ropes and winches so that actors could descend from, and reascend to, the "heavens."

Perhaps the greatest difference between dramatic performances in Shakespeare's time and ours was that in Shakespeare's England the roles of women were played by boys. (Some of these boys grew up to take male roles in their maturity.) There were no women in the acting companies, only in the audience. It had not always been so in the history of the English stage. There are records of women on English stages in the thirteenth and fourteenth centuries, two hundred years before Shakespeare's plays were performed. After the accession of James I in 1603, the queen of England and her ladies took part in entertainments at court called masques, and with the reopening of the theaters in 1660 at the restoration of Charles II, women again took their place on the public stage.

The chief competitors for the companies of adult actors such as the one to which Shakespeare belonged and for which he wrote were companies of exclusively boy actors. The competition was most intense in the early 1600s. There were then two principal children's companies: the Children of Paul's (the choirboys from St. Paul's Cathedral, whose private playhouse was near the cathedral); and the Children of the Chapel Royal (the choirboys from the monarch's private chapel, who performed at the Blackfriars theater built by Burbage in 1596, which Shakespeare's company had been stopped from using by local residents who objected to crowds). In *Hamlet* Shakespeare writes of "an aerie [nest] of children, little eyases [hawks], that cry out on the top of question and are most tyrannically clapped for 't. These are now the fashion and . . . berattle the common stages [attack the public theaters]." In the long run, the adult actors prevailed. The Children of Paul's dissolved around 1606. By about 1608 the Children of the Chapel Royal had been forced to stop playing at the Blackfriars theater, which was then taken over by the King's Men, Shakespeare's own troupe.

Acting companies and theaters of Shakespeare's time were organized in different ways. For example, Philip Henslowe owned the Rose and leased it to companies of actors, who paid him from their takings. Henslowe would act as manager of these companies, initially paying playwrights for their plays and buying properties, recovering his outlay from the actors. Shakespeare's company, however, managed itself, with the principal actors, Shakespeare among them, having the status of "sharers" and the right to a share in the takings, as well as the responsibility for a part of the expenses. Five of the sharers themselves, Shakespeare among them, owned the Globe. As actor, as sharer in an acting company and in ownership of theaters, and as playwright, Shakespeare was about as involved in the theatrical industry as one could imagine. Although Shakespeare and his fellows prospered, their status under the law was conditional upon the protection of powerful patrons. "Common players"—those who did not have patrons or masters—were classed in the language of the law with "vagabonds and sturdy beggars." So the actors had to secure for themselves the official rank of servants of patrons. Among the patrons under whose protection Shakespeare's company worked were the lord chamberlain and, after the accession of King James in 1603, the king himself.

We are now perhaps on the verge of learning a great deal more about the theaters in which Shakespeare and his contemporaries performed—or at least of opening up new questions about them. Already about 70 percent of the Rose has been excavated, as has about 10 percent of the second Globe, the one built in 1614. It is to be hoped that soon more will be available for study. These are exciting times for students of Shakespeare's stage.

The Publication of Shakespeare's Plays

Eighteen of Shakespeare's plays found their way into print during the playwright's lifetime, but there is nothing to suggest that he took any interest in their publication. These eighteen appeared separately in editions called quartos. Their pages were not much larger than the one you are now reading, and these little books were sold unbound for a few pence. The earliest of the quartos that still survive were printed in 1594, the year that both *Titus Andronicus* and a version of the play now called *2 King Henry VI* became available. While almost every one of these early quartos displays on its title page the name of the acting company that performed the play, only about half provide the name of the playwright, Shakespeare. The first quarto edition to bear the name Shakespeare on its title page is *Love's Labor's Lost* of 1598. A few of these quartos were popular with the book-buying public of Shakespeare's lifetime; for example, quarto *Richard II* went through five editions between 1597 and 1615. But most of the quartos were far from best-sellers; *Love's Labor's Lost* (1598), for instance, was not reprinted in quarto until 1631. After Shakespeare's death, two more of his plays appeared in quarto format: *Othello* in 1622 and *The Two Noble Kinsmen,* coauthored with John Fletcher, in 1634.

In 1623, seven years after Shakespeare's death, *Mr. William Shakespeares Comedies, Histories, & Tragedies* was published. This printing offered readers in a single book thirty-six of the thirty-eight plays now thought to have been written by Shakespeare, including eighteen that had never been printed before. And it offered them in a style that was then reserved for serious literature and scholarship. The plays were arranged in double columns on pages nearly a foot high. This large page size is called "folio," as opposed to the smaller "quarto," and the 1623 volume is usually called the Shakespeare First Folio. It is reputed to have sold for the lordly price of a pound. (One copy at the Folger Library is marked fifteen shillings—that is, three-quarters of a pound.)

In a preface to the First Folio entitled "To the great Variety of Readers," two of Shakespeare's former fellow actors in the King's Men, John Heminge and Henry Condell, wrote that they themselves had collected their dead companion's plays. They suggested that they had seen his own papers: "we have scarce received from him a blot in his papers." The title page of the Folio declared that the plays within it had been printed "according to the True Original Copies." Comparing the Folio to the quartos, Heminge and Condell disparaged the quartos, advising their readers that "before you were abused with divers stolen and surreptitious copies, maimed, and deformed by the frauds and stealths of injurious impostors." Many Shakespeareans of the eighteenth and nineteenth centuries believed Heminge and Condell and regarded the Folio plays as superior to anything in the quartos.

Once we begin to examine the Folio plays in detail, it becomes less easy to take at face value the word of

Heminge and Condell about the superiority of the Folio texts. For example, of the first nine plays in the Folio (one quarter of the entire collection), four were essentially reprinted from earlier quarto printings that Heminge and Condell had disparaged; and four have now been identified as printed from copies written in the hand of a professional scribe of the 1620s named Ralph Crane; the ninth, *The Comedy of Errors*, was apparently also printed from a manuscript, but one whose origin cannot be readily identified. Evidently then, eight of the first nine plays in the First Folio were not printed, in spite of what the Folio title page announces, "according to the True Original Copies," or Shakespeare's own papers, and the source of the ninth is unknown. Since today's editors have been forced to treat Heminge and Condell's pronouncements with skepticism, they must choose whether to base their own editions upon quartos or the Folio on grounds other than Heminge and Condell's story of where the quarto and Folio versions originated.

Editors have often fashioned their own narratives to explain what lies behind the quartos and Folio. They have said that Heminge and Condell meant to criticize only a few of the early quartos, the ones that offer much shorter and sometimes quite different, often garbled, versions of plays. Among the examples of these are the 1600 quarto of *Henry V* (the Folio offers a much fuller version) or the 1603 *Hamlet* quarto (in 1604 a different, much longer form of the play got into print as a quarto). Early in this century editors speculated that these questionable texts were produced when someone in the audience took notes from the plays' dialogue during performances and then employed "hack poets" to fill out the notes. The poor results were then sold to a publisher and presented in print as Shakespeare's plays. More recently this story has given way to another in which the shorter versions are said to be re-creations from memory of Shakespeare's plays by actors who wanted to stage them in the provinces but lacked manuscript copies. Most of the quartos offer much better texts than these so-called bad quartos. Indeed, in most of the quartos we find texts that are at least equal to or better than what is printed in the Folio. Many of this century's Shakespeare enthusiasts have persuaded themselves that most of the quartos were set into type directly from Shakespeare's own papers, although there is nothing on which to base this conclusion except the desire for it to be true. Thus speculation continues about how the Shakespeare plays got to be printed. All that we have are the printed texts.

The book collector who was most successful in bringing together copies of the quartos and the First Folio was Henry Clay Folger, founder of the Folger Shakespeare Library in Washington, D.C. While it is estimated that there survive around the world only about 230 copies of the First Folio, Mr. Folger was able to acquire more than seventy-five copies, as well as a large number of fragments, for the library that bears his name. He also amassed a substantial number of quartos. For example, only fourteen copies of the First Quarto of *Love's Labor's Lost* are known to exist, and three are at the Folger Shakespeare Library. As a consequence of Mr. Folger's labors, twentieth-century scholars visiting the Folger Library have been able to learn a great deal about sixteenth and seventeenth-century printing and, particularly, about the printing of Shakespeare's plays. And Mr. Folger did not stop at the First Folio, but collected many copies of later editions of Shakespeare, beginning with the Second Folio (1632), the Third (1663–64), and the Fourth (1685). Each of these later folios was based on its immediate predecessor and was edited anonymously. The first editor of Shakespeare whose name we know was Nicholas Rowe, whose first edition came out in 1709. Mr. Folger collected this edition and many, many more by Rowe's successors.

An Introduction to This Text

The play we call *Henry IV, Part 2* was printed in two different versions in the first quarter of the seventeenth century. One of these is in quarto, the other in the 1623 Folio. In 1600 there appeared the quarto (or pocket-size book) titled *The Second part of Henrie the fourth, continuing to his death, and coronation of Henrie the fift. With the humours of sir Iohn Falstaffe, and swaggering Pistoll.* This quarto edition (Q) exists in two different states (Qa and Qb). The second state (Qb) has two more leaves (four more pages) than the first (Qa). These additional pages contain an entire scene, the first scene of what we now call the third act. In order to add this scene to Q, its printer was also obliged to reprint the text that immediately surrounds 3.1—the end of the last scene of Act 2 (over 50 lines) and the beginning of the second scene of Act 3 (over 100 lines): all in all, about 165 lines.

The second version of *Henry IV, Part 2* appeared in the earliest collection of Shakespeare plays, now called the Shakespeare First Folio. In the Folio, this play is titled *The Second Part of Henry the Fourth, Containing his Death: and the Coronation of King Henry the Fift* (F). The small difference in title between Q and F belies major differences between the texts printed in each. Unlike Qa, all known states of F contain the first scene of the third act; because F, unlike Q, is divided into acts and scenes, this appears under the heading *"Actus Tertius. Scena Prima"* ("Third Act. First Scene"). F also contains eight passages (totaling about 170 lines) that are absent from Q, as well as more than sixty other shorter readings not in Q. At the same time F lacks about twenty-five lines and some seventy-five shorter readings that are found in Q. Furthermore, Q and F also differ from each other in their readings of over three hundred other words.

Most modern editions offer various combinations of the Q and F versions. But it is impossible in any edition to combine the whole of these two forms of the play because they often provide alternative readings that are mutually exclusive; for example, Q has Falstaff ask "do not the rebels need souldiers[?]" but F prints "want" for "need." In such cases (and there are a great many such cases) editors must choose whether to be guided by Q or by F.

Twentieth-century editors have decided which readings to prefer according to their theories about the origins of the early printed texts. Most recent editors have preferred Q's readings in the belief that it was printed directly from Shakespeare's own manuscript. These editors also regard F as being, in some respects, textually dependent on Q because they think a scribe behind the F text may well have based his transcription on a copy of Q as well as on an independent manuscript. Some of these editors go so far as to deny F any authority at all, except for the eight passages unique to it. Others grant it considerable authority and adopt not only its eight unique passages but also most of its additions to Q and many of the individual readings it substitutes for Q words—all in the belief that F presents a Shakespearean revision of the Q text and that F derives ultimately from a manuscript of this revision that was used in the theater as the basis for production. There is no editorial consensus.

As today's scholars reexamine the narratives about the origins of the printed texts, we discover that the evidence on which they are based is questionable, and we become more skeptical about ever identifying with any certainty how the play assumed the forms in which it was printed. In particular, the theory that the Q text originates in Shakespeare's own manuscript before it was adapted for staging is disturbed by the strong possibility that omissions from Q reflect either actors' abridgement or possibly, in some cases, censorship. The claim that F's text derives ultimately from the theater is troubled not only by the restoration to F of what may, in fact, be theatrical cuts but also by censorship of the F text that is both incomplete according to the 1606 Act that governed the use of profanity onstage and inconsistent with the provisions of that Act. We do not believe that we can depend on traditional editorial accounts of the origins of Q and F.*

The present edition is based on a fresh examination of the early printed texts rather than upon any modern edition. It offers its readers the Q printing of *Henry IV, Part 2.*† Our choice of Q does not rest on conjectures about its origin or about the origin of F. Rather, we prefer Q to F because of our knowledge that F was put into print under extremely difficult circumstances. We are nonetheless aware, from comparison of the lines common to Qa and Qb, that Q provides us with an imperfect text. Therefore we offer an *edition* of Q that prints such F readings and such emendations from previous editions as are, in the editors' judgments,

---

*For further discussion of textual problems in *Henry IV, Part 2*, we invite you to read the section titled "Textual Problems in *Henry IV, Part 2*" printed at the back of this book.

†We have also consulted the computerized text of Q provided by the Text Archive of the Oxford University Computing Centre, to which we are grateful.

necessary to repair what may be errors and deficiencies in Q. For those lines that appear in both Qa and Qb, we base our edition on the first printing of the lines (Qa) because we know that Qa must have been based directly on the printer's manuscript; Qb may have been printed from this manuscript but we cannot know that it was not printed from a copy of Qa.

Because we cannot know that scribal copying and difficulties in printing necessarily account for what is unique to the F text, we have also included in our edition almost all the words, lines, and passages that are unique to F. Of all the words that the printing of F adds to the version printed as Q (as opposed to words that the F printing substitutes for Q's words), we have omitted only the following from our edited text: F's repetition of "all" (2.1.75) and of "sir" at the end of 5.3.84; F's addition of "a" before "man" in the Q phrase "what man of good temper" (2.1.82–83); and F's extra-metrical addition of "an" to 2.3.2.

In order to enable its readers to tell the difference between the Q and F versions, the present edition uses a variety of signals:

(1) All the words in this edition that are printed only in the F version appear in pointed brackets(⟨ ⟩).

(2) All lines that are found only in Q and not in F are printed in square brackets ([ ]).

(3) Sometimes neither Q nor F seems to offer a satisfactory reading, and it is necessary to print a word different from what is offered by either. Such words (called "emendations" by editors) are printed within superior half-brackets (⌐ ⌐).

Whenever we change the wording of Q or F or add anything to their stage directions, we mark the change. We want our readers to be immediately aware when we have intervened. (Only when we correct an obvious typographical error in Q or F is the correction not marked in our text.) Whenever we change Q's or F's wording or punctuation so as to change meaning, we list the change in the textual notes at the back of the book, even if all we have done is fix an obvious error. Those who wish to find F's alternatives to Q readings will be able to find these also in the textual notes.

For the convenience of the reader, we have modernized the punctuation and the spelling of Q and F. Sometimes we go so far as to modernize certain old forms of words; for example, when *a* means *he,* we change it to *he;* we change *mo* to *more,* and *ye* to *you.* But it is not our practice in editing any of the plays to modernize words that sound distinctly different from modern forms. For example, when the early printed texts read *sith* or *apricocks* or *porpentine,* we have not modernized to *since, apricots, porcupine.* When the forms *an, and,* or *and if* appear instead of the modern form *if,* we have reduced *and* to *an* but have not changed any of these forms to their modern equivalent, *if.* We also modernize and, where necessary, correct passages in foreign languages, unless an error in the early printed text can be reasonably explained as a joke.

We regularize spellings of a number of the proper names, as is the usual practice in editions of the play. For example, Q sometimes uses the forms "Dowglas," "Westmerland," "Mourton," "Peyto," and "Falstalfe" but we consistently follow its spellings "Douglas," "Westmoreland," "Morton," "Peto," and "Falstaff."

This edition differs from many earlier ones in its efforts to aid the reader in imagining the play as a performance rather than as a series of actual events. Thus stage directions are written with reference to the stage. For example, when the Archbishop says to Westmoreland, "Then take, my Lord of Westmoreland, this schedule" (4.1.177), editors often print a stage direction calling for the Archbishop-actor to hand the Westmoreland-actor a "schedule," but onstage all the actors would actually exchange is a piece of paper, and so we add the direction *"giving Westmoreland a paper."* Whenever it is reasonably certain, in our view, that a speech is accompanied by a particular action, we provide a stage direction describing the action. (Occasional exceptions to this rule occur when the action is so obvious that to add a stage direction would insult the reader). Stage directions for the entrance of a character in mid-scene are, with rare exceptions, placed so that they immediately precede the character's participation in the scene, even though these entrances may appear somewhat earlier in the early printed texts. Whenever we move a stage direction, we record this change in the textual notes. Latin stage directions (e.g., *Exeunt*) are translated into English (e.g., *They exit*).

We expand the often severely abbreviated forms of names used as speech headings in early printed texts into the full names of the characters. We also regularize the speakers' names in speech headings, using only a single designation for each character, even though the early printed texts sometimes use a variety of designations. Variations in the speech headings of the early printed texts are recorded in the textual notes.

In the present edition, as well, we mark with a dash any change of address within a speech, unless a stage direction intervenes. When the -ed ending of a word is to be pronounced, we mark it with an accent. Like editors for the past two centuries, we print metrically linked lines in the following way:

ARCHBISHOP
  I do not doubt you.
WESTMORELAND   I am glad of it.

(4.1.325–26)

However, when there are a number of short verse-lines that can be linked in more than one way, we do not, with rare exceptions, indent any of them.

The Explanatory Notes

The notes that appear on the pages facing the text are designed to provide readers with the help that they may need to enjoy the play. Whenever the meaning of a word in the text is not readily accessible in a good contemporary dictionary, we offer the meaning in a note. Sometimes we provide a note even when the relevant meaning is to be found in the dictionary but when the word has acquired since Shakespeare's time other potentially confusing meanings. In our notes, we try to offer modern synonyms for Shakespeare's words. We also try to indicate to the reader the connection between the word in the play and the modern synonym. For example, Shakespeare sometimes uses the word *head* to mean *source,* but, for modern readers, there may be no connection evident between these two words. We provide the connection by explaining Shakespeare's usage as follows: "**head:** fountainhead, source." On some occasions, a whole phrase or clause needs explanation. Then we rephrase in our own words the difficult passage, and add at the end synonyms for individual words in the passage. When scholars have been unable to determine the meaning of a word or phrase, we acknowledge the uncertainty.

HENRY IV
Part 2

Henry IV's Ancestors and Descendants

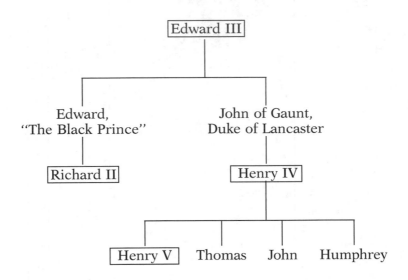

Characters in the Play

RUMOR, Presenter of the Induction

KING HENRY IV, formerly Henry Bolingbroke
PRINCE HAL, Prince of Wales and heir to the throne,
    later KING HENRY V

JOHN OF LANCASTER
THOMAS OF CLARENCE   } *younger sons of King Henry IV*
HUMPHREY OF GLOUCESTER

EARL OF NORTHUMBERLAND, Henry Percy
NORTHUMBERLAND'S WIFE
LADY PERCY, widow of Hotspur

Richard Scroop, ARCHBISHOP of York
LORD MOWBRAY
LORD HASTINGS
LORD BARDOLPH   } *in rebellion against*
TRAVERS   *King Henry IV*
MORTON
SIR JOHN COLEVILLE

EARL OF WESTMORELAND
EARL OF WARWICK
EARL OF SURREY
SIR JOHN BLUNT   } *supporters of King Henry IV*
GOWER
HARCOURT

LORD CHIEF JUSTICE

SIR JOHN FALSTAFF
POINS
BARDOLPH

3

PETO
PISTOL
FALSTAFF'S PAGE
HOSTESS of the tavern (also called Mistress Quickly)
DOLL TEARSHEET

JUSTICE ROBERT SHALLOW
JUSTICE SILENCE
DAVY, servant to Shallow

MOULDY
SHADOW
WART } *men of Gloucestershire*
FEEBLE
BULLCALF

FANG
SNARE } *London officers*

EPILOGUE

Drawers, Musicians, Beadles, Grooms, Messenger, Soldiers, Lords, Attendants, Porter, Servants

HENRY IV
Part 2

ACT 1

Induction. Following the battle of Shrewsbury (where King Henry and Prince Hal were victorious and Hotspur killed), Rumor spreads the false information that Hotspur was the victor and the King and Prince were killed.

---

2. **vent of hearing:** ear(s)

4. **post-horse:** a horse kept at an inn for the use of travelers; **still:** continually; **unfold:** reveal, disclose

12. **fearful:** terrible; **musters:** gatherings of soldiers

13. **big:** i.e., pregnant; **grief:** injury

15. **no such matter:** i.e., none of that is true; **pipe:** small wind instrument, like a flute or recorder

16. **jealousies:** suspicions

17. **of . . . stop:** i.e., so easily played **plain:** simple **stop:** finger hole or opening in a recorder or flute

18. **blunt:** rude, dull; **monster . . . heads:** Proverbial: "A **multitude** of people is a beast of many heads."

19. **still-discordant:** i.e., always in conflict (with a pun on **discordant** as "out of tune")

22. **my household:** i.e., those who attend or serve me (here, the theater audience)

23. **King Harry's victory:** i.e., Henry IV's **victory** over rebel forces, dramatized in *Henry IV, Part 1*

⟨*INDUCTION*⟩

Enter Rumor, painted full of tongues.

⌐RUMOR⌐

Open your ears, for which of you will stop
The vent of hearing when loud Rumor speaks?
I, from the orient to the drooping west,
Making the wind my post-horse, still unfold
The acts commencèd on this ball of earth.   5
Upon my tongues continual slanders ride,
The which in every language I pronounce,
Stuffing the ears of men with false reports.
I speak of peace while covert enmity
Under the smile of safety wounds the world.   10
And who but Rumor, who but only I,
Make fearful musters and prepared defense
Whiles the big year, swoll'n with some other grief,
Is thought with child by the stern tyrant war,
And no such matter? Rumor is a pipe   15
Blown by surmises, jealousies, conjectures,
And of so easy and so plain a stop
That the blunt monster with uncounted heads,
The still-discordant wav'ring multitude,
Can play upon it. But what need I thus   20
My well-known body to anatomize
Among my household? Why is Rumor here?
I run before King Harry's victory,

7

25. **Hotspur:** i.e., Henry Percy, son of the Earl of Northumberland

28. **office:** assigned part; duty, function

29. **Harry Monmouth:** i.e., Prince Hal, called **Monmouth** after his birthplace in Wales

31. **the Douglas:** i.e., Archibald, Earl of **Douglas**

35. **hold:** stronghold (The castle walls are made of **ragged** [that is, rough] **stone**, but there is wordplay on **ragged** as old and **worm-eaten**.)

37. **crafty-sick:** i.e., pretending to be sick; **posts:** messengers

41. **smooth . . . false:** i.e., flattering or pleasant misinformation

41–42. **worse . . . wrongs:** i.e., more harmful than painful truths

The Battle of Shrewsbury. (Ind. 24)
From John Speed, *A prospect of the most famous parts of the world . . .* (1631).

Who in a bloody field by Shrewsbury
Hath beaten down young Hotspur and his troops,   25
Quenching the flame of bold rebellion
Even with the rebels' blood. But what mean I
To speak so true at first? My office is
To noise abroad that Harry Monmouth fell
Under the wrath of noble Hotspur's sword,   30
And that the King before the Douglas' rage
Stooped his anointed head as low as death.
This have I rumored through the peasant towns
Between that royal field of Shrewsbury
And this worm-eaten ⌜hold⌝ of ragged stone,   35
(Where) Hotspur's father, old Northumberland,
Lies crafty-sick. The posts come tiring on,
And not a man of them brings other news
Than they have learnt of me. From Rumor's
     tongues   40
They bring smooth comforts false, worse than
     true wrongs.
                                   ⌜*Rumor*⌝ *exits.*

1.1 Northumberland, who had pleaded illness as an excuse for not appearing at the battle of Shrewsbury, learns that his son, Hotspur, is dead and that King Henry's troops are up in arms. He throws away his crutch and prepares to do battle.

---

1. **keeps:** guards
3. **What:** i.e., who
5. **attend:** await
6. **orchard:** garden (See illustration below.)
7. **Please . . . Honor:** a courteous phrase of request; **knock but:** i.e., only knock
8 SD. **a kerchief:** a linen headcloth, worn around the head when ill
11. **Should be:** i.e., threatens to be; **stratagem:** violent deed
12. **Contention:** strife, dispute

An orchard. (1.1.6; 5.3.1)
From Octavio Boldoni, *Theatrum temporaneum* . . . (1636).

⟨Scene ⌜1⌝⟩
Enter the Lord Bardolph at one door.

LORD BARDOLPH
  Who keeps the gate here, ho?

  ⌜*Enter the Porter.*⌝

                                    Where is the Earl?
PORTER
  What shall I say you are?
LORD BARDOLPH   Tell thou the Earl
  That the Lord Bardolph doth attend him here.   5
PORTER
  His Lordship is walked forth into the orchard.
  Please it your Honor knock but at the gate
  And he himself will answer.

Enter the Earl Northumberland, ⌜his head wrapped in a
  kerchief and supporting himself with a crutch.⌝

LORD BARDOLPH   Here comes the Earl.
                                   ⌜*Porter exits.*⌝

NORTHUMBERLAND
  What news, Lord Bardolph? Every minute now   10
  Should be the father of some stratagem.
  The times are wild. Contention, like a horse

13. **high feeding:** i.e., too-rich fodder
14. **bears down:** overwhelms; **him:** i.e., it
16. **certain:** reliable
17. **an:** i.e, if
20. **in the fortune:** i.e., through the success
21. **both the Blunts:** Sir Walter Blunt was killed by the Earl of **Douglas;** Sir John Blunt appears later in this play.
24. **brawn:** swine fattened for the table; **Sir John:** i.e., Falstaff
26. **followed:** i.e., followed through, successfully pursued
28. **fortunes:** i.e., successes (an allusion to the Roman military leader Julius Caesar, famous for his "I came, I saw, I overcame") See page 168.
29. **How is this derived:** i.e., how do you know this
33. **freely:** readily, openly; **these news:** i.e., this news
34. **who:** i.e., whom
36. **overrode:** overtook, outrode
37. **furnished:** provided
38. **haply:** perhaps; **retail:** repeat
40. **Sir John Umfrevile:** See longer note, page 247. **turned:** sent

Full of high feeding, madly hath broke loose
And bears down all before him.
LORD BARDOLPH   Noble earl,   15
I bring you certain news from Shrewsbury.
NORTHUMBERLAND
Good, an God will!
LORD BARDOLPH   As good as heart can wish.
The King is almost wounded to the death,
And, in the fortune of my lord your son,   20
Prince Harry slain outright; and both the Blunts
Killed by the hand of Douglas; young Prince John
And Westmoreland and Stafford fled the field;
And Harry Monmouth's brawn, the hulk Sir John,
Is prisoner to your son. O, such a day,   25
So fought, so followed, and so fairly won,
Came not till now to dignify the times
Since Caesar's fortunes.
NORTHUMBERLAND   How is this derived?
Saw you the field? Came you from Shrewsbury?   30
LORD BARDOLPH
I spake with one, my lord, that came from thence,
A gentleman well bred and of good name,
That freely rendered me these news for true.

Enter Travers.

NORTHUMBERLAND
Here comes my servant Travers, who I sent
On Tuesday last to listen after news.   35
LORD BARDOLPH
My lord, I overrode him on the way,
And he is furnished with no certainties
More than he haply may retail from me.
NORTHUMBERLAND
Now, Travers, what good tidings comes with you?
TRAVERS
My lord, Sir John Umfrevile turned me back   40

43. **forspent:** worn out
50. **armèd:** spurred
52. **starting:** i.e., leaping forward
54. **Staying . . . question:** i.e., waiting for no further discussion
60. **have not the day:** i.e., was not the victor
61–62. **for . . . barony:** i.e., I'll exchange my title for a trifle **point:** lace to hold up stockings
66. **hilding:** good-for-nothing
68. **at a venture:** at random, without thought
70. **title leaf:** i.e., title page, which often indicated the **nature** of the **volume** (line 71) See below.

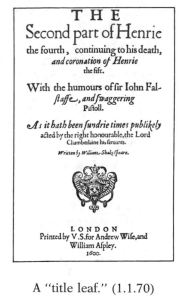

THE
Second part of Henrie
the fourth, continuing to his death,
and coronation of Henrie
the fift.

With the humours of fir Iohn Fal-
ſtaffe, and ſwaggering
Piſtoll.

As it hath been ſundrie times publikely
acted by the right honourable,the Lord
Chamberlaine his feruants.

Written by William Shakeſpeare.

LONDON
Printed by V.S.for Andrew Wiſe,and
William Aſpley.
1600.

A "title leaf." (1.1.70)
Title page of *Henry IV, Part 2,* 1600.

14

With joyful tidings and, being better horsed,
Outrode me. After him came spurring hard
A gentleman, almost forspent with speed,
That stopped by me to breathe his bloodied horse.
He asked the way to Chester, and of him   45
I did demand what news from Shrewsbury.
He told me that rebellion had bad luck
And that young Harry Percy's spur was cold.
With that he gave his able horse the head
And, bending forward, struck his armèd heels   50
Against the panting sides of his poor jade
Up to the rowel-head, and starting so
He seemed in running to devour the way,
Staying no longer question.
NORTHUMBERLAND   Ha? Again: 55
  Said he young Harry Percy's spur was cold?
  Of Hotspur, Coldspur? That rebellion
  Had met ill luck?
LORD BARDOLPH   My lord, I'll tell you what:
  If my young lord your son have not the day,   60
  Upon mine honor, for a silken point
  I'll give my barony. Never talk of it.
NORTHUMBERLAND
  Why should that gentleman that rode by Travers
  Give then such instances of loss?
LORD BARDOLPH   Who, he?   65
  He was some hilding fellow that had stol'n
  The horse he rode on and, upon my life,
  Spoke at a venture.

                Enter Morton.

                Look, here comes more news.
NORTHUMBERLAND
  Yea, this man's brow, like to a title leaf,   70
  Foretells the nature of a tragic volume.

72–73. **the strand . . . usurpation:** i.e., the beach on which the ocean has left lines in the sand (like wrinkles in a frowning brow) **flood:** ocean **witnessed usurpation:** i.e., evidence of its trespass

76. **his:** i.e., its

83. **Drew Priam's curtain:** i.e., opened Priam's bedcurtains (**Priam** was king of **Troy,** which was destroyed by the Greeks.) See below.

86. **my Percy's:** i.e., Hotspur's

89. **Stopping:** closing up, as with a stopper or plug

90. **to stop my ear indeed:** i.e., close my ear permanently

99. **is chancèd:** i.e., has happened

101. **his divination lies:** i.e., his guess is false

105. **spirit:** ability to perceive, mental power; **certain:** well-grounded

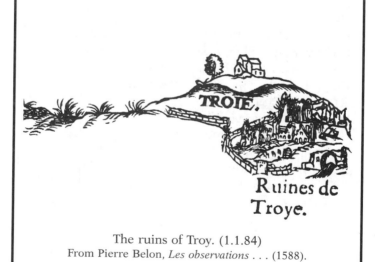

The ruins of Troy. (1.1.84)
From Pierre Belon, *Les observations . . .* (1588).

16

So looks the strand whereon the imperious flood
Hath left a witnessed usurpation.—
Say, Morton, didst thou come from Shrewsbury?
MORTON
    I ran from Shrewsbury, my noble lord,   75
    Where hateful death put on his ugliest mask
    To fright our party.
NORTHUMBERLAND   How doth my son and brother?
    Thou tremblest, and the whiteness in thy cheek
    Is apter than thy tongue to tell thy errand.   80
    Even such a man, so faint, so spiritless,
    So dull, so dead in look, so woebegone,
    Drew Priam's curtain in the dead of night
    And would have told him half his Troy was burnt;
    But Priam found the fire ere he his tongue,   85
    And I my Percy's death ere thou report'st it.
    This thou wouldst say: "Your son did thus and thus;
    Your brother thus; so fought the noble Douglas"—
    Stopping my greedy ear with their bold deeds.
    But in the end, to stop my ear indeed,   90
    Thou hast a sigh to blow away this praise,
    Ending with "Brother, son, and all are dead."
MORTON
    Douglas is living, and your brother yet,
    But for my lord your son—
NORTHUMBERLAND   Why, he is dead.   95
    See what a ready tongue suspicion hath!
    He that but fears the thing he would not know
    Hath, by instinct, knowledge from others' eyes
    That what he feared is chancèd. Yet speak,
        Morton.   100
    Tell thou an earl his divination lies,
    And I will take it as a sweet disgrace
    And make thee rich for doing me such wrong.
MORTON
    You are too great to be by me gainsaid,
    Your spirit is too true, your fears too certain.   105

106. **for:** in spite of

107. **strange:** reluctant

108. **fear:** a frightening thing

111. **belie:** misrepresent

114. **office:** duty, function

115. **sullen:** mournful

116. **tolling:** i.e., ringing slowly to announce the death of

119. **would:** i.e., wish

120. **state:** condition

121. **quittance:** reprisal, retaliation; **outbreathed:** out of breath

125. **In few:** i.e., in short, in brief

125–38. **spirit . . . field:** See longer note, page 247.

127. **bruited once:** i.e., once reported

128. **best-tempered:** i.e., of the finest temper (Steel is **tempered** through a process of heating and cooling that brings it to the proper degree of elasticity and strength.) **courage:** i.e., heart

129. **mettle:** spirit (with a pun on *metal*, which continues in the word **steeled**)

130. **abated:** blunted

131. **Turned on themselves:** i.e., bent (like weapons made of soft metal)

133. **Upon enforcement:** i.e., under force (specifically, propulsion)

134. **heavy:** sorrowful (with a pun on the word's usual meaning)

NORTHUMBERLAND
  Yet, for all this, say not that Percy's dead.
  I see a strange confession in thine eye.
  Thou shak'st thy head and hold'st it fear or sin
  To speak a truth. If he be slain, ⟨say so.⟩
  The tongue offends not that reports his death;   110
  And he doth sin that doth belie the dead,
  Not he which says the dead is not alive.
  Yet the first bringer of unwelcome news
  Hath but a losing office, and his tongue
  Sounds ever after as a sullen bell   115
  Remembered tolling a departing friend.
LORD BARDOLPH
  I cannot think, my lord, your son is dead.
MORTON, ⌜*to Northumberland*⌝
  I am sorry I should force you to believe
  That which I would to God I had not seen,
  But these mine eyes saw him in bloody state,   120
  Rend'ring faint quittance, wearied and outbreathed,
  To Harry Monmouth, whose swift wrath beat down
  The never-daunted Percy to the earth,
  From whence with life he never more sprung up.
  In few, his death, whose spirit lent a fire   125
  Even to the dullest peasant in his camp,
  Being bruited once, took fire and heat away
  From the best-tempered courage in his troops;
  For from his mettle was his party steeled,
  Which, once in him abated, all the rest   130
  Turned on themselves, like dull and heavy lead.
  And as the thing that's heavy in itself
  Upon enforcement flies with greatest speed,
  So did our men, heavy in Hotspur's loss,
  Lend to this weight such lightness with their fear   135
  That arrows fled not swifter toward their aim
  Than did our soldiers, aiming at their safety,

138. **Worcester:** i.e., the Earl of Worcester, brother of Northumberland

141. **three . . . King:** i.e., had killed three men disguised as King Henry (See *Henry IV, Part 1,* 5.3 and 5.4.)

142. **Gan:** began to: **vail his stomach:** i.e., subdue his appetite for battle; **grace:** countenance, condone (the shameful flight)

144. **took:** i.e., taken

146. **power:** army

147. **Under the conduct of:** i.e., led by

148. **the news at full:** i.e., all of **the news**

150. **In . . . physic:** i.e., **poison** can be medicinal; **these news:** i.e., this news

151. **Having . . . that:** i.e., that, if I had been well

152. **Being sick, have:** i.e., I being sick, has

154. **under life:** i.e., under the weight of his body

155. **Impatient of:** i.e., (when he is) unable to endure

156. **keeper's:** attendant's

157. **grief:** pain, suffering (used in line 158 to mean "sorrow")

160. **nice:** effeminate, unmanly

161. **scaly gauntlet:** i.e., a **gauntlet** made of small plates of armor (See page 78.)

162–63. **sickly coif:** i.e., cap worn by the sick

164. **guard:** protection, defense; **wanton:** frivolous

165. **fleshed with:** inflamed by, made eager by

167. **ragged'st:** roughest

171. **stage:** The metaphor of the **world** as a **stage** is continued through line 176, with the words **act** (line 172) and **scene** (line 175).

Fly from the field. Then was that noble Worcester
So soon ta'en prisoner; and that furious Scot,
The bloody Douglas, whose well-laboring sword   140
Had three times slain th'appearance of the King,
Gan vail his stomach and did grace the shame
Of those that turned their backs and in his flight,
Stumbling in fear, was took. The sum of all
Is that the King hath won and hath sent out   145
A speedy power to encounter you, my lord,
Under the conduct of young Lancaster
And Westmoreland. This is the news at full.
NORTHUMBERLAND
For this I shall have time enough to mourn.
In poison there is physic, and these news,   150
Having been well, that would have made me sick,
Being sick, have in some measure made me well.
And as the wretch whose fever-weakened joints,
Like strengthless hinges, buckle under life,
Impatient of his fit, breaks like a fire   155
Out of his keeper's arms, even so my limbs,
Weakened with grief, being now enraged with
    grief,
Are thrice themselves. Hence therefore, thou
    nice crutch.   ⌜*He throws down his crutch.*⌝ 160
A scaly gauntlet now with joints of steel
Must glove this hand. And hence, thou sickly
    coif.   ⌜*He removes his kerchief.*⌝
Thou art a guard too wanton for the head
Which princes, fleshed with conquest, aim to hit.   165
Now bind my brows with iron, and approach
The ragged'st hour that time and spite dare bring
To frown upon th'enraged Northumberland.
Let heaven kiss earth! Now let not Nature's hand
Keep the wild flood confined. Let order die,   170
And let this world no longer be a stage

172. **feed contention:** i.e., nourish controversy; **lingering:** i.e., long-drawn-out

173. **one . . . Cain:** i.e., a single murderous **spirit** (**Cain,** the **firstborn** son of Adam and Eve, murdered his brother Abel [Genesis 4.8–12].)

175. **courses:** proceedings; **rude:** violent

177. **strainèd:** forced, unnatural

179. **complices:** associates, comrades

181. **perforce:** necessarily

182. **cast th' event:** calculated the outcome (The metaphor of calculating is continued in **summed the accompt** [line 183].)

185. **make head:** raise an army; or, press forward; **presurmise:** i.e., beforehand conjecture or suspicion

186. **dole:** distribution, delivery (but also, perhaps, grief, sorrow)

189. **You were advised:** i.e., you knew

189–90. **capable/Of:** susceptible to

190. **forward:** ardent, eager

191–92. **where . . . ranged:** i.e., to the level where the greatest danger lay **trade of:** trafficking in

195. **stiff-borne:** i.e., resolutely maintained

197. **was like to be:** i.e., was likely to happen

198. **engagèd to:** involved in

200. **wrought out life:** i.e., preserved our lives to the end

202. **respect:** consideration

203. **o'erset:** overthrown, defeated

204. **put forth:** stake, wager (continuing the gambling metaphor of **loss, gain,** and **venture**); also, set out, go forward

To feed contention in a lingering act;
But let one spirit of the firstborn Cain
Reign in all bosoms, that, each heart being set
On bloody courses, the rude scene may end,   175
And darkness be the burier of the dead.
⌈LORD BARDOLPH⌉
[This strainèd passion doth you wrong, my lord.]
⌈MORTON⌉
Sweet earl, divorce not wisdom from your honor.
The lives of all your loving complices
⟨Lean⟩ on ⟨your⟩ health, the which, if you give o'er   180
To stormy passion, must perforce decay.
⟨You cast th' event of war, my noble lord,
And summed the accompt of chance before you
    said
"Let us make head." It was your presurmise   185
That in the dole of blows your son might drop.
You knew he walked o'er perils on an edge,
More likely to fall in than to get o'er.
You were advised his flesh was capable
Of wounds and scars, and that his forward spirit   190
Would lift him where most trade of danger
    ranged.
Yet did you say "Go forth," and none of this,
Though strongly apprehended, could restrain
The stiff-borne action. What hath then befall'n,   195
Or what ⌈did⌉ this bold enterprise bring forth,
More than that being which was like to be?⟩
LORD BARDOLPH
We all that are engagèd to this loss
Knew that we ventured on such dangerous seas
That if we wrought out life, 'twas ten to one;   200
And yet we ventured, for the gain proposed
Choked the respect of likely peril feared;
And since we are o'erset, venture again.
Come, we will all put forth, body and goods.

207. **gentle:** honorable; well-born; **up:** i.e., up in arms

208. **well-appointed powers:** i.e., well-equipped forces

209. **surety:** bond (The **double surety** may refer to that of soul and body [as in lines 221–22] or to the archbishop's temporal and spiritual authority.)

210. **corpse:** i.e., bodies

211. **But shadows:** i.e., only semblances; **shows:** illusory appearances; **to fight:** i.e., as fighters

215. **drink potions:** i.e., take medicine or poison; **that:** i.e., so that

216. **for their:** i.e., as for their

219. **the Bishop:** i.e., the Archbishop of York

220. **to religion:** i.e., into religion

221. **Supposed:** i.e., rightly believed

223. **enlarge his rising:** i.e., enhance his rebellion; or, attract followers; **with the blood:** i.e., by reminding people of **the blood** (The murder of **King Richard** II at **Pomfret** [i.e., Pontefract] Castle was instigated by his successor, King Henry IV.)

227. **bestride:** i.e., protect, defend (like a warrior standing over a fallen comrade)

228. **Bolingbroke:** King Henry IV (By giving the title of **King** to Richard and calling Henry by his family name, the Archbishop strengthens his case that **his quarrel** against Henry's kingship comes **from heaven.**)

229. **more and less:** i.e., highborn and lowborn

232. **counsel every man:** i.e., let each man give advice about; or, let us all consider

234. **posts:** messengers

MORTON

'Tis more than time.—And, my most noble lord,   205
I hear for certain, and dare speak the truth:
(The gentle Archbishop of York is up
With well-appointed powers. He is a man
Who with a double surety binds his followers.
My lord your son had only but the corpse,   210
But shadows and the shows of men, to fight;
For that same word "rebellion" did divide
The action of their bodies from their souls,
And they did fight with queasiness, constrained,
As men drink potions, that their weapons only   215
Seemed on our side. But, for their spirits and
     souls,
This word "rebellion," it had froze them up
As fish are in a pond. But now the Bishop
Turns insurrection to religion.   220
Supposed sincere and holy in his thoughts,
He's followed both with body and with mind,
And doth enlarge his rising with the blood
Of fair King Richard, scraped from Pomfret
     stones;   225
Derives from heaven his quarrel and his cause;
Tells them he doth bestride a bleeding land,
Gasping for life under great Bolingbroke;
And more and less do flock to follow him.)

NORTHUMBERLAND

I knew of this before, but, to speak truth,   230
This present grief had wiped it from my mind.
Go in with me and counsel every man
The aptest way for safety and revenge.
Get posts and letters, and make friends with speed.
Never so few, and never yet more need.   235

                              They exit.

1.2 Sir John Falstaff is confronted by the Lord Chief Justice. Since Falstaff has come away from Shrewsbury with the reputation of a warrior and has been commanded by the king to march to York to join Prince John, the Lord Chief Justice forbears to arrest him for the Gad's Hill robbery.

---

0 SD. **buckler:** small shield (See page 52.)
1. **Sirrah:** a term of address to a boy or a male social inferior
1–2. **to my water:** i.e., about my urine
4. **that owed it:** i.e., whose it is   **owed:** owned
5. **knew for:** i.e., knew about
6. **gird:** jeer
7. **foolish-compounded clay:** i.e., fool (For the notion that **man** is **clay,** see Genesis 2.7 and 3.19.)
8. **intends:** tends, inclines
9. **on:** i.e., about
14. **set me off:** i.e., make me conspicuous by contrast
15. **whoreson:** wretched (a generally abusive epithet); **mandrake:** a plant whose forked roots resemble the human torso (here referring to its small size) See page 120.
16. **wait:** follow; serve
17. **manned with an agate:** i.e., had an agate as my servant (An **agate** was a quartz crystal set in a ring, often carved with tiny figures.)
20. **juvenal:** i.e., juvenile, young man
21. **fledge:** covered with down
22. **off his cheek:** i.e., with a razor
23. **stick:** hesitate

(continued)

⟨Scene ⌜2⌝⟩
*Enter Sir John ⟨Falstaff,⟩ with his Page bearing his sword
and buckler.*

FALSTAFF   Sirrah, you giant, what says the doctor to my
water?

PAGE   He said, sir, the water itself was a good healthy
water, but, for the party that owed it, he might have
more diseases than he knew for.   5

FALSTAFF   Men of all sorts take a pride to gird at me.
The brain of this foolish-compounded clay, man, is
not able to invent anything that intends to laughter
more than I invent, or is invented on me. I am not
only witty in myself, but the cause that wit is in   10
other men. I do here walk before thee like a sow
that hath overwhelmed all her litter but one. If the
Prince put thee into my service for any other reason
than to set me off, why then I have no judgment.
Thou whoreson mandrake, thou art fitter to be   15
worn in my cap than to wait at my heels. I was never
manned with an agate till now, but I will inset you
neither in gold nor silver, but in vile apparel, and
send you back again to your master for a jewel. The
juvenal, the Prince your master, whose chin is not   20
yet fledge—I will sooner have a beard grow in the
palm of my hand than he shall get one off his cheek,
and yet he will not stick to say his face is a face
royal. God may finish it when He will. 'Tis not a hair
amiss yet. He may keep it still at a face royal, for a   25
barber shall never earn sixpence out of it, and yet
he'll be crowing as if he had writ man ever since his
father was a bachelor. He may keep his own grace,
but he's almost out of mine, I can assure him. What
said Master Dommelton about the satin for my   30
short cloak and my slops?

23–24. **face royal:** i.e., a princely **face** (with a pun at line 25 on the **royal** as a coin with the king's face stamped on it, and worth ten shillings)

25. **keep it still at:** i.e., continue to value it as

27. **writ man:** reached manhood

28–29. **keep . . . mine:** i.e., retain his title though he's lost my favor (punning on two meanings of **grace**)

31. **slops:** wide, baggy breeches

33. **assurance:** guarantee; **Bardolph:** one of Falstaff's men, not the Lord Bardolph of scene 1

34. **band:** bond; **security:** surety or guarantee

35–36. **damned . . . hotter:** an allusion to the rich **glutton** in Luke 16.19–31, who, burning in hell, begged for water to cool **his tongue**

36. **Achitophel:** i.e., traitor (in 2 Samuel 15–17, King David's counselor who conspires with David's son Absalom against the king)

37. **yea-forsooth:** perhaps, hypocritical; or, perhaps, lower-class or Puritan (See longer note, page 247.)

37–38. **bear . . . in hand:** systematically deceive, delude (from the French *maintenir*)

38. **stand upon:** attach importance to

39. **smoothy-pates:** See longer note to 1.2.37. **high shoes:** i.e., shoes with high heels and soles, worn by dandies

40. **keys:** i.e., **keys** to lock up their (supposed) hoards of gold

40–41. **is through . . . taking up:** i.e., has reached agreement with them for an **honest** purchase

42. **I had as lief:** I'd just as soon

43. **stop it:** i.e., close it up

(continued)

PAGE He said, sir, you should procure him better
assurance than Bardolph. He would not take his
band and yours. He liked not the security.

FALSTAFF Let him be damned like the glutton! Pray   35
God his tongue be hotter! A whoreson Achitophel, a
⟨rascally⟩ yea-forsooth knave, to bear a gentleman in
hand and then stand upon security! The whoreson
smoothy-pates do now wear nothing but high shoes
and bunches of keys at their girdles; and if a man is   40
through with them in honest taking up, then they
must stand upon security. I had as lief they would
put ratsbane in my mouth as offer to stop it with
"security." I looked he should have sent me two-
and-twenty yards of satin, as I am a true knight, and   45
he sends me "security." Well, he may sleep in
security, for he hath the horn of abundance, and the
lightness of his wife shines through it, and yet
cannot he see though he have his own lantern to
light him. Where's Bardolph?   50

PAGE He's gone in Smithfield to buy your Worship a
horse.

FALSTAFF I bought him in Paul's, and he'll buy me a
horse in Smithfield. An I could get me but a wife in
the stews, I were manned, horsed, and wived.   55

Enter Lord Chief Justice ⟨and Servant.⟩

PAGE, ⌜*to Falstaff*⌝ Sir, here comes the nobleman that
committed the Prince for striking him about Bardolph.

FALSTAFF Wait close. I will not see him.
⌜*They begin to exit.*⌝

CHIEF JUSTICE, ⌜*to Servant*⌝ What's he that goes there?   60

SERVANT Falstaff, an 't please your Lordship.

CHIEF JUSTICE He that was in question for the robbery?

SERVANT He, my lord; but he hath since done good

44. **looked he should:** i.e., expected he would

46–50. **he may sleep . . . light him:** i.e., he sleeps in foolish complacency, since his wife is unfaithful to him (See longer note, page 248.)

51. **in Smithfield:** i.e., into **Smithfield,** a London district known as a market for livestock

53–55. **I . . . wived:** Proverbial: "Who goes to Westminster for a wife, to Paul's for a man, and to Smithfield for a horse may meet with a whore, a knave, and a jade." **Paul's:** i.e., St. Paul's Cathedral (See page 238.) **An:** i.e., if **stews:** brothels **manned:** provided with a servant

57. **committed:** sentenced to prison (See longer note to 1.2.56–58, page 249.)

59. **close:** hidden

61. **an 't please:** i.e., if it please (a polite expression)

62. **in question for:** i.e., examined about

65. **charge:** command (of soldiers)

74. **Is:** i.e., are

78. **to be on:** i.e., to support

79. **tell:** state; know

80. **make:** regard, represent

81. **mistake:** misunderstand (Falstaff pretends that the servant means "identify wrongly.")

84. **in my throat:** i.e., deeply and deliberately

86. **give me leave:** i.e., permit me

90. **grows to:** i.e., is an integral part of

92. **hunt counter:** In hunting, a dog goes **counter** when it follows the trail in the wrong direction. **Avaunt:** begone! (a word used to send away devils)

97. **abroad:** out in public; out of doors

98. **advice:** i.e., medical **advice**

service at Shrewsbury, and, as I hear, is now going
with some charge to the Lord John of Lancaster. 65
CHIEF JUSTICE What, to York? Call him back again.
SERVANT Sir John Falstaff!
FALSTAFF Boy, tell him I am deaf.
PAGE You must speak louder. My master is deaf.
CHIEF JUSTICE I am sure he is, to the hearing of 70
anything good.—Go pluck him by the elbow. I must
speak with him.
SERVANT, ⌜*plucking Falstaff's sleeve*⌝ Sir John!
FALSTAFF What, a young knave and begging? Is there
not wars? Is there not employment? Doth not the 75
King lack subjects? Do not the rebels need soldiers?
Though it be a shame to be on any side but one, it is
worse shame to beg than to be on the worst side,
were it worse than the name of rebellion can tell
how to make it. 80
SERVANT You mistake me, sir.
FALSTAFF Why sir, did I say you were an honest man?
Setting my knighthood and my soldiership aside, I
had lied in my throat if I had said so.
SERVANT I pray you, sir, then set your knighthood and 85
your soldiership aside, and give me leave to tell you,
you lie in your throat if you say I am any other than
an honest man.
FALSTAFF I give thee leave to tell me so? I lay aside that
which grows to me? If thou gett'st any leave of me, 90
hang me; if thou tak'st leave, thou wert better be
hanged. You hunt counter. Hence! Avaunt!
SERVANT Sir, my lord would speak with you.
CHIEF JUSTICE Sir John Falstaff, a word with you.
FALSTAFF My good lord. God give your Lordship good 95
time of ⟨the⟩ day. I am glad to see your Lordship
abroad. I heard say your Lordship was sick. I hope
your Lordship goes abroad by advice. Your Lord-

100. **smack:** taste, flavor; **ague:** chills and fevers (Many editions here follow the Folio and print "age" rather than the Quarto's "an ague.")

102. **reverend:** respectful

111. **this ... apoplexy:** i.e., a wretched paralysis (**This same** was used to express irritation, contempt, or familiarity.)

112. **I pray you:** i.e., please (a polite phrase)

117. **What:** i.e., why; **Be it:** i.e., let it be

118. **it original:** i.e., its origin

120. **his:** i.e., its; **in Galen:** i.e., in one of Galen's medical treatises (**Galen** was Claudius Galenus, a second-century A.D. anatomist, physiologist, and physician.) See page xl.

125. **marking:** paying attention; **withal:** i.e., with

126. **punish ... heels:** i.e., imprison you; or, put you in the stocks; **amend:** improve

129. **Job:** the much-afflicted central figure in the biblical Book of **Job,** proverbial for his patience and his poverty

130–31. **minister ... imprisonment:** i.e., imprison me

131. **in respect of:** i.e., because I suffer from

133. **make ... scruple:** i.e., have a tiny doubt **dram:** tiniest bit (literally, an apothecaries' weight of 60 grains)   **scruple:** doubt (also, an apothecaries' weight of 20 grains)

ship, though not clean past your youth, have yet
some smack of an ague in you, some relish of the   100
saltness of time in you, and I most humbly beseech
your Lordship to have a reverend care of your
health.

CHIEF JUSTICE   Sir John, I sent for you before your
expedition to Shrewsbury.   105

FALSTAFF   An 't please your Lordship, I hear his Majesty
is returned with some discomfort from Wales.

CHIEF JUSTICE   I talk not of his Majesty. You would not
come when I sent for you.

FALSTAFF   And I hear, moreover, his Highness is fallen   110
into this same whoreson apoplexy.

CHIEF JUSTICE   Well, God mend him. I pray you let me
speak with you.

FALSTAFF   This apoplexy, as I take it, is a kind of
lethargy, an 't please your Lordship, a kind of   115
sleeping in the blood, a whoreson tingling.

CHIEF JUSTICE   What tell you me of it? Be it as it is.

FALSTAFF   It hath it original from much grief, from
study, and perturbation of the brain. I have read the
cause of his effects in Galen. It is a kind of deafness.   120

CHIEF JUSTICE   I think you are fallen into the disease,
for you hear not what I say to you.

FALSTAFF   Very well, my lord, very well. Rather, an 't
please you, it is the disease of not listening, the
malady of not marking, that I am troubled withal.   125

CHIEF JUSTICE   To punish you by the heels would amend
the attention of your ears, and I care not if I do
become your physician.

FALSTAFF   I am as poor as Job, my lord, but not so
patient. Your Lordship may minister the potion of   130
imprisonment to me in respect of poverty, but how
I should be your patient to follow your prescrip-
tions, the wise may make some dram of a scruple,
or indeed a scruple itself.

135–36. **matters . . . life:** charges against you carrying the death penalty

138. **this land-service:** i.e., military service

150. **gall:** irritate

152. **night's . . . Hill:** In *Henry IV, Part 1* Falstaff robs merchants at **Gad's Hill.**

154. **o'erposting that action:** i.e., escaping from the consequences of the robbery (literally, "riding quickly over **that action**")

156–57. **Wake . . . wolf:** Proverbial: "It is not good waking a sleeping dog."

158. **to smell a fox:** i.e., to be suspicious (Proverbial: "As rank as a fox.")

161. **wassail candle:** perhaps, a large candle burned on feast nights

162. **of wax:** i.e., all made of wax (with a pun on **wax** as "grow, expand"); **approve:** prove, confirm, demonstrate

164. **his effect:** i.e., its effect

165. **gravy:** fat from cooking meat

167. **ill angel:** i.e., evil spirit

168. **Your . . . light:** a complex pun on **ill,** on **angel,** and on **light** (See longer note, page 249, and picture, page 180.)

170. **weighing:** (1) judging; (2) measuring my weight

CHIEF JUSTICE I sent for you, when there were matters 135
    against you for your life, to come speak with me.
FALSTAFF As I was then advised by my learned counsel
    in the laws of this land-service, I did not come.
CHIEF JUSTICE Well, the truth is, Sir John, you live in
    great infamy.   140
FALSTAFF He that buckles himself in my belt cannot
    live in less.
CHIEF JUSTICE Your means are very slender, and your
    waste is great.
FALSTAFF I would it were otherwise. I would my means 145
    were greater and my waist slender.
CHIEF JUSTICE You have misled the youthful prince.
FALSTAFF The young prince hath misled me. I am the
    fellow with the great belly, and he my dog.
CHIEF JUSTICE Well, I am loath to gall a new-healed 150
    wound. Your day's service at Shrewsbury hath a
    little gilded over your night's exploit on Gad's Hill.
    You may thank th' unquiet time for your quiet
    o'erposting that action.
FALSTAFF My lord.   155
CHIEF JUSTICE But since all is well, keep it so. Wake not
    a sleeping wolf.
FALSTAFF To wake a wolf is as bad as ⟨to⟩ smell a fox.
CHIEF JUSTICE What, you are as a candle, the better
    part burnt out.   160
FALSTAFF A wassail candle, my lord, all tallow. If I did
    say of wax, my growth would approve the truth.
CHIEF JUSTICE There is not a white hair in your face but
    should have his effect of gravity.
FALSTAFF His effect of gravy, gravy, gravy.   165
CHIEF JUSTICE You follow the young prince up and
    down like his ill angel.
FALSTAFF Not so, my lord. Your ill angel is light, but I
    hope he that looks upon me will take me without
    weighing. And yet in some respects I grant I cannot 170

171. **go:** (1) walk; (2) pass as current

172. **costermongers':** a term of abuse (literally, one who sells fruit or vegetables from a barrow)

172–73. **bearherd:** keeper of a tame bear (See page 224.)

173. **pregnancy:** quick-wittedness

178. **the heat of our livers:** i.e., our passions (See longer note to 1.2.178–79, **livers, galls,** page 250.)

179. **galls:** i.e., gallbladders

180. **vaward:** vanguard

183. **characters:** characteristics (literally, **written** or printed letters of the alphabet)

186. **wind:** i.e., breath; **single:** poor

191–92. **something a:** i.e., a somewhat

192. **For:** i.e., as for

193. **halloing:** calling to the hounds; **approve:** prove, confirm

196. **caper with:** compete in dancing with; **marks:** i.e., coins (a "mark" was worth about thirteen shillings)

197. **For the box of:** i.e., as for the blow on

199. **sensible:** (1) intelligent; (2) capable of experiencing physical sensation

200. **checked:** reproved, rebuked

201. **Marry:** indeed (originally an oath on the name of the Virgin Mary)

202. **sack:** costly dry Spanish wine, such as sherry

go. I cannot tell. Virtue is of so little regard in these
costermongers' times that true valor is turned bearherd; pregnancy is made a tapster, and ⟨hath⟩ his
quick wit wasted in giving reckonings. All the other
gifts appurtenant to man, as the malice of ⟨this⟩ age   175
shapes ⟨them, are⟩ not worth a gooseberry. You that
are old consider not the capacities of us that are
young. You do measure the heat of our livers with
the bitterness of your galls, and we that are in the
vaward of our youth, I must confess, are wags too.   180
CHIEF JUSTICE   Do you set down your name in the scroll
of youth, that are written down old with all the
characters of age? Have you not a moist eye, a dry
hand, a yellow cheek, a white beard, a decreasing
leg, an increasing belly? Is not your voice broken,   185
your wind short, your chin double, your wit single,
and every part about you blasted with antiquity?
And will you yet call yourself young? Fie, fie, fie, Sir
John.
FALSTAFF   My lord, I was born [about three of the clock   190
in the afternoon,] with a white head and something
a round belly. For my voice, I have lost it with
halloing and singing of anthems. To approve my
youth further, I will not. The truth is, I am only old
in judgment and understanding. And he that will   195
caper with me for a thousand marks, let him lend
me the money, and have at him. For the box of the
⟨ear⟩ that the Prince gave you, he gave it like a rude
prince, and you took it like a sensible lord. I have
checked him for it, and the young lion repents.   200
⌜*Aside.*⌝ Marry, not in ashes and sackcloth, but in
new silk and old sack.
CHIEF JUSTICE   Well, God send the Prince a better
companion.
FALSTAFF   God send the companion a better prince. I   205
cannot rid my hands of him.

212. **look you:** i.e., be sure that you

216. **would:** i.e., wish

217. **spit white:** perhaps, in contrast to spitting blood or phlegm (The phrase is much debated.)

221–22. **will needs say:** i.e., insist upon saying

230. **furnish me forth:** i.e., supply me with what I need

232. **bear crosses:** (1) carry money (a "cross" being a coin stamped with a cross); (2) put up with adversity (with perhaps wordplay on the familiar biblical verse "whosoever beareth not his cross and cometh after me cannot be my disciple" [Luke 14.27, Geneva Bible])

234. **three-man beetle:** i.e., a mallet so heavy that it takes three men to wield it

237. **the pox:** i.e., syphilis; **pinches:** torments

238. **both the degrees:** i.e., both youth and age; **prevent:** forestall, anticipate

241. **groats:** i.e., small coins (literally, coins worth four pennies)

A "cross." (1.2.232)
From Edward Hawkins, *The silver coins of England . . .* (1841).

CHIEF JUSTICE Well, the King hath severed you ⟨and
   Prince Harry.⟩ I hear you are going with Lord John
   of Lancaster against the Archbishop and the Earl of
   Northumberland.   210

FALSTAFF Yea, I thank your pretty sweet wit for it. But
   look you pray, all you that kiss my Lady Peace at
   home, that our armies join not in a hot day, for, by
   the Lord, I take but two shirts out with me, and I
   mean not to sweat extraordinarily. If it be a hot day   215
   and I brandish anything but a bottle, I would I
   might never spit white again. There is not a dangerous action can peep out his head but I am thrust
   upon it. Well, I cannot last ever. [But it was always
   yet the trick of our English nation, if they have a   220
   good thing, to make it too common. If you will
   needs say I am an old man, you should give me rest.
   I would to God my name were not so terrible to the
   enemy as it is. I were better to be eaten to death
   with a rust than to be scoured to nothing with   225
   perpetual motion.]

CHIEF JUSTICE Well, be honest, be honest, and God
   bless your expedition.

FALSTAFF Will your Lordship lend me a thousand
   pound to furnish me forth?   230

CHIEF JUSTICE Not a penny, not a penny. You are too
   impatient to bear crosses. Fare you well. Commend
   me to my cousin Westmoreland.
            ⌜*Lord Chief Justice and his Servant exit.*⌝

FALSTAFF If I do, fillip me with a three-man beetle. A
   man can no more separate age and covetousness   235
   than he can part young limbs and lechery; but the
   gout galls the one, and the pox pinches the other,
   and so both the degrees prevent my curses.—Boy!

PAGE Sir.

FALSTAFF What money is in my purse?   240

PAGE Seven groats and two pence.

249. **hair of:** i.e., hair on
250. **A pox of:** i.e., a plague on, curses on
253. **halt:** limp; **for my color:** i.e., as my pretext or excuse
254. **wit:** mind, intelligence
256. **commodity:** expediency, profit

1.3 At York, the Archbishop discusses with Mowbray, Hastings, and Lord Bardolph whether they can defeat the king's forces if their ally Northumberland, whose forces are strongest, does not appear. After comforting themselves by observing that the king's army is divided so as to fight on three fronts, they set out to win the common people to their cause.

---

0 SD. **Earl Marshal:** an important officer of the state charged with arranging ceremonies, also called **Lord Marshal** (line 5)
6. **allow:** accept, approve
7. **would . . . satisfied:** i.e., wish more assurance or better answers about
8. **in our means:** i.e., given our resources
9. **forehead . . . enough:** i.e., sufficient audacity
11. **upon the file:** i.e., according to our rolls

FALSTAFF I can get no remedy against this consumption of the purse. Borrowing only lingers and lingers it out, but the disease is incurable. ⌜*Giving*
papers to the Page.⌝ Go bear this letter to my Lord   245
of Lancaster, this to the Prince, this to the Earl
of Westmoreland, and this to old Mistress Ursula,
whom I have weekly sworn to marry since I perceived the first white hair of my chin. About it. You
know where to find me. ⌜*Page exits.*⌝ A pox of this   250
gout! Or a gout of this pox, for the one or the other
plays the rogue with my great toe. 'Tis no matter if I
do halt. I have the wars for my color, and my
pension shall seem the more reasonable. A good wit
will make use of anything. I will turn diseases to   255
commodity.

                                        ⌜*He exits.*⌝

⟨Scene ⌜3⌝⟩

Enter th' Archbishop ⌜of York,⌝ Thomas Mowbray (Earl
Marshal), the Lord Hastings, and ⟨Lord⟩ Bardolph.

ARCHBISHOP
  Thus have you heard our cause and known our
    means,
  And, my most noble friends, I pray you all
  Speak plainly your opinions of our hopes.
  And first, Lord Marshal, what say you to it?   5
MOWBRAY
  I well allow the occasion of our arms,
  But gladly would be better satisfied
  How in our means we should advance ourselves
  To look with forehead bold and big enough
  Upon the power and puissance of the King.   10
HASTINGS
  Our present musters grow upon the file

12. **men of choice:** i.e., choice men

13. **supplies:** reinforcements; **largely:** abundantly

18. **hold up head:** i.e., offer a successful resistance

26. **aids incertain:** i.e., uncertain support

28. **cause:** case (See longer note, page 250.)

29. **lined:** reinforced, strengthened

30. **Eating . . . supply:** i.e., feeding himself on insubstantial promises (See longer note, page 250.)

31. **project:** i.e., anticipation; **a power:** an army

35. **winking:** closing his eyes

36. **by your leave:** a polite phrase meaning, e.g., "if you'll allow me to speak"

37. **forms:** images, representations

38–40. **Yes . . . hope:** perhaps, "yes, in the present situation, it does do harm to live **in hope**" (Lines 38–39 are confusing and often emended.) **quality:** occasion **on foot:** in active existence

King Henry IV.
From John Speed, *The theatre of the empire of Great Britaine* . . . (1627 [i.e., 1631]).

To five-and-twenty thousand men of choice,
And our supplies live largely in the hope
Of great Northumberland, whose bosom burns
With an incensèd fire of injuries.　　　　　　　15
LORD BARDOLPH
　The question, then, Lord Hastings, standeth thus:
　Whether our present five-and-twenty thousand
　May hold up head without Northumberland.
HASTINGS
　With him we may.
LORD BARDOLPH　　Yea, marry, there's the point.　20
　But if without him we be thought too feeble,
　My judgment is we should not step too far
　⟨Till we had his assistance by the hand.
　For in a theme so bloody-faced as this,
　Conjecture, expectation, and surmise　　　　　25
　Of aids incertain should not be admitted.⟩
ARCHBISHOP
　'Tis very true, Lord Bardolph, for indeed
　It was young Hotspur's cause at Shrewsbury.
LORD BARDOLPH
　It was, my lord; who lined himself with hope,
　Eating the air and promise of supply,　　　　30
　Flatt'ring himself in project of a power
　Much smaller than the smallest of his thoughts,
　And so, with great imagination
　Proper to madmen, led his powers to death
　And, winking, leapt into destruction.　　　　35
HASTINGS
　But, by your leave, it never yet did hurt
　To lay down likelihoods and forms of hope.
LORD BARDOLPH
　⟨Yes, if this present quality of war—
　Indeed the instant action, a cause on foot—
　Lives so in hope, as in an early spring　　　　40
　We see th' appearing buds, which to prove fruit

42. **Hope . . . despair:** perhaps, "we have less guarantee of **hope** than of **despair**"

44. **plot:** site for the building; **model:** architect's design (See longer note to 1.3.43–64, page 251.)

45. **figure:** design, drawing

46. **rate:** calculate

47. **ability:** i.e., the ability to pay

49. **offices:** rooms (especially for household work or service); **at least:** i.e., at worst

54. **Consent upon:** come to an agreement about (This line initiates wordplay on building terms that also apply to the current political plot. **Foundation,** e.g., means both "the base on which a house is structured" and "the principles on which an action is founded.")

55. **surveyors:** (1) architects (2) those with oversight or supervision; **estate:** means, ability (to pay)

57. **weigh against:** counterbalance; **his opposite:** i.e., its adversary ([1] the arguments against building; [2] the opposition of our enemies)

58. **in paper:** i.e., merely on **paper**

62. **Gives o'er:** i.e., gives up; **part-created cost:** unfinished costly thing

63. **naked:** defenseless, exposed

66–67. **we . . . expectation:** i.e., we have every man that we could possibly expect

69. **equal with:** match

72. **as . . . brawl:** i.e., in view of the number of present disturbances

73. **heads:** bodies of men

74. **Glendower:** i.e., Owen Glendower, leader of the Welsh, who conspired with the rebels (See *Henry IV, Part 1.*) **perforce:** necessarily

Hope gives not so much warrant as despair
That frosts will bite them. When we mean to build,
We first survey the plot, then draw the model,
And when we see the figure of the house,   45
Then must we rate the cost of the erection,
Which if we find outweighs ability,
What do we then but draw anew the model
In fewer offices, or at least desist
To build at all? Much more in this great work,   50
Which is almost to pluck a kingdom down
And set another up, should we survey
The plot of situation and the model,
Consent upon a sure foundation,
Question surveyors, know our own estate,   55
How able such a work to undergo,
To weigh against his opposite. Or else)
We fortify in paper and in figures,
Using the names of men instead of men,
Like one that draws the model of an house   60
Beyond his power to build it, who, half through,
Gives o'er and leaves his part-created cost
A naked subject to the weeping clouds
And waste for churlish winter's tyranny.

HASTINGS
Grant that our hopes, yet likely of fair birth,   65
Should be stillborn and that we now possessed
The utmost man of expectation,
I think we are (a) body strong enough,
Even as we are, to equal with the King.

LORD BARDOLPH
What, is the King but five-and-twenty thousand?   70

HASTINGS
To us no more, nay, not so much, Lord Bardolph,
For his divisions, as the times do brawl,
(Are) in three heads: one power against the French,
And one against Glendower; perforce a third

75. **take up:** encounter, oppose

76. **sound:** resound

78. **several strengths:** i.e., separate forces

84. **like:** i.e., likely

85. **Duke of Lancaster:** i.e., Prince John (Historically the title did not belong to him.)

87. **substituted:** deputed, delegated

90. **occasion . . . arms:** i.e., reason for our taking up **arms**

92. **surfeited:** i.e., fallen sick through overindulgence

94. **vulgar heart:** i.e., the **heart** of the common people (See longer note to 1.3.93–94, page 251.)

95. **fond many:** i.e., foolish multitude

98. **being . . . desires:** i.e., **now** that you are dressed up in what you wished for

102. **glutton bosom:** i.e., gluttonous stomach

103. **thou . . . up:** Proverb: "The dog is turned to his own vomit again" (quoted in 2 Peter 2.22).

Must take up us. So is the unfirm king   75
In three divided, and his coffers sound
With hollow poverty and emptiness.
ARCHBISHOP
That he should draw his several strengths together
And come against us in full puissance
Need not to be dreaded.   80
HASTINGS   If he should do so,
⟨He leaves his back unarmed, the French and Welsh⟩
Baying him at the heels. Never fear that.
LORD BARDOLPH
Who is it like should lead his forces hither?
HASTINGS
The Duke of Lancaster and Westmoreland;   85
Against the Welsh, himself and Harry Monmouth;
But who is substituted against the French
I have no certain notice.
⟨ARCHBISHOP   Let us on,
And publish the occasion of our arms.   90
The commonwealth is sick of their own choice.
Their over-greedy love hath surfeited.
An habitation giddy and unsure
Hath he that buildeth on the vulgar heart.
O thou fond many, with what loud applause   95
Didst thou beat heaven with blessing Bolingbroke
Before he was what thou wouldst have him be.
And being now trimmed in thine own desires,
Thou, beastly feeder, art so full of him
That thou provok'st thyself to cast him up.   100
So, so, thou common dog, didst thou disgorge
Thy glutton bosom of the royal Richard,
And now thou wouldst eat thy dead vomit up
And howl'st to find it. What trust is in these
    times?   105
They that, when Richard lived, would have him die
Are now become enamored on his grave.

115. **draw:** assemble; **set on:** go forward

"The power and puissance of the King." (1.3.10)
From Raphael Holinshed, *The historie of England* (1577).

Thou, that threw'st dust upon his goodly head
When through proud London he came sighing on
After th' admirèd heels of Bolingbroke,   110
Criest now "O earth, yield us that king again,
And take thou this!" O thoughts of men accursed!
Past and to come seems best; things present,
    worst.⟩
⟨MOWBRAY⟩
Shall we go draw our numbers and set on?   115
HASTINGS
We are time's subjects, and time bids begone.
                                                They exit.

HENRY IV
Part 2

ACT 2

2.1   Sir John is arrested for the debt he owes Mistress Quickly. He persuades her to drop the charges and to lend him an additional ten pounds.

---

1. **entered the action:** brought the suit before the court
3. **yeoman:** assistant; **lusty:** valiant, courageous
4. **stand to 't:** fight courageously
9. **entered him:** i.e., started the suit against him
11. **chance:** perhaps
16. **foin:** lunge, stab (one of many words in these speeches that may carry sexual meanings, among them **stabbed, weapon,** and **thrust**)
18. **close:** grapple
20. **An . . . him:** i.e., if I only hit him with my **fist**
21. **view:** Most editors print "vice," the Folio variant, which means "firm grip."
22. **undone:** ruined; **going:** i.e., leaving for the war (without paying me)

A buckler. (1.2.0 SD)
From Louis de Gaya, *A treatise of the arms . . .* (1678).

⟨ACT 2⟩

⟨Scene 1⟩

Enter Hostess ⌐Quickly⌐ of the tavern ⟨with two Officers,
Fang and Snare,⟩ ⌐who lags behind.⌐

HOSTESS   Master Fang, have you entered the action?
FANG   It is entered.
HOSTESS   Where's your yeoman? Is 't a lusty yeoman?
  Will he stand to 't?
FANG, ⌐calling⌐   Sirrah! Where's Snare?   5
HOSTESS   O Lord, ay, good Master Snare.
SNARE, ⌐catching up to them⌐   Here, here.
FANG   Snare, we must arrest Sir John Falstaff.
HOSTESS   Yea, good Master Snare, I have entered him
  and all.   10
SNARE   It may chance cost some of us our lives, for he
  will stab.
HOSTESS   Alas the day, take heed of him. He stabbed me
  in mine own house, ⟨and that⟩ most beastly, in good
  faith. He cares not what mischief he does. If his   15
  weapon be out, he will foin like any devil. He will
  spare neither man, woman, nor child.
FANG   If I can close with him, I care not for his thrust.
HOSTESS   No, nor I neither. I'll be at your elbow.
FANG   An I but fist him once, an he come but within my   20
  view—
HOSTESS   I am undone by his going. I warrant you, he's

53

23. **infinitive:** perhaps her error for "infinite"; **score:** account for goods obtained on credit

24. **sure:** i.e., securely

25. **continuantly:** perhaps her mistake for "continuately" (meaning "without interruption") See longer note, page 251. **Pie Corner:** a corner in Smithfield where cooks' shops stood

26. **saving your manhoods:** a (probably comic) version of the phrase "saving your reverence," used to introduce a remark that might be offensive

27. **indited:** perhaps her error for "invited"

27–28. **Lubber's . . . Street:** i.e., the Libbard's (i.e., Leopard's) Head Inn in Lombard Street

29. **exion:** her error for "action"

30–31. **to his answer:** i.e., to reply to my charges

31. **mark:** i.e., marks (coins worth about thirteen shillings); **long one:** perhaps, large reckoning

33–34. **fubbed off:** i.e., fobbed off, cheated

38. **malmsey-nose:** i.e., red-nosed (his nose inflamed by excessive drinking)

39. **offices:** duties

40. **do me:** i.e., do

42. **whose mare's dead:** proverbial for "what's wrong?"

46. **Cut me:** i.e., cut

47. **quean:** a term of abuse for a woman

48. **channel:** gutter

50. **bastardly:** perhaps a blending of "dastardly" and "bastard"

51. **honeysuckle:** perhaps "homicidal"

53. **honeyseed:** perhaps "homicide"

54. **man-queller:** murderer

an infinitive thing upon my score. Good Master
Fang, hold him sure. Good Master Snare, let him
not 'scape. He comes ⟨continuantly⟩ to Pie Corner,   25
saving your manhoods, to buy a saddle, and he is
indited to dinner to the Lubber's Head in Lumbert
Street, to Master Smooth's the silkman. I pray you,
since my exion is entered, and my case so openly
known to the world, let him be brought in to his   30
answer. A hundred mark is a long one for a poor
lone woman to bear, and I have borne, and borne,
and borne, and have been fubbed off, and fubbed
off, and fubbed off from this day to that day, that it is
a shame to be thought on. There is no honesty in   35
such dealing, unless a woman should be made an
ass and a beast to bear every knave's wrong. Yonder
he comes, and that arrant malmsey-nose knave,
Bardolph, with him. Do your offices, do your of
fices, Master Fang and Master Snare, do me, do me,   40
do me your offices.

Enter Sir John ⟨Falstaff⟩ and Bardolph, and the ⌜Page.⌝

FALSTAFF   How now, whose mare's dead? What's the
   matter?
FANG   ⟨Sir John,⟩ I arrest you at the suit of Mistress
   Quickly.   45
FALSTAFF   Away, varlets!—Draw, Bardolph. Cut me off
   the villain's head. Throw the quean in the
   channel.   ⌜*They draw.*⌝
HOSTESS   Throw me in the channel? I'll throw thee in
   the channel. Wilt thou, wilt thou, thou bastardly   50
   rogue?—Murder, murder!—Ah, thou honeysuckle
   villain, wilt thou kill God's officers and the King's?
   Ah, thou honeyseed rogue, thou art a honeyseed, a
   man-queller, and a woman-queller.
FALSTAFF   Keep them off, Bardolph.   55

56. **rescue:** perhaps the legal use of the word, meaning to remove a person forcibly from legal custody

58. **wot:** wilt; **ta:** thou

59. **hempseed:** i.e., gallows-bird, someone worthy of hanging

60. **scullion:** menial servant (an abusive epithet); **rampallian:** scoundrel

60–61. **fustilarian:** perhaps a comic form of "fustilugs," a fat frowsy woman

61. **tickle your catastrophe:** i.e., beat your behind

64. **stand to me:** support me, take my side

65. **What:** an interjection introducing a question or exclamation

72. **Eastcheap:** a London street filled with markets and taverns (See pages xvi–xvii.)

79. **ride . . . mare:** i.e., haunt you at night like a nightmare

80. **like:** i.e., likely; **ride the mare:** Since **mare** was used contemptuously to mean "woman," the phrase is probably sexual.

81. **vantage . . . up:** i.e., position from which to mount

83. **temper:** mental constitution, habitual disposition

85–86. **come by her own:** obtain what is rightfully hers

OFFICERS A rescue, a rescue!

HOSTESS Good people, bring a rescue or two.—Thou
wot, wot thou? Thou wot, wot ta? Do, do, thou
rogue. Do, thou hempseed.

PAGE Away, you scullion, you rampallian, you fustil- 60
arian! I'll tickle your catastrophe.

Enter Lord Chief Justice and his Men.

CHIEF JUSTICE
What is the matter? Keep the peace here, ho!

HOSTESS Good my lord, be good to me. I beseech you
stand to me.

CHIEF JUSTICE
How now, Sir John? What, are you brawling here? 65
Doth this become your place, your time, and
business?
You should have been well on your way to York.—
Stand from him, fellow. Wherefore hang'st thou
upon him? 70

HOSTESS O my most worshipful lord, an 't please your
Grace, I am a poor widow of Eastcheap, and he is
arrested at my suit.

CHIEF JUSTICE For what sum?

HOSTESS It is more than for some, my lord; it is for all I 75
have. He hath eaten me out of house and home. He
hath put all my substance into that fat belly of his.
⌜*To Falstaff.*⌝ But I will have some of it out again, or I
will ride thee o' nights like the mare.

FALSTAFF I think I am as like to ride the mare if I have 80
any vantage of ground to get up.

CHIEF JUSTICE How comes this, Sir John? ⟨Fie,⟩ what
man of good temper would endure this tempest of
exclamation? Are you not ashamed to enforce a
poor widow to so rough a course to come by her 85
own?

90. **parcel-gilt goblet:** i.e., a **goblet** with a gilt inner surface; **Dolphin chamber:** the name of a room in her inn

91. **sea-coal:** i.e., coal (as distinguished from char-coal)

92. **Wheeson:** dialect for "Whitsun" (the seventh week after Easter); **broke:** cut open

93. **liking:** comparing; **singing-man of Windsor:** See longer note, page 251.

95. **my lady thy wife:** Since Falstaff is a knight, his **wife** would be called **"my lady."**

96. **Goodwife:** i.e., Mrs.

97. **Gossip:** i.e., friend (here used as a term of address)

98. **mess:** small amount

100. **whereby:** whereupon

101. **ill:** harmful; **green:** recent, raw

103. **familiarity:** her mistake for "familiar"

104. **madam:** one designation for the wife of a knight

106. **book-oath:** oath sworn on the Bible

110. **in good case:** well off, wealthy

111. **distracted her:** driven her insane

118. **level:** balanced

FALSTAFF What is the gross sum that I owe thee?

HOSTESS Marry, if thou wert an honest man, thyself
and the money too. Thou didst swear to me upon a
parcel-gilt goblet, sitting in my Dolphin chamber at   90
the round table by a sea-coal fire, upon Wednesday
in Wheeson week, when the Prince broke thy head
for liking his father to a singing-man of Windsor,
thou didst swear to me then, as I was washing thy
wound, to marry me and make me my lady thy wife.   95
Canst thou deny it? Did not Goodwife Keech, the
butcher's wife, come in then and call me Gossip
Quickly, coming in to borrow a mess of vinegar,
telling us she had a good dish of prawns, whereby
thou didst desire to eat some, whereby I told thee   100
they were ill for a green wound? And didst thou not,
when she was gone downstairs, desire me to be no
more so familiarity with such poor people, saying
that ere long they should call me madam? And didst
thou not kiss me and bid me fetch thee thirty   105
shillings? I put thee now to thy book-oath. Deny it if
thou canst.

FALSTAFF My lord, this is a poor mad soul, and she says
up and down the town that her eldest son is like
you. She hath been in good case, and the truth is,   110
poverty hath distracted her. But, for these foolish
officers, I beseech you I may have redress against
them.

CHIEF JUSTICE Sir John, Sir John, I am well acquainted
with your manner of wrenching the true cause the   115
false way. It is not a confident brow, nor the throng
of words that come with such more than impudent
sauciness from you, can thrust me from a level
consideration. You have, as it appears to me, practiced upon the easy-yielding spirit of this woman,   120
[and made her serve your uses both in purse and in
person.]

127. **current:** genuine (i.e., having the quality of **sterling money**)

128. **sneap:** i.e., rebuke

130. **make curtsy:** i.e., bow

131–32. **my . . . remembered:** i.e., remembering the respect I owe you

132. **suitor:** suppliant

135. **as having power:** i.e., as if empowered or entitled

136. **in . . . reputation:** in a way (1) suitable to your reputation, or (2) that will reflect well on you

147. **fain:** content (as my only option); **plate:** silver or gold utensils

149. **Glasses:** i.e., drinking vessels of glass; **only drinking:** i.e., only acceptable way to drink; **for:** i.e., as for

150. **slight drollery:** i.e., comic painting on thin fabric

150–51. **the Prodigal:** i.e. the Prodigal Son (Luke 15.11–32) See page 198.

151. **German hunting:** perhaps, a scene of boar hunting or of St. Hubert, converted while hunting the stag; **waterwork:** imitation tapestry

152. **bed-hangers:** i.e., bed-hangings, pieces of tapestry used as bed-curtains

HOSTESS   Yea, in truth, my lord.

CHIEF JUSTICE   Pray thee, peace.—Pay her the debt you
   owe her, and unpay the villainy you have done with   125
   her. The one you may do with sterling money, and
   the other with current repentance.

FALSTAFF   My lord, I will not undergo this sneap without reply. You call honorable boldness "impudent
   sauciness." If a man will make curtsy and say   130
   nothing, he is virtuous. No, my lord, my humble
   duty remembered, I will not be your suitor. I say to
   you, I do desire deliverance from these officers,
   being upon hasty employment in the King's affairs.

CHIEF JUSTICE   You speak as having power to do wrong;   135
   but answer in th' effect of your reputation, and
   satisfy the poor woman.

FALSTAFF   Come hither, hostess.

⌜*He speaks aside to the Hostess.*⌝

Enter a Messenger, ⟨Master Gower.⟩

CHIEF JUSTICE   Now, Master Gower, what news?

GOWER
   The King, my lord, and Harry Prince of Wales   140
   Are near at hand. The rest the paper tells.

⌜*He gives the Chief Justice a paper to read.*⌝

FALSTAFF, ⌜*to the Hostess*⌝   As I am a gentleman!

HOSTESS   Faith, you said so before.

FALSTAFF   As I am a gentleman. Come. No more words
   of it.   145

HOSTESS   By this heavenly ground I tread on, I must be
   fain to pawn both my plate and the tapestry of my
   dining chambers.

FALSTAFF   Glasses, glasses, is the only drinking. And for
   thy walls, a pretty slight drollery, or the story of the   150
   Prodigal or the German hunting in waterwork is
   worth a thousand of these bed-hangers and these

154. **an 'twere:** i.e., if it were; **humors:** moods
156. **draw the action:** i.e., withdraw the suit
160. **nobles:** i.e., coins worth about seven shillings
(**Twenty nobles** would be about seven pounds.)
162. **make other shift:** i.e., try somewhere else
163. **still:** always
164. **though I:** i.e., even if I have to
168. **Hook on:** i.e., don't get separated from her
176. **tonight:** i.e., last night
177. **Basingstoke:** a town southwest of London
181. **foot:** foot soldiers; **horse:** cavalry troops

A seventeenth-century view of Falstaff and the Hostess.
From *The wits, or Sport upon sport . . .* (1662).

fly-bitten ⟨tapestries.⟩ Let it be ten pound, if thou
canst. Come, an 'twere not for thy humors, there's
not a better wench in England. Go wash thy face,   155
and draw the action. Come, thou must not be in this
humor with me. Dost not know me? Come, come. I
know thou wast set on to this.

HOSTESS Pray thee, Sir John, let it be but twenty
nobles. I' faith, I am loath to pawn my plate, so God   160
save me, la.

FALSTAFF Let it alone. I'll make other shift. You'll be a
fool still.

HOSTESS Well, you shall have it, though I pawn my
gown. I hope you'll come to supper. You'll pay   165
me all together?

FALSTAFF Will I live? ⌜*Aside to Bardolph.*⌝ Go with her,
with her. Hook on, hook on.

HOSTESS Will you have Doll Tearsheet meet you at
supper?   170

FALSTAFF No more words. Let's have her.
              Hostess, ⌜*Fang, Snare, Bardolph, Page,*
                              and others⌝ *exit.*

CHIEF JUSTICE, ⌜*to Gower*⌝ I have heard better news.

FALSTAFF, ⌜*to Chief Justice*⌝ What's the news, my ⟨good⟩
lord?

CHIEF JUSTICE, ⌜*to Gower*⌝ Where lay the King   175
tonight?

GOWER At ⟨Basingstoke,⟩ my lord.

FALSTAFF, ⌜*to Chief Justice*⌝ I hope, my lord, all's
well. What is the news, my lord?

CHIEF JUSTICE, ⌜*to Gower*⌝ Come all his forces back?   180

GOWER
No. Fifteen hundred foot, five hundred horse
Are marched up to my Lord of Lancaster
Against Northumberland and the Archbishop.

185. **presently:** immediately
191. **wait upon:** accompany
193. **being:** i.e., since
194. **take . . . up:** i.e., recruit **soldiers**
198. **they . . . not:** i.e., my manners are not suitable
200. **tap for tap:** i.e., tit for tat; **fair:** i.e., on good terms
201. **lighten thee:** i.e., spiritually enlighten you (with wordplay on "take off some of your weight")

2.2 Learning that Falstaff will be dining that night in Eastcheap, Prince Hal and Poins decide to disguise themselves as waiters and observe him.

---

3. **attached:** seized; **so high blood:** i.e., such exalted lineage
4–5. **discolors . . . greatness:** perhaps, makes me blush
6. **show:** look; **vilely:** i.e., vile; **small beer:** weak, watery beer
7. **loosely studied:** negligently educated

FALSTAFF, ⌈*to Chief Justice*⌉
   Comes the King back from Wales, my noble lord?
CHIEF JUSTICE, ⌈*to Gower*⌉
   You shall have letters of me presently.   185
   Come. Go along with me, good Master Gower.
FALSTAFF   My lord!
CHIEF JUSTICE   What's the matter?
FALSTAFF   Master Gower, shall I entreat you with me to
   dinner?   190
GOWER   I must wait upon my good lord here. I thank
   you, good Sir John.
CHIEF JUSTICE   Sir John, you loiter here too long, being
   you are to take soldiers up in counties as you go.
FALSTAFF   Will you sup with me, Master Gower?   195
CHIEF JUSTICE   What foolish master taught you these
   manners, Sir John?
FALSTAFF   Master Gower, if they become me not, he was
   a fool that taught them me.—This is the right
   fencing grace, my lord: tap for tap, and so part fair.   200
CHIEF JUSTICE   Now the Lord lighten thee. Thou art a
   great fool.
                       ⟨*They* ⌈*separate and*⌉ *exit.*⟩

                       ⟨Scene 2⟩
            Enter the Prince ⌈*and*⌉ *Poins.*

PRINCE   Before God, I am exceeding weary.
POINS   Is 't come to that? I had thought weariness durst
   not have attached one of so high blood.
PRINCE   Faith, it does me, though it discolors the com-
   plexion of my greatness to acknowledge it. Doth it   5
   not show vilely in me to desire small beer?
POINS   Why, a prince should not be so loosely studied
   as to remember so weak a composition.

9. **Belike:** perhaps; **got:** begotten, conceived

11. **creature:** See longer note, page 252.

11–12. **these . . . considerations:** (1) i.e., my considering such **humble** things; (2) **these humble** things that I think about

15. **with these:** Most editors print F's "viz. these," which means "namely, these."

17–18. **for superfluity:** i.e., as an extra

18. **that:** i.e., Poins's **inventory of . . . shirts; tennis-court:** an enclosed oblong court or building for playing "real tennis" (i.e., "royal tennis") as opposed to lawn tennis

19–20. **it . . . there:** i.e., when you don't play tennis it means you are low on clean shirts   **keepest:** carry on, maintain   **racket:** uproar, disturbance (with wordplay on **racket** as the light bat used in playing tennis)

21–24. **the rest . . . kingdom:** perhaps, your vices have led to your pawning your shirts or using them to swaddle your illegitimate children (See longer note, page 252.)

25–26. **in the fault:** i.e., to blame

26. **whereupon:** on which account; **kindreds:** families

29. **idly:** (1) lazily; (2) foolishly

34. **breeding:** (1) parentage; (2) education

36. **Go to:** an expression of impatience; **stand:** i.e., encounter without flinching; **push:** blow; thrust

38. **meet:** suitable, fitting

40. **for fault of:** in default of, for want of

42. **Very hardly:** i.e., with great difficulty

PRINCE   Belike then my appetite was not princely got,
for, by my troth, I do now remember the poor   10
creature small beer. But indeed these humble considerations make me out of love with my greatness.
What a disgrace is it to me to remember thy name,
or to know thy face tomorrow, or to take note how
many pair of silk stockings thou hast—with these,   15
and those that were thy peach-colored ⟨ones⟩—or to
bear the inventory of thy shirts, as, one for superfluity and another for use. But that the tennis-court
keeper knows better than I, for it is a low ebb of
linen with thee when thou keepest not racket there,   20
as thou hast not done a great while, because the rest
of the low countries have ⟨made a shift to⟩ eat up thy
holland; [and God knows whether those that bawl
out the ruins of thy linen shall inherit His kingdom;
but the midwives say the children are not in the   25
fault, whereupon the world increases and kindreds
are mightily strengthened.]
POINS   How ill it follows, after you have labored so
hard, you should talk so idly! Tell me, how many
good young princes would do so, their fathers being   30
so sick as yours at this time is?
PRINCE   Shall I tell thee one thing, Poins?
POINS   Yes, faith, and let it be an excellent good thing.
PRINCE   It shall serve among wits of no higher breeding
than thine.   35
POINS   Go to. I stand the push of your one thing that
you will tell.
PRINCE   Marry, I tell thee it is not meet that I should be
sad, now my father is sick—albeit I could tell to
thee, as to one it pleases me, for fault of a better, to   40
call my friend, I could be sad, and sad indeed too.
POINS   Very hardly, upon such a subject.

45. **Let the end try the man:** Proverbial: "The end tries all."

48. **ostentation:** display

55. **keeps the roadway:** i.e., holds to the common way (of thinking)

57. **accites:** arouses

59. **lewd:** worthless, unprincipled

60. **engraffed:** closely attached

62. **spoke on:** i.e., spoken of

64. **second brother:** i.e., younger brother (and therefore without property)

65. **proper . . . hands:** i.e., a good man in a fight

69. **Christian:** i.e., a normal boy

69–70. **if . . . ape:** i.e., how Falstaff has turned him into a monkey (presumably by dressing him gaudily)

74. **blushing:** a mocking reference to Bardolph's drink-flushed face; **Wherefore:** why

PRINCE   By this hand, thou thinkest me as far in the
     devil's book as thou and Falstaff for obduracy and
     persistency. Let the end try the man. But I tell thee,   45
     my heart bleeds inwardly that my father is so sick;
     and keeping such vile company as thou art hath in
     reason taken from me all ostentation of sorrow.

POINS   The reason?

PRINCE   What wouldst thou think of me if I should   50
     weep?

POINS   I would think thee a most princely hypocrite.

PRINCE   It would be every man's thought, and thou art
     a blessed fellow to think as every man thinks. Never
     a man's thought in the world keeps the roadway   55
     better than thine. Every man would think me an
     hypocrite indeed. And what accites your most wor-
     shipful thought to think so?

POINS   Why, because you have been so lewd and so
     much engraffed to Falstaff.   60

PRINCE   And to thee.

POINS   By this light, I am well spoke on. I can hear it
     with mine own ears. The worst that they can say of
     me is that I am a second brother, and that I am a
     proper fellow of my hands, and those two things, I   65
     confess, I cannot help. By the Mass, here comes
     Bardolph.

Enter Bardolph and ⌐Page.⌐

PRINCE   And the boy that I gave Falstaff. He had him
     from me Christian, and look if the fat villain have
     not transformed him ape.   70

BARDOLPH   God save your Grace.

PRINCE   And yours, most noble Bardolph.

POINS, ⌐*to Bardolph*⌐   Come, you virtuous ass, you bash-
     ful fool, must you be blushing? Wherefore blush
     you now? What a maidenly man-at-arms are you   75

76–77. **get a pottle-pot's maidenhead:** i.e., drain a two-quart tankard of ale

78. **e'en now:** i.e., just a moment ago

78–79. **a red lattice:** i.e., an alehouse window

88. **Althea:** The Page confuses two mythological stories, **Althea's dream** about keeping a **firebrand** (line 89) burning and Hecuba's dream of giving birth to a **firebrand.**

90. **A crown's worth:** i.e., five shillings' worth

93. **cankers:** cankerworms (larvae that destroy flower buds) See picture below.

99. **good respect:** i.e., proper ceremony

100. **Martlemas:** i.e., Martinmas, the feastday of St. Martin celebrated on November 11 (Because Martinmas was a traditional time to slaughter cattle for the winter, the day was associated with beef, as was Falstaff, who, in *Henry IV, Part 1*, is called "my sweet beef.")

104. **this wen:** this excrescence or tumor (i.e., Falstaff)

105. **holds his place:** i.e., maintains his (privileged) position

108. **Every . . . that:** i.e., he makes sure that everyone knows his title

A cankerworm. (2.2.93)
From John Johnstone, [*Opera aliquot*] [1650–62].

become! Is 't such a matter to get a pottle-pot's
maidenhead?

PAGE   He calls me ⌜e'en now,⌝ my lord, through a red
lattice, and I could discern no part of his face from
the window. At last I spied his eyes, and methought   80
he had made two holes in the ale-wife's ⟨new⟩
petticoat and so peeped through.

PRINCE   Has not the boy profited?

BARDOLPH, ⌜to Page⌝   Away, you whoreson upright ⟨rab-
bit⟩, away!   85

PAGE   Away, you rascally Althea's dream, away!

PRINCE   Instruct us, boy. What dream, boy?

PAGE   Marry, my lord, Althea dreamt she was delivered
of a firebrand, and therefore I call him her dream.

PRINCE   A crown's worth of good interpretation. There   90
'tis, boy.   ⌜He gives the Page money.⌝

POINS   O, that this ⟨good⟩ blossom could be kept from
cankers! Well, there is sixpence to preserve thee.
                        ⌜He gives the Page money.⌝

BARDOLPH   An you do not make him ⟨be⟩ hanged among
you, the gallows shall have wrong.   95

PRINCE   And how doth thy master, Bardolph?

BARDOLPH   Well, my ⟨good⟩ lord. He heard of your
Grace's coming to town. There's a letter for you.
                        ⌜He gives the Prince a paper.⌝

POINS   Delivered with good respect. And how doth the
Martlemas your master?   100

BARDOLPH   In bodily health, sir.

POINS   Marry, the immortal part needs a physician, but
that moves not him. Though that be sick, it dies not.

PRINCE   I do allow this wen to be as familiar with me as
my dog, and he holds his place, for look you how he   105
writes.   ⌜He shows the letter to Poins.⌝

POINS ⌜reads the superscription⌝ *John Falstaff, knight.*
Every man must know that as oft as he has occasion

109. **name himself:** announce his own name

112. **takes upon him:** pretends

113. **conceive:** understand

113–14. **ready . . . cap:** The image is of a borrower eagerly doffing his **cap** to a lender. The phrase may be proverbial.

115. **fetch it:** i.e., derive their ancestry

116. **Japheth:** Genesis 10.1–5 traces the European peoples back to **Japheth,** one of Noah's three sons.

123. **brevity in breath:** wordplay on **brevity** as "shortness"

124. **commend me:** i.e., offer my greetings

127. **at idle times:** i.e., in times of idleness

129. **by yea and no:** a Puritan oath (See Matthew 5.34–37: "Swear not at all, . . . but let your communication be yea, yea; nay, nay.")

136. **twenty of:** a vague phrase for "a large number of"

A tavern.
From August Casimir Redel, *Apophtegmata symbolica* . . . [n.d.].

to name himself, even like those that are kin to the
King, for they never prick their finger but they say   110
"There's some of the King's blood spilt." "How
comes that?" says he that takes upon him not to
conceive. The answer is as ready as a ⌜borrower's⌝
cap: "I am the King's poor cousin, sir."

PRINCE Nay, they will be kin to us, or they will fetch it   115
from Japheth. But ⟨to⟩ the letter: ⌜*Reads.*⌝ *Sir John*
Falstaff, knight, to the son of the King nearest his
father, Harry Prince of Wales, greeting.

POINS Why, this is a certificate.

PRINCE Peace!   120
⌜*Reads.*⌝ *I will imitate the honorable Romans in*
brevity.

POINS He sure means brevity in breath, short-winded.

⌜PRINCE *reads*⌝ *I commend me to thee, I commend thee,*
and I leave thee. Be not too familiar with Poins, for he   125
misuses thy favors so much that he swears thou art to
marry his sister Nell. Repent at idle times as thou
mayst, and so farewell.
         Thine by yea and no, which is as much as
         to say, as thou usest him,   130
              Jack Falstaff with my ⟨familiars,⟩
              John with my brothers and sisters, and
              Sir John with all Europe.

POINS My lord, I'll steep this letter in sack and make
him eat it.   135

PRINCE That's to make him eat twenty of his words.
But do you use me thus, Ned? Must I marry your
sister?

POINS God send the wench no worse fortune! But I
never said so.   140

PRINCE Well, thus we play the fools with the time, and
the spirits of the wise sit in the clouds and mock us.
⌜*To Bardolph.*⌝ Is your master here in London?

BARDOLPH Yea, my lord.

146. **frank:** pigsty

147. **the old place:** Lines 145–47 have suggested to many that Falstaff's tavern is to be imagined as the Boar's Head, a sixteenth-century **Eastcheap** tavern.

149. **Ephesians:** i.e., drinking companions; **the old church:** St. Paul's Epistle to the Ephesians concludes its instructions about how members of the "new church" should live: "And be not drunk with wine, wherein is excess, but be fulfilled with the Spirit" (5.18).

153. **pagan:** i.e., prostitute (See page 128.)

154. **proper:** respectable, honest

156–57. **the town bull:** a bull kept in turn by the cattle breeders of a village

166. **should be some road:** i.e., must be as commonly available as a highway

167–68. **the way . . . London:** i.e., the busy Great North Road

169. **bestow himself:** i.e., behave

172. **jerkins:** close-fitting jackets

173. **drawers:** waiters, tapsters

174. **heavy descension:** grave or significant descent

175. **Jove's case:** The king of the Roman gods transformed himself into a **bull** in order to abduct Europa. (See page 216.)

177. **weigh:** be of equal value or importance

PRINCE   Where sups he? Doth the old boar feed in the   145
old frank?

BARDOLPH   At the old place, my lord, in Eastcheap.

PRINCE   What company?

PAGE   Ephesians, my lord, of the old church.

PRINCE   Sup any women with him?   150

PAGE   None, my lord, but old Mistress Quickly and
Mistress Doll Tearsheet.

PRINCE   What pagan may that be?

PAGE   A proper gentlewoman, sir, and a kinswoman of
my master's.   155

PRINCE   Even such kin as the parish heifers are to the
town bull.—Shall we steal upon them, Ned, at
supper?

POINS   I am your shadow, my lord. I'll follow you.

PRINCE   Sirrah—you, boy—and Bardolph, no word to   160
your master that I am yet come to town. There's for
your silence.   ⌜*He gives money.*⌝

BARDOLPH   I have no tongue, sir.

PAGE   And for mine, sir, I will govern it.

PRINCE   Fare you well. Go.   ⌜*Bardolph and Page exit.*⌝   165
This Doll Tearsheet should be some road.

POINS   I warrant you, as common as the way between
Saint Albans and London.

PRINCE   How might we see Falstaff bestow himself
tonight in his true colors, and not ourselves be   170
seen?

POINS   Put on two leathern jerkins and aprons, and
wait upon him at his table as drawers.

PRINCE   From a god to a bull: a heavy descension. It
was Jove's case. From a ⟨prince⟩ to a 'prentice: a low   175
transformation that shall be mine, for in everything
the purpose must weigh with the folly. Follow me,
Ned.

They exit.

2.3 Northumberland is persuaded by his daughter-in-law, Hotspur's widow, to abandon the other rebels.

---

1. **daughter:** i.e., daughter-in-law
2. **Give even way unto:** i.e., allow free scope to
4. **them:** i.e., **the times** (line 3); **to Percy:** i.e., to me (Northumberland's family name is "Percy.")
5. **given over:** i.e., given up (trying to persuade you)
8. **but my going, nothing:** i.e., nothing except my going
11. **more endeared:** i.e., bound or obligated by greater affection
14. **powers:** forces
17. **For yours, the:** i.e., as for yours, may the
18–19. **it . . . heaven:** perhaps, his honor shone like **the sun** in a clear sky
20. **chivalry:** men-at-arms
21. **glass:** looking glass, mirror
23. **He . . . gait:** i.e., the only men who did not imitate his walk were men without legs
24. **thick:** perhaps, rapidly and loudly (The contrast seems to be with the **perfection** [line 27] of speaking **low and tardily** [line 26], i.e., softly and slowly.)
27. **abuse:** bad or improper usage

⟨Scene 3⟩
*Enter Northumberland, his wife, and the wife to
Harry Percy.*

NORTHUMBERLAND
  I pray thee, loving wife and gentle daughter,
  Give even way unto my rough affairs.
  Put not you on the visage of the times
  And be, like them, to Percy troublesome.
LADY NORTHUMBERLAND
  I have given over. I will speak no more.   5
  Do what you will; your wisdom be your guide.
NORTHUMBERLAND
  Alas, sweet wife, my honor is at pawn,
  And, but my going, nothing can redeem it.
LADY PERCY
  O yet, for God's sake, go not to these wars.
  The time was, father, that you broke your word   10
  When you were more ⟨endeared⟩ to it than now,
  When your own Percy, when my heart's dear Harry,
  Threw many a northward look to see his father
  Bring up his powers; but he did long in vain.
  Who then persuaded you to stay at home?   15
  There were two honors lost, yours and your son's.
  For yours, the God of heaven brighten it.
  For his, it stuck upon him as the sun
  In the gray vault of heaven, and by his light
  Did all the chivalry of England move   20
  To do brave acts. He was indeed the glass
  Wherein the noble youth did dress themselves.
  ⟨He had no legs that practiced not his gait;
  And speaking thick, which nature made his blemish,
  Became the accents of the valiant;   25
  For those that could speak low and tardily
  Would turn their own perfection to abuse

29. **affections of delight:** inclinations toward pleasure

30. **humors of blood:** i.e., caprices of passion

31. **mark:** object of attention; **copy:** pattern, example; **book:** i.e., book of instructions

36. **In disadvantage:** i.e., in an unfavorable situation; **abide a field:** i.e., face a battle

38. **defensible:** capable of making a defense

40. **nice:** strict

45. **Monmouth's:** i.e., Prince Hal's

46–47. **Beshrew your heart:** a mild oath

49. **new lamenting:** i.e., lamenting anew; **ancient:** former

55. **of their . . . taste:** i.e., tested their strength

56. **get . . . vantage of:** i.e., obtain mastery over

60. **so suffered:** i.e., allowed to **try** his own strength; **came:** became

Gantelet

A gauntlet. (1.1.161)
From Louis de Gaya, *Traité des armes, des machines de guerre . . .* (1678).

To seem like him. So that in speech, in gait,
In diet, in affections of delight,
In military rules, humors of blood,   30
He was the mark and glass, copy and book,
That fashioned others. And him—O wondrous him!
O miracle of men!—him did you leave,
Second to none, unseconded by you,
To look upon the hideous god of war   35
In disadvantage, to abide a field
Where nothing but the sound of Hotspur's name
Did seem defensible. So you left him.
Never, O never, do his ghost the wrong
To hold your honor more precise and nice   40
With others than with him. Let them alone.
The Marshal and the Archbishop are strong.
Had my sweet Harry had but half their numbers,
Today might I, hanging on Hotspur's neck,
Have talked of Monmouth's grave.⟩   45
NORTHUMBERLAND   Beshrew your
    heart,
Fair daughter, you do draw my spirits from me
With new lamenting ancient oversights.
But I must go and meet with danger there,   50
Or it will seek me in another place
And find me worse provided.
LADY NORTHUMBERLAND   O, fly to Scotland
Till that the nobles and the armèd commons
Have of their puissance made a little taste.   55
LADY PERCY
If they get ground and vantage of the King,
Then join you with them like a rib of steel
To make strength stronger; but, for all our loves,
First let them try themselves. So did your son;
He was so suffered. So came I a widow,   60
And never shall have length of life enough

64. **recordation to:** commemoration of
67. **still-stand:** i.e., standstill
68. **Fain:** gladly
70. **resolve for:** i.e., decide to go to; **am I:** i.e., will I be

2.4 At Mistress Quickly's inn in Eastcheap, a fight erupts after Falstaff's ensign, Pistol, insults Doll Tearsheet. The disguised Prince Hal and Poins hear Falstaff's demeaning comments about them. Hal and Falstaff are summoned to the war.

———————

2. **applejohns:** i.e., old apples with withered skins
6–7. **putting . . . hat:** i.e., standing bareheaded as a sign of respect
10. **cover:** i.e., lay the cloth for the meal (As lines 1–21 are spoken, the "drawers" may be bringing on tables and chairs.)
11. **noise:** band of musicians
12. **Dispatch:** make haste
14. **straight:** straightway, immediately

To rain upon remembrance with mine eyes
That it may grow and sprout as high as heaven
For recordation to my noble husband.

NORTHUMBERLAND
Come, come, go in with me. 'Tis with my mind   65
As with the tide swelled up unto his height,
That makes a still-stand, running neither way.
Fain would I go to meet the Archbishop,
But many thousand reasons hold me back.
I will resolve for Scotland. There am I   70
Till time and vantage crave my company.

They exit.

⟨Scene 4⟩
Enter ⌜*Francis and another*⌝ *Drawer.*

FRANCIS   What the devil hast thou brought there—
applejohns? Thou knowest Sir John cannot endure
an applejohn.

⟨SECOND⟩ DRAWER   Mass, thou sayst true. The Prince
once set a dish of applejohns before him and told   5
him there were five more Sir Johns and, putting off
his hat, said "I will now take my leave of these six
dry, round, old, withered knights." It angered him
to the heart. But he hath forgot that.

FRANCIS   Why then, cover and set them down, and see if   10
thou canst find out Sneak's noise. Mistress Tearsheet would fain hear some music. [Dispatch. The
room where they supped is too hot. They'll come in
straight.

Enter Will.]

⌜WILL⌝   Sirrah, here will be the Prince and Master   15
Poins anon, and they will put on two of our jerkins

19. **old utis:** i.e., great fun

23. **temperality, pulsidge:** her mistakes for "temper" and "pulse"

27. **canaries:** i.e., canary (sweet wine); **searching:** penetrating, probing

30. **Hem:** perhaps a hiccup or a belch

33. **When . . . court:** A popular ballad, known as *Sir Launcelot du Lake,* began: "When Arthur first in court began, And was approvèd king."

34. **jordan:** chamber pot

37. **calm:** i.e., qualm (a fit of faintness or nausea)

38. **sect:** perhaps, sex; or, perhaps, occupation (as a prostitute)

38–39. **An . . . sick:** perhaps, if they are ever **calm** it is because they are **sick**

40. **muddy rascal:** i.e., dirty scoundrel (Falstaff replies, line 42, as if **rascal** had its meaning of "lean, inferior deer," and was thus not applicable to him.)

Tapping a hogshead. (2.4.64)
From Guillaume de La Perrière, *La morosophie* . . . (1553).

and aprons, and Sir John must not know of it.
Bardolph hath brought word.
⌜SECOND⌝ DRAWER By the Mass, here will be old utis. It
will be an excellent stratagem.   20
FRANCIS I'll see if I can find out Sneak.
                           He exits ⌜*with the Second Drawer.*⌝

       Enter ⟨*Hostess*⟩ *and Doll Tearsheet.*

HOSTESS I' faith, sweetheart, methinks now you are in
an excellent good temperality. Your pulsidge beats
as extraordinarily as heart would desire, and your
color, I warrant you, is as red as any rose, in good   25
truth, la. But, i' faith, you have drunk too much
canaries, and that's a marvellous searching wine,
and it perfumes the blood ere one can say "What's
this?" How do you now?
DOLL Better than I was. Hem.   30
HOSTESS Why, that's well said. A good heart's worth
gold. Lo, here comes Sir John.

       Enter Sir John ⟨*Falstaff.*⟩

FALSTAFF, ⌜*singing*⌝
       When Arthur first in court—
⌜*To Will.*⌝ Empty the jordan.   ⌜*Will exits.*⌝
       And was a worthy king—   35
How now, Mistress Doll?
HOSTESS Sick of a calm, yea, good faith.
FALSTAFF So is all her sect. An they be once in a calm,
they are sick.
DOLL A pox damn you, you muddy rascal. Is that all the   40
comfort you give me?
FALSTAFF You make fat rascals, Mistress Doll.
DOLL I make them? Gluttony and diseases make ⟨them⟩;
I make them not.

46. **catch of:** i.e., are infected by

49. **Yea . . . jewels:** possible wordplay on **catch** as "seize, take hold of" (i.e., you do indeed **catch** our jewelry)

50. **ouches:** ornamental brooches or buckles (with possible wordplay on "scabs, sores")

50–54. **to serve . . . bravely:** Falstaff plays with military language (**serve, breach, pike, surgery, charged chambers**) that also has reference to sex and to venereal disease and its treatment. **chambers:** small cannon

55. **conger:** big eel

58. **rheumatic:** her error, perhaps, for "splenetic" or "choleric" (i.e., irritable)

59. **confirmities:** her error for "infirmities"

60. **What the good-year:** i.e., "what the devil"

61. **weaker vessel:** proverbial, from 1 Peter 3.7, which refers to "the wife" as **"the weaker vessel"**

64. **hogshead:** cask of wine (See page 82.)

64–65. **whole . . . stuff:** i.e., a shipload of Bordeaux wine (A **venture** referred to the goods put at risk.)

65. **hulk:** ship

70. **Ancient:** i.e., ensign (the lowest ranking commissioned officer in the infantry)

72. **swaggering:** i.e., blustering, bullying

75. **I'll:** i.e., I will have

FALSTAFF   If the cook help to make the gluttony, you   45
    help to make the diseases, Doll. We catch of you,
    Doll, we catch of you. Grant that, my poor virtue,
    grant that.
DOLL   Yea, joy, our chains and our jewels.
FALSTAFF   Your brooches, pearls, and ouches—for to   50
    serve bravely is to come halting off, you know; to
    come off the breach with his pike bent bravely, and
    to surgery bravely, to venture upon the charged
    chambers bravely—
[DOLL   Hang yourself, you muddy conger, hang yourself!]   55
HOSTESS   By my troth, this is the old fashion. You two
    never meet but you fall to some discord. You are
    both, i' good truth, as rheumatic as two dry toasts.
    You cannot one bear with another's confirmities.
    What the good-year! One must bear, and ⌜to Doll⌝   60
    that must be you. You are the weaker vessel, as they
    say, the emptier vessel.
DOLL   Can a weak empty vessel bear such a huge full
    hogshead? There's a whole merchant's venture of
    Bordeaux stuff in him. You have not seen a hulk   65
    better stuffed in the hold.—Come, I'll be friends
    with thee, Jack. Thou art going to the wars, and
    whether I shall ever see thee again or no, there is
    nobody cares.

Enter Drawer.

DRAWER   Sir, Ancient Pistol's below and would speak   70
    with you.
DOLL   Hang him, swaggering rascal! Let him not come
    hither. It is the foul-mouthed'st rogue in England.
HOSTESS   If he swagger, let him not come here. No, by
    my faith, I must live among my neighbors. I'll no   75
    swaggerers. I am in good name and fame with the

83. **mine ancient:** i.e., my ensign (The Hostess responds, line 85, as if **ancient** here meant "old.")

84. **Tilly-vally:** an exclamation of impatience

86. **debuty:** i.e., deputy (a petty official standing in for the alderman)

89. **by:** i.e., nearby

91. **civil:** well-bred, polite; **are . . . name:** i.e., have a bad reputation

92. **whereupon:** i.e., why

95. **companions:** fellows (a contemptuous term)

98. **tame cheater:** decoy in a con game (who did not **swagger** for fear of scaring off his prey)

100. **swagger:** quarrel; **Barbary hen:** i.e., guinea fowl (known for its mild manner)

103. **Cheater:** The Hostess may assume that the word carries its original meaning of "escheator," an officer of the king appointed by the Lord Treasurer.

very best. Shut the door. There comes no swaggerers here. I have not lived all this while to have
swaggering now. Shut the door, I pray you.

FALSTAFF Dost thou hear, hostess?　　　　　　　　　　80

HOSTESS Pray you pacify yourself, Sir John. There
comes no swaggerers here.

FALSTAFF Dost thou hear? It is mine ancient.

HOSTESS Tilly-vally, Sir John, ne'er tell me. And your
ancient swaggerer comes not in my doors. I was　　85
before Master Tisick the debuty t' other day, and, as
he said to me—'twas no longer ago than Wednesday last, i' good faith—"Neighbor Quickly," says
he—Master Dumb, our minister, was by then—
"Neighbor Quickly," says he, "receive those that　90
are civil, for," said he, "you are in an ill name."
Now he said so, I can tell whereupon. "For," says
he, "you are an honest woman, and well thought
on. Therefore take heed what guests you receive.
Receive," says he, "no swaggering companions."　95
There comes none here. You would bless you to
hear what he said. No, I'll no swaggerers.

FALSTAFF He's no swaggerer, hostess, a tame cheater, i'
faith. You may stroke him as gently as a puppy
greyhound. He'll not swagger with a Barbary hen if　100
her feathers turn back in any show of resistance.—
Call him up, drawer.　　　　　⌜*Drawer exits.*⌝

HOSTESS "Cheater" call you him? I will bar no honest
man my house, nor no cheater, but I do not love
swaggering. By my troth, I am the worse when one　105
says "swagger." Feel, masters, how I shake; look
you, I warrant you.

DOLL So you do, hostess.

HOSTESS Do I? Yea, in very truth, do I, an 'twere an
aspen leaf. I cannot abide swaggerers.　　　　　110

112. **Pistol:** The ensign's name gives rise to word-play on its meaning as a weapon that discharges and thus on its sexual connotations.

112–14. **I charge . . . hostess:** perhaps, I will pledge you if you will pay for the drink

117. **pistol-proof:** i.e., safe from sexual assault and from Pistol himself; **not hardly:** i.e., by no means

118. **offend:** harm

122. **Mistress Dorothy:** i.e., Doll

124, 126. **companion, mate:** terms of contempt

125. **lack-linen:** i.e., shirtless

126–27. **meat . . . master:** This way of describing a woman in a sexual relation became proverbial, but perhaps originated in this play.

129. **bung:** thieves' slang for **cutpurse** or pick-pocket

131. **chaps:** i.e., jaws; **cuttle:** i.e., cutter, bully

132. **basket-hilt . . . juggler:** i.e., worn-out imposter (A **basket-hilt** was a basket-shaped web for protecting the swordsman's hand.)

134. **points:** tagged laces or cords (perhaps for attaching armor); **Much:** a derisive exclamation indicating incredulity

135. **God . . . but:** i.e., if God lets me live; **murder:** i.e., destroy

141. **Captain:** Pistol is, of course, several ranks below captain.

Enter Ancient Pistol, ⟨Bardolph, and⟩ ⌐Page.⌐

PISTOL God save you, Sir John.

FALSTAFF Welcome, Ancient Pistol. Here, Pistol, I
charge you with a cup of sack. Do you discharge
upon mine hostess.

PISTOL I will discharge upon her, Sir John, with two 115
bullets.

FALSTAFF She is pistol-proof. Sir, you shall not hardly
offend her.

HOSTESS Come, I'll drink no proofs nor no bullets. I'll
drink no more than will do me good, for no man's 120
pleasure, I.

PISTOL Then, to you, Mistress Dorothy! I will charge
you.

DOLL Charge me? I scorn you, scurvy companion.
What, you poor, base, rascally, cheating lack-linen 125
mate! Away, you mouldy rogue, away! I am meat for
your master.

PISTOL I know you, Mistress Dorothy.

DOLL Away, you cutpurse rascal, you filthy bung, away!
By this wine, I'll thrust my knife in your mouldy 130
chaps an you play the saucy cuttle with me. Away,
you bottle-ale rascal, you basket-hilt stale juggler,
you. Since when, I pray you, sir? God's light, with
two points on your shoulder? Much!

PISTOL God let me not live but I will murder your ruff 135
for this.

[FALSTAFF No more, Pistol. I would not have you go off
here. Discharge yourself of our company, Pistol.]

HOSTESS No, good Captain Pistol, not here, sweet captain! 140

DOLL Captain? Thou abominable damned cheater, art
thou not ashamed to be called captain? An captains

143. **truncheon:** i.e., beat (with a truncheon)

148. **stewed prunes:** a dish associated with brothels

151. **before . . . ill sorted:** i.e., before it got into bad company (**Occupy** had come to mean "copulate.")

156. **of her:** i.e., on her

158–59. **Pluto's damnèd lake:** perhaps, the River Styx in the mythological underworld, of which **Pluto** was king (Pistol's speech is characterized by mangled lines of poetry, archaic language, and scraps of verse from other plays.)

159. **Erebus:** usually, in classical mythology, the place of darkness through which the dead must pass; here, perhaps, the son of Chaos

162. **Hiren:** the name of the sword of the romance hero Amadis du Gaul

163. **Peesell:** i.e., pizzle (an animal's penis)

164. **beseek:** i.e., beseech; **aggravate:** her mistake perhaps for "moderate"

165. **humors:** See longer note, page 253.

166–67. **hollow . . . day:** These lines parody Marlowe's *Tamburlaine, Part II* (c. 1587): "Holla, ye pampered jades of Asia! What, can ye draw but twenty miles a day . . . ?"

168. **Caesars, cannibals:** See longer note, page 253. **Troyant:** i.e., Trojan (Trojans and **Greeks** were bitter enemies in the so-called Trojan War.)

169. **Cerberus:** in Greek mythology, the monstrous three-headed dog guarding the gateway to the underworld (See page 100.)

170. **welkin:** sky; **fall foul for toys:** i.e., quarrel over trifles

174. **anon:** i.e., soon

were of my mind, they would truncheon you out for
taking their names upon you before you have
earned them. You a captain? You slave, for what? 145
For tearing a poor whore's ruff in a bawdy house?
He a captain! Hang him, rogue. He lives upon
mouldy stewed prunes and dried cakes. A captain?
God's light, these villains will make the word as
odious [as the word "occupy," which was an excel- 150
lent good word before it was ill sorted.] Therefore
captains had need look to 't.

BARDOLPH, ⌜to Pistol⌝ Pray thee go down, good ancient.

FALSTAFF Hark thee hither, Mistress Doll.

PISTOL, ⌜to Bardolph⌝ Not I. I tell thee what, Corporal 155
Bardolph, I could tear her. I'll be revenged of her.

PAGE Pray thee go down.

PISTOL I'll see her damned first to Pluto's damnèd
lake, by this hand, to th' infernal deep with Erebus
and tortures vile also. Hold hook and line, say I. 160
Down, down, dogs! Down, ⟨Fates!⟩ Have we not
Hiren here?   ⌜He draws his sword.⌝

HOSTESS Good Captain Peesell, be quiet. 'Tis very late,
i' faith. I beseek you now, aggravate your choler.

PISTOL These be good humors indeed. Shall pack- 165
horses and hollow pampered jades of Asia, which
cannot go but thirty mile a day, compare with
Caesars and with cannibals and Troyant Greeks?
Nay, rather damn them with King Cerberus, and let
the welkin roar. Shall we fall foul for toys?   170

HOSTESS By my troth, captain, these are very bitter
words.

BARDOLPH Begone, good ancient. This will grow to a
brawl anon.

PISTOL ⟨Die⟩ men like dogs! Give crowns like pins! Have 175
we not Hiren here?

177. **there's . . . here:** The word **Hiren,** a corruption of the name "Irene," is understood by the Hostess as referring to a woman.

180. **feed . . . Calipolis:** a parody of a line from the play *The Battle of Alcazar* (c. 1594)

181. **give 's:** i.e., give us

181–82. **Si . . . contento:** i.e., if fortune torments me, hope contents me (in a mixture of Italian and Spanish)

182. **broadsides:** i.e., discharges of artillery from a ship of war

183. **give fire:** shoot

185. **full points:** complete stops; **etceteras nothings:** Both words were sometimes used to refer to the vagina.

187. **neaf:** fist

188. **seven stars:** the Pleiades

190. **fustian:** worthless, pretentious

191–92. **Galloway nags:** i.e., common prostitutes (literally, small horses from Scotland, but **nags** were also prostitutes)

193. **Quoit:** i.e., throw (as if he were a quoit)

193–94. **shove-groat shilling:** the coin used in playing **shove-groat** (a table game like shuffleboard)

198. **imbrue:** drench with blood

200. **untwind:** i.e., untwine

200–01. **Sisters Three:** i.e., Fates (one of whom, **Atropos,** cuts the thread of one's life) See page 102.

202. **toward:** about to happen

206–7. **keeping house:** i.e., running the tavern

207. **tirrits:** i.e., terrors, fits of fear

HOSTESS   O' my word, captain, there's none such here.
What the good-year, do you think I would deny her?
For God's sake, be quiet.

PISTOL   Then feed and be fat, my fair Calipolis. Come,   180
give 's some sack. *Si fortune me tormente, sperato
me contento.* Fear we broadsides? No, let the fiend
give fire. Give me some sack, and, sweetheart, lie
thou there. ⌐*Laying down his sword.*⌐ Come we to
full points here? And are etceteras nothings?   185

FALSTAFF   Pistol, I would be quiet.

PISTOL   Sweet knight, I kiss thy neaf. What, we have
seen the seven stars.

DOLL   For God's sake, thrust him downstairs. I cannot
endure such a fustian rascal.   190

PISTOL   "Thrust him downstairs"? Know we not Galloway nags?

FALSTAFF   Quoit him down, Bardolph, like a shove-
groat shilling. Nay, an he do nothing but speak
nothing, he shall be nothing here.   195

BARDOLPH   Come, get you downstairs.

PISTOL, ⌐*taking up his sword*⌐ What, shall we have
incision? Shall we imbrue? Then death rock me
asleep, abridge my doleful days. Why then, let
grievous, ghastly, gaping wounds untwind the Sis-   200
ters Three. Come, Atropos, I say.

HOSTESS   Here's goodly stuff toward!

FALSTAFF   Give me my rapier, boy.

DOLL   I pray thee, Jack, I pray thee do not draw.

FALSTAFF, ⌐*to Pistol*⌐ Get you downstairs. ⌐*They fight.*⌐   205

HOSTESS   Here's a goodly tumult. I'll forswear keeping
house afore I'll be in these tirrits and frights. So,
murder, I warrant now. Alas, alas, put up your
naked weapons, put up your naked weapons.
                              ⌐*Bardolph and Pistol exit.*⌐

DOLL   I pray thee, Jack, be quiet. The rascal's gone. Ah,   210
you whoreson little valiant villain, you.

213. **shrewd:** sharp, severe

220. **chops:** fat cheeks

221, 222. **Hector, Agamemnon:** military heroes and leaders in the Trojan War (See page 208.)

223. **Nine Worthies:** nine famous men from history and mythology

224–25. **toss . . . blanket:** a rough form of punishment

227. **canvass:** i.e., toss

228. **music is:** i.e., musicians are

232. **like a church:** probably referring to Falstaff's size or his immobility

233. **tidy:** plump; **Bartholomew boar-pig:** i.e., roast pig sold at Bartholomew Fair

234. **foining:** copulating (literally, thrusting with a sharp weapon)

237–38. **death's-head:** i.e., a memento mori, a reminder of one's mortality (literally, a skull) See below.

239. **what . . . of:** i.e., how would you describe the prince (See longer note to **humors**, 2.4.165, page 253.)

A death's-head ring. (2.4.237–38)
From James Orchard Halliwell-Phillipps, *Some account of the antiquities . . . in the possession of James Orchard Halliwell . . .* (1852).

HOSTESS, ⌐*to Falstaff*⌐ Are you not hurt i' th' groin?
Methought he made a shrewd thrust at your belly.

⌐*Enter Bardolph.*⌐

FALSTAFF Have you turned him out o' doors?
BARDOLPH Yea, sir. The rascal's drunk. You have hurt 215
him, sir, i' th' shoulder.
FALSTAFF A rascal to brave me!
DOLL Ah, you sweet little rogue, you. Alas, poor ape,
how thou sweat'st! Come, let me wipe thy face.
Come on, you whoreson chops. Ah, rogue, i' faith, I 220
love thee. Thou art as valorous as Hector of Troy,
worth five of Agamemnon, and ten times better
than the Nine Worthies. Ah, villain!
FALSTAFF Ah, rascally slave! I will toss the rogue in a
blanket. 225
DOLL Do, an thou darest for thy heart. An thou dost, I'll
canvass thee between a pair of sheets.

Enter ⌐*Musicians and Francis.*⌐

PAGE The music is come, sir.
FALSTAFF Let them play.—Play, sirs.—Sit on my knee,
Doll. A rascal bragging slave! The rogue fled from 230
me like quicksilver.
DOLL I' faith, and thou followed'st him like a church.
Thou whoreson little tidy Bartholomew boar-pig,
when wilt thou leave fighting a-days and foining a-
nights and begin to patch up thine old body for 235
heaven?

Enter ⌐*behind them*⌐ *Prince and Poins* ⟨*disguised.*⟩

FALSTAFF Peace, good Doll. Do not speak like a death's-
head; do not bid me remember mine end.
DOLL Sirrah, what humor's the Prince of?
FALSTAFF A good shallow young fellow, he would have 240

241. **pantler:** household officer responsible for the bread; **chipped:** i.e., cut the crust off

245. **Tewkesbury:** a market town in Gloucestershire, famous for its **mustard** balls

246. **conceit:** i.e., imagination, wit

250. **drinks . . . flap-dragons:** perhaps, **drinks** brandy on which flaming **candles' ends** float

251. **wild mare:** i.e., seesaw

252. **joint stools:** stools made of parts fitted together

253–54. **sign of the Leg:** perhaps, sign over a bootmaker's shop

254. **bate:** i.e., discord

255. **gambol:** playful

257. **admits him:** i.e., includes him among his friends

260. **nave:** wordplay on Falstaff's knavery and his roundness

261. **have . . . off:** punishment for defaming the royal family

262. **before:** in front of

263–64. **Look . . . parrot:** perhaps, see how the old man is having his head scratched   **elder:** (1) old man; (2) elder tree   **poll:** head (with perhaps a reference to the familiar name for the **parrot**)

268–69. **Saturn . . . conjunction:** wordplay on **Saturn** as the Roman god (and the planet) connected with old age and melancholy and **Venus** as the goddess (and planet) connected with youth and love

270. **fiery . . . man:** i.e., Bardolph, whose drink-flushed face is like the **fiery trigon,** the conjunction of the "fiery" constellations Aries, Leo, and Sagittarius

(continued)

made a good pantler; he would 'a chipped bread
well.

DOLL They say Poins has a good wit.

FALSTAFF He a good wit? Hang him, baboon. His wit's
as thick as Tewkesbury mustard. There's no more 245
conceit in him than is in a mallet.

DOLL Why does the Prince love him so then?

FALSTAFF Because their legs are both of a bigness, and
he plays at quoits well, and eats conger and fennel,
and drinks off candles' ends for flap-dragons, and 250
rides the wild mare with the boys, and jumps upon
joint stools, and swears with a good grace, and
wears his boots very smooth like unto the sign of
the Leg, and breeds no bate with telling of discreet
stories, and such other gambol faculties he has that 255
show a weak mind and an able body, for the which
the Prince admits him; for the Prince himself is
such another. The weight of a hair will turn ⟨the⟩
scales between their avoirdupois.

PRINCE, ⌜*aside to Poins*⌝ Would not this nave of a wheel 260
have his ears cut off?

POINS Let's beat him before his whore.

PRINCE Look whe'er the withered elder hath not his
poll clawed like a parrot.

POINS Is it not strange that desire should so many years 265
outlive performance?

FALSTAFF Kiss me, Doll.

PRINCE, ⌜*aside to Poins*⌝ Saturn and Venus this year in
conjunction! What says th' almanac to that?

POINS And look whether the fiery trigon, his man, be 270
not lisping to his ⟨master's⟩ old tables, his notebook,
his counsel keeper.

FALSTAFF, ⌜*to Doll*⌝ Thou dost give me flattering busses.

DOLL By my troth, I kiss thee with a most constant
heart. 275

FALSTAFF I am old, I am old.

271–72. **lisping . . . keeper:** i.e., courting Mistress Quickly (**Tables** [i.e., writing tablet], **notebook,** and **counsel keeper** refer to her role as his confidante.)

273. **busses:** kisses

279. **stuff:** material; **kirtle:** gown

285. **harken . . . end:** i.e., wait and see (proverbial)

288–89. **A . . . brother:** Falstaff pretends that he is seeing men who simply look like the Prince and Poins. **Poins his:** i.e., Poins's

290. **globe . . . continents:** wordplay on **continents** as "land masses," as "containers," and as "contents"

301. **by . . . blood:** Falstaff swears by Doll's wanton **flesh** and **corrupt blood.**

305. **take . . . heat:** Proverbial: "Strike while the iron is hot."

306. **candle-mine:** i.e., mine of tallow for making candles

308. **honest:** chaste

311. **hear me:** i.e., hear what I said about you earlier

DOLL   I love thee better than I love e'er a scurvy young
     boy of them all.

FALSTAFF   What stuff wilt ⟨thou⟩ have a kirtle of? I shall
     receive money o' Thursday; ⟨thou⟩ shalt have a cap   280
     tomorrow. A merry song! Come, it grows late. We'll
     to bed. Thou 'lt forget me when I am gone.

DOLL   By my troth, thou 'lt set me a-weeping an thou
     sayst so. Prove that ever I dress myself handsome till
     thy return. Well, harken a' th' end.   285

FALSTAFF   Some sack, Francis.

PRINCE, POINS, ⌜*coming forward*⌝   Anon, anon, sir.

FALSTAFF   Ha? A bastard son of the King's?—And art
     not thou Poins his brother?

PRINCE   Why, thou globe of sinful continents, what a   290
     life dost thou lead?

FALSTAFF   A better than thou. I am a gentleman. Thou
     art a drawer.

PRINCE   Very true, sir, and I come to draw you out by
     the ears.   295

HOSTESS   O, the Lord preserve thy ⟨good⟩ Grace! By my
     troth, welcome to London. Now the Lord bless that
     sweet face of thine. O Jesu, are you come from
     Wales?

FALSTAFF, ⌜*to Prince*⌝   Thou whoreson mad compound   300
     of majesty, by this light flesh and corrupt blood,
     thou art welcome.

DOLL   How? You fat fool, I scorn you.

POINS   My lord, he will drive you out of your revenge
     and turn all to a merriment if you take not the heat.   305

PRINCE, ⌜*to Falstaff*⌝   You whoreson candle-mine, you,
     how vilely did you speak of me ⟨even⟩ now before
     this honest, virtuous, civil gentlewoman!

HOSTESS   God's blessing of your good heart, and so she
     is, by my troth.   310

FALSTAFF, ⌜*to Prince*⌝   Didst thou hear me?

312–13. **you knew . . . Hill:** In *Henry IV, Part 1* Falstaff excuses his failure to fight the disguised prince by claiming he knew the prince even in disguise.

328. **is to:** i.e., should

333. **to close:** i.e., in order to come to terms

338. **pricked down:** i.e., picked out, marked

339. **privy kitchen:** i.e., own personal **kitchen**

340. **malt-worms:** i.e., drunkards; **For:** i.e., as for

341, 342. **good angel, devil:** two guiding forces (as in morality plays)

343. **For:** as regards (as also in lines 344 and 345)

345. **burns:** infects (with venereal disease)

346. **for that:** i.e., for lending money (See longer note, page 253.)

Cerberus. (2.4.169)
From Vincenzo Cartari, *Imagines deorum . . .* (1581).

PRINCE Yea, and you knew me as you did when you ran away by Gad's Hill. You knew I was at your back, and spoke it on purpose to try my patience.

FALSTAFF No, no, no, not so. I did not think thou wast 315 within hearing.

PRINCE I shall drive you, then, to confess the wilfull abuse, and then I know how to handle you.

FALSTAFF No abuse, Hal, o' mine honor, no abuse.

PRINCE Not to dispraise me and call me pantler and 320 bread-chipper and I know not what?

FALSTAFF No abuse, Hal.

POINS No abuse?

FALSTAFF No abuse, Ned, i' th' world, honest Ned, none. I dispraised him before the wicked, (⌜to 325 Prince⌝) that the wicked might not fall in love with thee; in which doing, I have done the part of a careful friend and a true subject, and thy father is to give me thanks for it. No abuse, Hal.—None, Ned, none. No, faith, boys, none. 330

PRINCE See now whether pure fear and entire coward-ice doth not make thee wrong this virtuous gentle-woman to close with us. Is she of the wicked, is thine hostess here of the wicked, or is thy boy of the wicked, or honest Bardolph, whose zeal burns in 335 his nose, of the wicked?

POINS Answer, thou dead elm, answer.

FALSTAFF The fiend hath pricked down Bardolph ir recoverable, and his face is Lucifer's privy kitchen, where he doth nothing but roast malt-worms. For 340 the boy, there is a good angel about him, but the devil blinds him too.

PRINCE For the women?

FALSTAFF For one of them, she's in hell already and burns poor souls. For th' other, I owe her money, 345 and whether she be damned for that I know not.

348–49. **quit for:** i.e., (1) absolved of; (2) deprived of; (3) repaid for

350–51. **suffering . . . law:** i.e., (1) allowing meat to be served during Lent; (2) allowing prostitution in your inn

352. **howl:** i.e., in hell

353. **vitlars:** i.e., victuallers, keepers of eating houses

363. **posts:** i.e., messengers (arriving on post-horses)

366. **Bareheaded:** a sign of their disarray (A hat was a standard item of male dress.)

368. **feel . . . blame:** i.e., feel guilty, blameworthy

370. **commotion:** sedition, insurrection; **south:** i.e., south wind (which brings storms)

371. **Borne:** laden

The Fates. (2.4.200–01)
From Vincenzo Cartari, *Imagines deorum* . . . (1581).

HOSTESS No, I warrant you.

FALSTAFF No, I think thou art not. I think thou art quit
for that. Marry, there is another indictment upon
thee for suffering flesh to be eaten in thy house 350
contrary to the law, for the which I think thou wilt
howl.

HOSTESS All vitlars do so. What's a joint of mutton or
two in a whole Lent?

PRINCE, ⌜*to Doll*⌝ You, gentlewoman. 355

DOLL What says your Grace?

FALSTAFF His grace says that which his flesh rebels
against.

Peto knocks at door.

HOSTESS Who knocks so loud at door? Look to th' door
there, Francis. �os *Francis exits.* ⌝ 360

⟨*Enter Peto.*⟩

PRINCE Peto, how now, what news?

PETO
The King your father is at Westminster,
And there are twenty weak and wearied posts
Come from the north, and as I came along
I met and overtook a dozen captains, 365
Bareheaded, sweating, knocking at the taverns
And asking everyone for Sir John Falstaff.

PRINCE
By heaven, Poins, I feel me much to blame
So idly to profane the precious time
When tempest of commotion, like the south 370
Borne with black vapor, doth begin to melt
And drop upon our bare unarmèd heads.—
Give me my sword and cloak.—Falstaff, good
night. *Prince,* ⌜*Peto,*⌝ *and Poins exit.*

FALSTAFF Now comes in the sweetest morsel of the 375
night, and we must hence and leave it unpicked.

380. **presently:** at once
381. **stay:** wait
385. **undeserver:** i.e., unworthy man
387. **post:** hastily
392. **peasecod time:** i.e., the season for peas
400. **blubbered:** i.e., her eyes flooded with tears

A tavern or a brothel.
From *Le centre de l'amour* . . . [1650?].

(⌐*Knocking. Bardolph exits.*¬) More knocking at the
door? (⌐*Bardolph returns.*¬) How now, what's the
matter?

BARDOLPH
  You must away to court, sir, presently.   380
  A dozen captains stay at door for you.

FALSTAFF, ⌐*to Page*¬ Pay the musicians, sirrah.—
  Farewell, hostess.—Farewell, Doll. You see, my
  good wenches, how men of merit are sought after.
  The undeserver may sleep when the man of action   385
  is called on. Farewell, good wenches. If I be not sent
  away post, I will see you again ere I go.

DOLL   I cannot speak. If my heart be not ready to
  burst—well, sweet Jack, have a care of thyself.

FALSTAFF   Farewell, farewell.   390
          He exits ⌐with Bardolph, Page, and Musicians.¬

HOSTESS   Well, fare thee well. I have known thee these
  twenty-nine years, come peasecod time, but an
  honester and truer-hearted man—well, fare thee
  well.

BARDOLPH, ⌐*within*¬ Mistress Tearsheet!   395

HOSTESS   What's the matter?

BARDOLPH, ⌐*within*¬   Bid Mistress Tearsheet come to my
  master.

HOSTESS   O, run, Doll, run, run, good Doll. [Come.—
  She comes blubbered.—Yea! Will you come, Doll?]   400
                                        They exit.

HENRY IV
Part 2

ACT 3

3.1 An ill and anxious King Henry IV consults with Warwick.

---

0 SD. **nightgown:** i.e., dressing gown (In the Quarto the stage direction reads *"Enter the King in his night-gowne alone."* Since the king immediately sends someone to deliver a message, the word "alone" in the direction probably signals that the king is attended only by his page. For an analogous use of *alone* in a Quarto stage direction, see the textual note to 1.2.0 SD, page 257.)

2. **o'erread:** read through

6. **soft:** mild, gentle

9. **cribs:** hovels

10. **uneasy:** uncomfortable; **thee:** i.e., yourself

13. **state:** splendor, magnificence

15. **dull:** (1) drowsy; (2) foolish

17. **watch-case:** perhaps, a place where one stands watch; **'larum:** i.e., alarm

20. **rude:** turbulent

21. **visitation:** violent assault

⟨ACT 3⟩

⟨Scene 1⟩
Enter the King in his nightgown ⟨with a Page.⟩

KING
Go call the Earls of Surrey and of Warwick;
But, ere they come, bid them o'erread these letters
And well consider of them. Make good speed.
⌜*Page ⟨exits.⟩*⌝
How many thousand of my poorest subjects
Are at this hour asleep! O sleep, O gentle sleep,   5
Nature's soft nurse, how have I frighted thee,
That thou no more wilt weigh my eyelids down
And steep my senses in forgetfulness?
Why rather, sleep, liest thou in smoky cribs,
Upon uneasy pallets stretching thee,   10
And hushed with buzzing night-flies to thy slumber,
Than in the perfumed chambers of the great,
Under the canopies of costly state,
And lulled with sound of sweetest melody?
O thou dull god, why liest thou with the vile   15
In loathsome beds and leavest the kingly couch
A watch-case or a common 'larum bell?
Wilt thou upon the high and giddy ⟨mast⟩
Seal up the shipboy's eyes and rock his brains
In cradle of the rude imperious surge   20
And in the visitation of the winds,

22. **Who:** i.e., which
24. **deafing:** deafening
25. **That:** i.e., so that; **hurly:** uproar, tumult
26. **partial:** biased, unfair
29. **With . . . boot:** i.e., with, in addition, everything helpful to bring about sleep **appliances:** things applied as a means to an end **to boot:** in addition
30. **low:** i.e., humble persons, commoners
31. **Uneasy . . . crown:** Proverbial: "Crowns have cares."
32. **good morrows:** a salutation used in the morning
33. **Is it good morrow:** i.e., is it morning
39. **rank:** festering
41. **distempered:** ill
42. **his:** i.e., its
43. **little:** i.e., a little
46. **revolution . . . times:** i.e., changes brought about through time (but with wordplay on **revolution** as a violent overthrow of a ruler or government)
47. **continent:** land, earth

Who take the ruffian ⟨billows⟩ by the top,
Curling their monstrous heads and hanging them
With deafing clamor in the slippery clouds
That with the hurly death itself awakes? 25
Canst thou, O partial sleep, give ⟨thy⟩ repose
To the wet ⟨sea-boy⟩ in an hour so rude,
And, in the calmest and most stillest night,
With all appliances and means to boot,
Deny it to a king? Then, happy low, lie down. 30
Uneasy lies the head that wears a crown.

Enter Warwick, Surrey and Sir John Blunt.

WARWICK
Many good morrows to your Majesty.
KING Is it good morrow, lords?
WARWICK 'Tis one o'clock, and past.
KING
Why then, good morrow to you all, my lords. 35
Have you read o'er the letter that I sent you?
WARWICK We have, my liege.
KING
Then you perceive the body of our kingdom
How foul it is, what rank diseases grow,
And with what danger near the heart of it. 40
WARWICK
It is but as a body yet distempered,
Which to his former strength may be restored
With good advice and little medicine.
My Lord Northumberland will soon be cooled.
KING
O God, that one might read the book of fate 45
And see the revolution of the times
Make mountains level, and the continent,
Weary of solid firmness, melt itself
Into the sea, and other times to see

50–51. **beachy . . . hips:** The image here is of the shoreline worn like a **girdle** around the **hips** of the sea-god Neptune; when the ocean recedes, the beach expands.

55. **crosses:** troubles, misfortunes

56. **the book:** i.e., the **book of fate** (line 45)

57. **gone:** i.e., past (The story that he tells in lines 57–80 was dramatized by Shakespeare in *Richard II*.)

61. **This Percy:** i.e., Northumberland

63. **under my foot:** at my disposal

64 **to . . . Richard:** i.e., to Richard's face

65. **by:** i.e., nearby, standing by

66. **Nevil:** Historically, the earldom of Warwick at this time was held by the Beauchamp (not the Nevil) family.

69. **checked:** rebuked; **rated:** chided

74. **bowed the state:** i.e., forced **the state** into submission

77–78. **foul . . . corruption:** The image is of an abscess reaching maturation and breaking.

79. **this same time's:** i.e., today's

82. **Figuring:** portraying; **deceased:** past

The beachy girdle of the ocean   50
Too wide for Neptune's hips; how chance's mocks
And changes fill the cup of alteration
With divers liquors! [O, if this were seen,
The happiest youth, viewing his progress through,
What perils past, what crosses to ensue,   55
Would shut the book and sit him down and die.]
'Tis not ten years gone
Since Richard and Northumberland, great friends,
Did feast together, and in two ⟨years⟩ after
Were they at wars. It is but eight years since   60
This Percy was the man nearest my soul,
Who like a brother toiled in my affairs
And laid his love and life under my foot,
Yea, for my sake, even to the eyes of Richard
Gave him defiance. But which of you was by—   65
⌜*To Warwick.*⌝ You, cousin Nevil, as I may
    remember—
When Richard, with his eye brimful of tears,
Then checked and rated by Northumberland,
Did speak these words, now proved a prophecy?   70
"Northumberland, thou ladder by the which
My cousin Bolingbroke ascends my throne"—
Though then, God knows, I had no such intent,
But that necessity so bowed the state
That I and greatness were compelled to kiss—   75
"The time shall come," thus did he follow it,
"The time will come that foul sin, gathering head,
Shall break into corruption"—so went on,
Foretelling this same time's condition
And the division of our amity.   80

WARWICK
There is a history in all men's lives
Figuring the natures of the times deceased,
The which observed, a man may prophesy,
With a near aim, of the main chance of things

85. **who:** i.e., which

86. **intreasurèd:** i.e., stored up as if a treasure

88. **necessary . . . this:** i.e., inevitable pattern of cause and effect

94. **necessities:** things unavoidable

96. **cries out on:** exclaims against

101. **Please . . . Grace:** a courteous phrase of request

103. **powers:** forces

106. **A certain instance:** i.e., indisputable evidence

108. **unseasoned:** late, unseasonable

111. **inward:** civil; **out of hand:** finished with

112. **unto the Holy Land:** i.e., go on a crusade to Jerusalem (From 1095 to c. 1450 a series of wars—the Crusades—were fought by Christians to recover the **Holy Land** from the Muslims. At the end of *Richard II*, King Henry promised to fight such a war in order to gain God's forgiveness for having played a part in Richard's death. *Henry IV, Part 1* opened with Henry's interrupted attempt to mount a crusade.) See illustration, page 200.

As yet not come to life, who in their seeds 85
And weak beginning lie intreasurèd.
Such things become the hatch and brood of time,
And by the necessary form of this,
King Richard might create a perfect guess
That great Northumberland, then false to him, 90
Would of that seed grow to a greater falseness,
Which should not find a ground to root upon
Unless on you.
KING   Are these things then necessities?
Then let us meet them like necessities. 95
And that same word even now cries out on us.
They say the Bishop and Northumberland
Are fifty thousand strong.
WARWICK   It cannot be, my lord.
Rumor doth double, like the voice and echo, 100
The numbers of the feared. Please it your Grace
To go to bed. Upon my soul, my lord,
The powers that you already have sent forth
Shall bring this prize in very easily.
To comfort you the more, I have received 105
A certain instance that Glendower is dead.
Your Majesty hath been this fortnight ill,
And these unseasoned hours perforce must add
Unto your sickness.
KING   I will take your counsel. 110
And were these inward wars once out of hand,
We would, dear lords, unto the Holy Land.

They exit.

3.2   On his journey through Gloucestershire, Falstaff selects recruits for the army and decides that, on his return, he will fleece his old friend, Justice Shallow.

2–3. **by the rood:** a mild oath on **the rood,** the cross as a symbol of Christian faith

3. **cousin:** kinsman

5. **bedfellow:** i.e., wife

8. **a black ousel:** i.e., she is not **fairest,** but has dark hair or skin (and, according to the standards of the time, is therefore less "fair," or beautiful) **ousel:** blackbird

9. **By yea and no:** a Puritan oath (See note to 2.2.129.)

13. **Inns o' Court:** the **inns** of the legal profession in London, which admitted, trained, and examined men to practice at the bar (See page 130.)

14. **Clement's Inn:** one of the lesser inns (The four major inns were Inner Temple, Middle Temple, Grey's Inn, and Lincoln's Inn.)

16. **Lusty:** (1) lively, cheerful; (2) lustful

23. **swinge-bucklers:** swashbucklers, rowdies

25. **bona robas:** i.e., wenches (See longer note, page 253.)

25–26. **at commandment:** at our bidding

27. **page . . . Mowbray:** This bit of fictional history has attached itself to both the historical Sir John Fastolfe and to Sir John Oldcastle. (For Oldcastle and Falstaff, see "Historical Background," page 295.)

29. **anon:** soon

31. **see:** i.e., saw (Using **see** for the past tense, once acceptable, was old-fashioned in Shakespeare's day.)

33. **crack:** lad, young rogue

⟨Scene 2⟩

Enter Justice Shallow and Justice Silence.

SHALLOW   Come on, come on, come on. Give me your
    hand, sir, give me your hand, sir. An early stirrer, by
    the rood. And how doth my good cousin Silence?
SILENCE   Good morrow, good cousin Shallow.
SHALLOW   And how doth my cousin your bedfellow?   5
    And your fairest daughter and mine, my goddaugh-
    ter Ellen?
SILENCE   Alas, a black ousel, cousin Shallow.
SHALLOW   By yea and no, sir. I dare say my cousin
    William is become a good scholar. He is at Oxford   10
    still, is he not?
SILENCE   Indeed, sir, to my cost.
SHALLOW   He must then to the Inns o' Court shortly. I
    was once of Clement's Inn, where I think they will
    talk of mad Shallow yet.   15
SILENCE   You were called "Lusty Shallow" then,
    cousin.
SHALLOW   By the Mass, I was called anything, and I
    would have done anything indeed too, and roundly
    too. There was I, and little John Doit of Stafford-   20
    shire, and black George Barnes, and Francis Pick-
    bone, and Will Squele, a Cotswold man. You had
    not four such swinge-bucklers in all the Inns o'
    Court again. And I may say to you, we knew where
    the bona robas were and had the best of them all at   25
    commandment. Then was Jack Falstaff, now Sir
    John, a boy, and page to Thomas Mowbray, Duke of
    Norfolk.
SILENCE   This Sir John, cousin, that comes hither anon
    about soldiers?   30
SHALLOW   The same Sir John, the very same. I see him
    break Scoggin's head at the court gate, when he
    was a crack not thus high; and the very same day did

40. **Death . . . all:** See Psalm 89.48: "What man liveth and shall not see death?" (Geneva Bible)

41. **How:** i.e., what was the price of; **Stamford:** a market town north of London where three great fairs were held each year (The Quarto prints "Samforth," an apparently fictional place name.)

48. **He . . . shoot:** i.e., he shot well; **John o' Gaunt:** father of King Henry IV

50. **clapped i' th' clout:** i.e., hit the center of the target; **at twelve score:** i.e., from 240 yards

51. **carried . . . shaft:** i.e., shot a heavy arrow in a direct line

51–52. **a . . . half:** i.e., over a distance of **fourteen** to **fourteen and a half** score yards (280 to 290 yards)

54. **Thereafter . . . be:** i.e., depending on their quality

61. **esquire:** landowner

64. **commends him:** offers his greetings

65. **tall:** valiant

"He . . . shot a fine shoot." (3.2.47–48)
From Gilles Corrozet, *Hecatongraphie* . . . (1543).

I fight with one Sampson Stockfish, a fruiterer, behind Grey's Inn. Jesu, Jesu, the mad days that I have spent! And to see how many of my old acquaintance are dead. 35

SILENCE We shall all follow, cousin.

SHALLOW Certain, 'tis certain, very sure, very sure. Death, as the Psalmist saith, is certain to all. All shall die. How a good yoke of bullocks at ⟨Stamford⟩ Fair? 40

SILENCE By my troth, ⟨cousin,⟩ I was not there.

SHALLOW Death is certain. Is old Dooble of your town living yet? 45

SILENCE Dead, sir.

SHALLOW Jesu, Jesu, dead! He drew a good bow, and dead? He shot a fine shoot. John o' Gaunt loved him well, and betted much money on his head. Dead! He would have clapped i' th' clout at twelve score, and carried you a forehand shaft a fourteen and fourteen and a half, that it would have done a man's heart good to see. How a score of ewes now? 50

SILENCE Thereafter as they be, a score of good ewes may be worth ten pounds. 55

SHALLOW And is old Dooble dead?

SILENCE Here come two of Sir John Falstaff's men, as I think.

Enter Bardolph and one with him.

⟨SHALLOW⟩ Good morrow, honest gentlemen.

BARDOLPH I beseech you, which is Justice Shallow? 60

SHALLOW I am Robert Shallow, sir, a poor esquire of this county and one of the King's justices of the peace. What is your good pleasure with me?

BARDOLPH My captain, sir, commends him to you, my captain, Sir John Falstaff, a tall gentleman, by heaven, and a most gallant leader. 65

67. **knew him:** i.e., knew him to be

68. **backsword man:** fencer with a **backsword** (a sword with a single cutting edge)

70–71. **accommodated:** furnished, supplied

75–76. **It . . . accommodo:** Like a schoolboy, Shallow derives the English word from its Latin root. Also, in the manner schoolboys were taught, he cites the first-person singular form of the Latin verb.

87. **like:** are getting on, are doing

91–92. **in commission:** i.e., serving as a justice of the peace

94. **of the peace:** i.e., a magistrate (but playing on **peace** as "silence")

97. **sufficient:** competent, capable

A mandrake. (1.2.15; 3.2.326)
From *The grete herball* . . . [1529].

SHALLOW　He greets me well, sir. I knew him a good
　　backsword man. How doth the good knight? May I
　　ask how my lady his wife doth?

BARDOLPH　Sir, pardon. A soldier is better ⟨accommo-　70
　　dated⟩ than with a wife.

SHALLOW　It is well said, in faith, sir, and it is well said
　　indeed too. "Better accommodated." It is good,
　　yea, indeed is it. Good phrases are surely, and ever
　　were, very commendable. "Accommodated." It　75
　　comes of *accommodo.* Very good, a good phrase.

BARDOLPH　Pardon, sir, I have heard the word—
　　"phrase" call you it? By this day, I know not the
　　phrase, but I will maintain the word with my sword
　　to be a soldierlike word, and a word of exceeding　80
　　good command, by heaven. "Accommodated," that
　　is when a man is, as they say, accommodated, or
　　when a man is being whereby he may be thought to
　　be accommodated, which is an excellent thing.

Enter Falstaff.

SHALLOW　It is very just. Look, here comes good Sir　85
　　John.—Give me your good hand, give me your
　　Worship's good hand. By my troth, you like well and
　　bear your years very well. Welcome, good Sir John.

FALSTAFF　I am glad to see you well, good Master
　　Robert Shallow.—Master ⟨Sure-card,⟩ as I think?　90

SHALLOW　No, Sir John. It is my cousin Silence, in
　　commission with me.

FALSTAFF　Good Master Silence, it well befits you
　　should be of the peace.

SILENCE　Your good Worship is welcome.　95

FALSTAFF　Fie, this is hot weather, gentlemen. Have you
　　provided me here half a dozen sufficient men?

SHALLOW　Marry, have we, sir. Will you sit?
　　　　　　　　　　　　⌐*They sit at a table.*⌐

100. **roll:** scroll of names

106. **an it please you:** a deferential phrase of address

108. **of good friends:** i.e., from a good family

113. **singular:** i.e., singularly, uncommonly

115. **Prick him:** choose him (by marking his name)

116. **pricked:** (1) provoked, nagged; (2) soured or mouldy (said of wine or beer); (3) endowed with genitals

117. **old dame:** perhaps wife, perhaps mother

118. **undone . . . one:** i.e., now ruined through the lack of someone; **husbandry:** farming (but with possible wordplay on "husband")

122. **spent:** consumed; used up; exhausted

125. **other:** i.e., others

128. **like:** i.e., likely; **cold:** indifferent, apathetic

FALSTAFF Let me see them, I beseech you.

SHALLOW Where's the roll? Where's the roll? Where's 100
the roll? Let me see, let me see, let me see. So, so,
so, so, so. So, so. Yea, marry, sir.—Rafe Mouldy!—
Let them appear as I call, let them do so, let them
do so.

⌐*Enter Mouldy, followed by Shadow, Wart, Feeble,
and Bullcalf.* ⌐

Let me see, where is Mouldy? 105

MOULDY, ⌐*coming forward*⌐ Here, an it please you.

SHALLOW What think you, Sir John? A good-limbed
fellow, young, strong, and of good friends.

FALSTAFF Is thy name Mouldy?

MOULDY Yea, an 't please you. 110

FALSTAFF 'Tis the more time thou wert used.

SHALLOW Ha, ha, ha, most excellent, i' faith! Things
that are mouldy lack use. Very singular good, in
faith. Well said, Sir John, very well said.

⟨FALSTAFF Prick him.⟩ 115

⌐*Shallow marks the scroll.*⌐

MOULDY I was pricked well enough before, an you
could have let me alone. My old dame will be
undone now for one to do her husbandry and her
drudgery. You need not to have pricked me. There
are other men fitter to go out than I. 120

FALSTAFF Go to. Peace, Mouldy. You shall go. Mouldy,
it is time you were spent.

MOULDY Spent?

SHALLOW Peace, fellow, peace. Stand aside. Know you
where you are?—For th' other, Sir John. Let me 125
see.—Simon Shadow!

FALSTAFF Yea, marry, let me have him to sit under.
He's like to be a cold soldier.

SHALLOW Where's Shadow?

131. **Shadow . . . thou:** the first of a series of puns on son/sun

134. **shadow:** Lines 133–36 contain multiple wordplay on **shadow** as, e.g., "portrait, image," "a delusive semblance" (contrasted with **substance**), "a remnant" or "a form from which the substance has departed," "a small insignificant portion," and "protection from the sun."

135–36. **much of:** perhaps used ironically to mean "little of"

138. **serve:** (1) suffice; (2) do military service

139. **shadows:** i.e., mere names of men (for which the captain could pocket the pay)

146. **ragged:** rough (with wordplay on his **ragged** clothes)

148–50. **It . . . more:** i.e., he is so **ragged** and pinned together that he looks like a house constructed with wooden pegs (wordplay on **prick** as "fasten together with pins," on **frame** as [1] construction and [2] body, and on **stands upon pins** as [1] depends on **pins,** [2] **stands** on pegs, and [3] is supported by skinny legs)

158. **pricked:** (1) attired, dressed; (2) impaled (with sexual innuendo)

159. **battle:** battalion, army

SHADOW, ⌜*coming forward*⌝   Here, sir.   130
FALSTAFF   Shadow, whose son art thou?
SHADOW   My mother's son, sir.
FALSTAFF   Thy mother's son! Like enough, and thy
   father's shadow. So the son of the female is the
   shadow of the male. It is often so, indeed, but much   135
   of the father's substance.
SHALLOW   Do you like him, Sir John?
FALSTAFF   Shadow will serve for summer. Prick him,
   for we have a number of shadows ⟨to⟩ fill up the
   muster book.   140
SHALLOW   Thomas Wart!
FALSTAFF   Where's he?
WART, ⌜*coming forward*⌝   Here, sir.
FALSTAFF   Is thy name Wart?
WART   Yea, sir.   145
FALSTAFF   Thou art a very ragged wart.
SHALLOW   Shall I prick him ⟨down,⟩ Sir John?
FALSTAFF   It were superfluous, for ⟨his⟩ apparel is built
   upon his back, and the whole frame stands upon
   pins. Prick him no more.   150
SHALLOW   Ha, ha, ha. You can do it, sir, you can do it. I
   commend you well.—Francis Feeble!
FEEBLE, ⌜*coming forward*⌝   Here, sir.
SHALLOW   What trade art thou, Feeble?
FEEBLE   A woman's tailor, sir.   155
SHALLOW   Shall I prick him, sir?
FALSTAFF   You may, but if he had been a man's tailor,
   he'd ha' pricked you.—Wilt thou make as many
   holes in an enemy's battle as thou hast done in a
   woman's petticoat?   160
FEEBLE   I will do my good will, sir. You can have no
   more.
FALSTAFF   Well said, good woman's tailor, well said,
   courageous Feeble. Thou wilt be as valiant as the

165. **magnanimous:** courageous

171. **put him to:** i.e., enlist him as

172. **thousands:** perhaps, **thousands** of vermin

180. **prick me:** i.e., stick, wound

181. **again:** i.e., in response

187. **whoreson:** vile

188. **ringing in:** i.e., **ringing** the church bells

188–89. **his coronation day:** i.e., the anniversary of the day the King was crowned

190. **gown:** dressing gown

191–92. **take . . . order:** i.e., make . . . arrangements

192. **ring for thee:** i.e., ring the bells in your place (but also, ring the bells for your funeral)

194. **two more called:** There is some confusion in this scene about how many men are **called** and how many Falstaff is to recruit.

198. **tarry:** i.e., wait for

wrathful dove or most magnanimous mouse.— 165
Prick the woman's tailor well, Master Shallow,
deep, Master Shallow.

FEEBLE I would Wart might have gone, sir.

FALSTAFF I would thou wert a man's tailor, that thou
mightst mend him and make him fit to go. I cannot 170
put him to a private soldier that is the leader of so
many thousands. Let that suffice, most forcible
Feeble.

FEEBLE It shall suffice, sir.

FALSTAFF I am bound to thee, reverend Feeble.—Who 175
is ⟨the⟩ next?

SHALLOW Peter Bullcalf o' th' green.

FALSTAFF Yea, marry, let's see Bullcalf.

BULLCALF, ⌜coming forward⌝ Here, sir.

FALSTAFF Fore God, a likely fellow. Come, prick ⟨me⟩ 180
Bullcalf till he roar again.

BULLCALF O Lord, good my lord captain—

FALSTAFF What, dost thou roar before thou art
pricked?

BULLCALF O Lord, sir, I am a diseased man. 185

FALSTAFF What disease hast thou?

BULLCALF A whoreson cold, sir, a cough, sir, which I
caught with ringing in the King's affairs upon his
coronation day, sir.

FALSTAFF Come, thou shalt go to the wars in a gown. 190
We will have away thy cold, and I will take such
order that thy friends shall ring for thee.—Is here
all?

SHALLOW Here is two more called than your number.
You must have but four here, sir, and so I pray you 195
go in with me to dinner.

FALSTAFF Come, I will go drink with you, but I cannot
tarry dinner. I am glad to see you, by my troth,
Master Shallow.

200. **since:** the time when

207. **away with:** i.e., tolerate, endure

227. **Corporate:** his mistake for "corporal"; **stand:** i.e., act as

228. **four Harry ten-shillings:** i.e., one pound (In Elizabethan England, money issued under Henry VII was worth one-half its original value. One Harry ten-shilling was worth five shillings.)

230. **had as lief:** i.e., would just as soon

233. **Else:** otherwise

A prostitute. (2.2.153)
From *Roxburghe ballads* . . . (printed 1895).

SHALLOW   O, Sir John, do you remember since we lay   200
   all night in the windmill in Saint George's Field?
FALSTAFF   No more of that, ⟨good⟩ Master Shallow, ⟨no
   more of that.⟩
SHALLOW   Ha, 'twas a merry night. And is Jane Night-
   work alive?   205
FALSTAFF   She lives, Master Shallow.
SHALLOW   She never could away with me.
FALSTAFF   Never, never. She would always say she could
   not abide Master Shallow.
SHALLOW   By the Mass, I could anger her to th' heart.   210
   She was then a bona roba. Doth she hold her own
   well?
FALSTAFF   Old, old, Master Shallow.
SHALLOW   Nay, she must be old. She cannot choose but
   be old. Certain, she's old, and had Robin Nightwork   215
   by old Nightwork before I came to Clement's Inn.
SILENCE   That's fifty-five year ago.
SHALLOW   Ha, cousin Silence, that thou hadst seen that
   that this knight and I have seen!—Ha, Sir John, said
   I well?   220
FALSTAFF   We have heard the chimes at midnight, Mas-
   ter Shallow.
SHALLOW   That we have, that we have, that we have. In
   faith, Sir John, we have. Our watchword was "Hem,
   boys." Come, let's to dinner, come, let's to dinner.   225
   Jesus, the days that we have seen! Come, come.
                ⌐*Shallow, Silence, and Falstaff rise and*⌐ *exit.*
BULLCALF   Good Master Corporate Bardolph, stand my
   friend, and here's four Harry ten-shillings in
   French crowns for you. ⌐*He gives Bardolph money.*⌐
   In very truth, sir, I had as lief be hanged, sir, as go.   230
   And yet, for mine own part, sir, I do not care, but
   rather because I am unwilling, and, for mine own
   part, have a desire to stay with my friends. Else, sir,
   I did not care, for mine own part, so much.

239. **forty:** i.e., forty shillings (two pounds)

242–47. **A man . . . next:** This speech is a series of proverbs and popular phrases. **quit:** free, clear (Proverbial: Death pays all debts.)

260. **past service:** i.e., too **mouldy** to put on the table (with wordplay on military **service**)

261–62. **will none of:** i.e., don't want

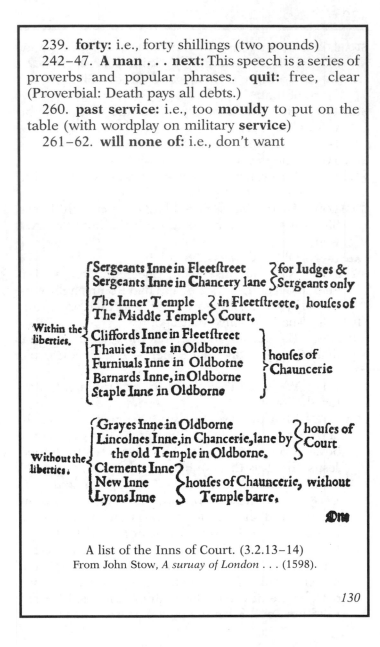

A list of the Inns of Court. (3.2.13–14)
From John Stow, *A suruay of London* . . . (1598).

BARDOLPH   Go to. Stand aside.   235
MOULDY   And, good Master Corporal Captain, for my
old dame's sake, stand my friend. She has nobody to
do anything about her when I am gone, and she is
old and cannot help herself. You shall have forty,
sir.   ⌈*He gives money.*⌉   240
BARDOLPH   Go to. Stand aside.
FEEBLE   By my troth, I care not. A man can die but
once. We owe God a death. I'll ne'er bear a base
mind. An 't be my destiny, so; an 't be not, so. No
man's too good to serve 's prince, and let it go   245
which way it will, he that dies this year is quit for
the next
BARDOLPH   Well said. Th' art a good fellow.
FEEBLE   Faith, I'll bear no base mind.

Enter Falstaff and the Justices.

FALSTAFF   Come, sir, which men shall I have?   250
SHALLOW   Four of which you please.
BARDOLPH, ⌈*aside to Falstaff*⌉   Sir, a word with you. I
have three pound to free Mouldy and Bullcalf.
FALSTAFF   Go to, well.
SHALLOW   Come, Sir John, which four will you have?   255
FALSTAFF   Do you choose for me.
SHALLOW   Marry, then, Mouldy, Bullcalf, Feeble, and
Shadow.
FALSTAFF   Mouldy and Bullcalf! For you, Mouldy, stay
at home till you are past service.—And for your   260
part, Bullcalf, grow till you come unto it. I will
none of you.   ⌈*Mouldy and Bullcalf exit.*⌉
SHALLOW   Sir John, Sir John, do not yourself wrong.
They are your likeliest men, and I would have you
served with the best.   265
FALSTAFF   Will you tell me, Master Shallow, how to
choose a man? Care I for the limb, the thews, the

268. **assemblance:** appearance

270–71. **charge you and discharge you:** i.e., load and fire his weapon

271–72. **with the motion . . . hammer:** i.e., as rapidly and as precisely as a pewter-maker uses his small hammer

272–73. **come . . . bucket:** The meaning is unclear. "To gibbet" is to hang as on the gallows. A **brewer's bucket** is a beam on which something can be hung or carried. The emphasis is on swiftness of motion.

273–74. **half-faced fellow:** i.e., man so thin he shows up only in profile (like a face on a coin)

279. **Put me a caliver:** i.e., put a light musket

281. **Hold:** Here! Take it!

282. **Thas, thas, thas:** Perhaps Bardolph, like a drill sergeant, is shouting out the rhythm of Wart's marching. (The Folio prints "Thus, thus, thus.")

283. **manage me:** i.e., manage, wield

285. **chopped:** i.e., chapped; **shot:** marksman

286. **scab:** scoundrel (but alluding to its meaning as a skin disease and thus related to **Wart**)

287. **tester:** slang term for a sixpence

289. **Mile End Green:** used as a drilling ground for the London militia; **lay:** lived, lodged

290–91. **Sir . . . show:** i.e., in the annual archery exhibition (called **Arthur's show**), Shallow took the name of Arthur's fool

291. **quiver:** nimble, active

292. **manage you his piece:** i.e., wield his weapon

293–97. **about . . . come:** Shallow describes the marksman's movements as he shoots, moves back to reload, then forward again to shoot. **Bounce:** boom, bang

stature, bulk and big assemblance of a man? Give
me the spirit, Master Shallow. Here's Wart. You see
what a ragged appearance it is. He shall charge you   270
and discharge you with the motion of a pewterer's
hammer, come off and on swifter than he that
gibbets on the brewer's bucket. And this same half-
faced fellow, Shadow, give me this man. He presents no mark to the enemy. The foeman may with   275
as great aim level at the edge of a penknife. And for
a retreat, how swiftly will this Feeble, the woman's
tailor, run off! O, give me the spare men, and spare
me the great ones.—Put me a caliver into Wart's
hand, Bardolph.   280
BARDOLPH, ⌜*giving Wart a musket*⌝ Hold, Wart. Traverse.
    Thas, thas, thas.
FALSTAFF, ⌜*to Wart*⌝ Come, manage me your caliver: so,
    very well, go to, very good, exceeding good. O, give
    me always a little, lean, old, chopped, bald shot.   285
    Well said, i' faith, Wart. Th' art a good scab. Hold,
    there's a tester for thee.   ⌜*He gives Wart money.*⌝
SHALLOW He is not his craft's master. He doth not do it
    right. I remember at Mile End Green, when I lay at
    Clement's Inn—I was then Sir Dagonet in Arthur's   290
    show—there was a little quiver fellow, and he
    would manage you his piece thus. ⌜*Shallow per-
    forms with the musket.*⌝ And he would about and
    about, and come you in, and come you in. "Rah,
    tah, tah," would he say. "Bounce," would he say,   295
    and away again would he go, and again would he
    come. I shall ne'er see such a fellow.
FALSTAFF These fellows will do well, Master Shal-
    low.—God keep you, Master Silence. I will not use
    many words with you. Fare you well, gentlemen   300
    both. I thank you. I must a dozen mile tonight.—
    Bardolph, give the soldiers coats.

309. **I have spoke at a word:** perhaps, "I mean what I say"; or, perhaps, "I spoke too hastily"

312. **As:** when; **fetch off:** get the better of, cheat

317. **Turnbull Street:** a disreputable London street

318. **duer:** more duly, more fully; **than ... tribute:** i.e., than is **tribute** paid to the Sultan of Turkey

323. **forlorn:** meager, thin

324. **thick sight:** i.e., dull vision; **invincible:** i.e., invisible (See longer note, page 253.)

325. **genius:** embodiment

326. **mandrake:** a root thought to be a sexual stimulant (See also the note to 1.2.15, and picture, page 120.)

328. **overscutched huswives:** i.e., worn-out prostitutes (**Huswives** here means "hussies" rather than "housewives.")

330. **fancies or ... good-nights:** perhaps, improvised tunes or serenades

330–31. **Vice's dagger:** i.e., thin stick (literally, a wooden **dagger** carried by a comic stage character called the **Vice**)

332. **sworn brother:** i.e., best friend (as if they had **sworn** an oath to defend each other)

334. **tilt-yard:** See pages xxxvi–xxxvii. **he burst his head:** i.e., John of Gaunt cut Shallow's **head**

336. **beat ... name:** i.e., **beat** a **gaunt** man

SHALLOW   Sir John, the Lord bless you. God prosper
your affairs. God send us peace. At your return, visit
our house. Let our old acquaintance be renewed.   305
Peradventure I will with you to the court.
FALSTAFF   Fore   God,   would   you   would,   ⟨Master
Shallow.⟩
SHALLOW   Go to. I have spoke at a word. God keep you.
FALSTAFF   Fare you well, gentle gentlemen.   310
                           ⌐*Shallow and Silence*⌐ *exit.*
On, Bardolph. Lead the men away.
                           | *All but Falstaff exit.* |
As I return, I will fetch off these justices. I do see
the bottom of Justice Shallow. Lord, Lord, how
subject we old men are to this vice of lying. This
same starved justice hath done nothing but prate to   315
me of the wildness of his youth and the feats he hath
done about Turnbull Street, and every third word a
lie, duer paid to the hearer than the Turk's tribute. I
do remember him at Clement's Inn, like a man
made after supper of a cheese paring. When he was   320
naked, he was, for all the world, like a forked radish
with a head fantastically carved upon it with a
knife. He was so forlorn that his dimensions to
any thick sight were invincible. He was the very
genius of famine, [yet lecherous as a monkey,   325
and the whores called him "mandrake."] He came
⟨ever⟩ in the rearward of the fashion, [and sung
those tunes to the overscutched huswives that he
heard the carmen whistle, and swore they were his
fancies or his good-nights.] And now is this Vice's   330
dagger become a squire, and talks as familiarly
of John o' Gaunt as if he had been sworn brother
to him, and I'll be sworn he ne'er saw him but
once in the tilt-yard, and then he burst his head
for crowding among the Marshal's men. I saw it   335
and told John o' Gaunt he beat his own name, for

337. **thrust him:** i.e., put Shallow

338. **treble hautboy:** the slenderest of the double-reed instruments known as "hautboys," precursors of modern-day oboes (Its **case** would be long and thin.) See below.

340. **beefs:** fat oxen; **be acquainted:** a reference to Shallow's "Let our old acquaintance be renewed" (line 305)

341–42. **a philosopher's two stones:** i.e., a source of inexhaustible wealth (There were two kinds of **philosopher's stones:** one that purportedly changed lead to gold and another, an elixir, that gave perfect health. Some editors think **stones** also means "testicles.")

342–43. **the young . . . pike:** i.e., little fish are eaten by big fish (proverbial)

Hautboy. (3.2.338)
From Balthasar Küchler, *Repraesentatio der . . . Ritterspil* (1611).

you might have thrust him and all his apparel into
an eel-skin; the case of a treble hautboy was a
mansion for him, a court. And now has he land and
beefs. Well, I'll be acquainted with him if I return, 340
and 't shall go hard but I'll make him a philosopher's two stones to me. If the young dace be a
bait for the old pike, I see no reason in the law of
nature but I may snap at him. Let time shape, and
there an end. 345

⌜*He exits.*⌝

HENRY IV
Part 2

ACT 4

4.1 The leaders of the rebellion reach Gaultree Forest, where they present their grievances to Westmoreland. After Prince John promises redress for the grievances, the army of the rebellion is dismissed. John then arrests the Archbishop, Mowbray, and Hastings.

---

3. **discoverers:** scouts, spies

11–12. **Here . . . quality:** i.e., he would like to be **here** accompanied by suitably powerful forces **powers:** forces **sortance:** agreement, correspondence **quality:** position in society

14. **ripe:** i.e., bring to ripeness

16. **overlive:** survive

17. **opposite:** opponent

18. **touch ground:** hit bottom (like a ship running aground)

⟨ACT 4⟩

___

⟨Scene 1⟩

Enter the Archbishop ⌜*of York,*⌝ *Mowbray,* ⌜*Lord*⌝
Bardolph, Hastings, ⌜*and their officers*⌝ *within the Forest
of Gaultree.*

ARCHBISHOP What is this forest called?
HASTINGS
  'Tis Gaultree Forest, an 't shall please your Grace.
ARCHBISHOP
  Here stand, my lords, and send discoverers forth
  To know the numbers of our enemies.
HASTINGS
  We have sent forth already.   5
ARCHBISHOP   'Tis well done.
  My friends and brethren in these great affairs,
  I must acquaint you that I have received
  New-dated letters from Northumberland,
  Their cold intent, tenor, and substance, thus: 10
  Here doth he wish his person, with such powers
  As might hold sortance with his quality,
  The which he could not levy; whereupon
  He is retired, to ripe his growing fortunes,
  To Scotland, and concludes in hearty prayers   15
  That your attempts may overlive the hazard
  And fearful meeting of their opposite.
MOWBRAY
  Thus do the hopes we have in him touch ground
  And dash themselves to pieces.

141

21. **off a mile:** i.e., a mile away
22. **form:** military formation
25. **just proportion:** exact number
26. **sway:** move
27. **well-appointed:** well-equipped; **fronts:** confronts
30. **The . . . Lancaster:** i.e., Prince John (See note to 1.3.85.)
32. **What . . . coming:** i.e., why you have come
35. **If that:** i.e., if
36. **routs:** mobs
37. **guarded with rage:** perhaps, escorted by the figure of Rage
38. **countenanced:** patronized, favored
39. **commotion:** sedition, insurrection
40. **his:** i.e., its; **most proper shape:** i.e., the **shape** rightly belonging to it
42. **Had not been:** i.e., would not be

Enter Messenger.

HASTINGS   Now, what news?   20
MESSENGER
   West of this forest, scarcely off a mile,
   In goodly form comes on the enemy,
   And, by the ground they hide, I judge their number
   Upon or near the rate of thirty thousand.
MOWBRAY
   The just proportion that we gave them out.   25
   Let us sway on and face them in the field.

Enter Westmoreland.

ARCHBISHOP
   What well-appointed leader fronts us here?
MOWBRAY
   I think it is my Lord of Westmoreland.
WESTMORELAND
   Health and fair greeting from our general,
   The Prince Lord John and Duke of Lancaster.   30
ARCHBISHOP
   Say on, my Lord of Westmoreland, in peace,
   What doth concern your coming.
WESTMORELAND   Then, my lord,
   Unto your Grace do I in chief address
   The substance of my speech. If that rebellion   35
   Came like itself, in base and abject routs,
   Led on by bloody youth, guarded with rage,
   And countenanced by boys and beggary—
   I say, if damned commotion so ⌜appeared⌝
   In his true, native, and most proper shape,   40
   You, reverend father, and these noble lords
   Had not been here to dress the ugly form
   Of base and bloody insurrection
   With your fair honors. You, Lord Archbishop,

45. **see:** diocese; **civil:** well-governed

47. **good letters:** scholarship

48. **investments:** vestments, robes; **figure:** represent

50. **Wherefore:** why; **so . . . yourself:** i.e., transform yourself so injuriously (with an allusion to "badly translating" one language into another)

55. **point:** trumpet signal (See page 146.)

60. **bleed:** wordplay on bleeding from the wounds of war and bloodletting as a cure for **fever**

63. **take . . . as:** i.e., do not here assume the role of

66. **show:** look, appear

67. **rank:** bloated and overfed

70. **in . . . weighed:** The image here is of weighing two objects against each other in a balance scale. (See below.) **justly:** exactly

73. **griefs:** grievances

75. **enforced:** forced; **most quiet there:** perhaps, complete peace therein (in **the stream of time**)

76. **occasion:** the course of events

78. **articles:** i.e., an indictment

A balance scale. (4.1.70)
From Silvestro Pietrasanta, . . . *Symbola heroica* (1682).

Whose see is by a civil peace maintained,   45
Whose beard the silver hand of peace hath touched,
Whose learning and good letters peace hath tutored,
Whose white investments figure innocence,
The dove and very blessèd spirit of peace,
Wherefore do you so ill translate yourself   50
Out of the speech of peace, that bears such grace,
Into the harsh and boist'rous tongue of war,
Turning your books to graves, your ink to blood,
Your pens to lances, and your tongue divine
To a loud trumpet and a point of war?   55

ARCHBISHOP
Wherefore do I this? So the question stands.
Briefly, to this end: we are all diseased
(And with our surfeiting and wanton hours
Have brought ourselves into a burning fever,
And we must bleed for it; of which disease   60
Our late King Richard, being infected, died.
But, my most noble Lord of Westmoreland,
I take not on me here as a physician,
Nor do I as an enemy to peace
Troop in the throngs of military men,   65
But rather show awhile like fearful war
To diet rank minds sick of happiness
And purge th' obstructions which begin to stop
Our very veins of life. Hear me more plainly.
I have in equal balance justly weighed   70
What wrongs our arms may do, what wrongs we
     suffer,
And find our griefs heavier than our offenses.
We see which way the stream of time doth run
And are enforced from our most quiet there   75
By the rough torrent of occasion,
And have the summary of all our griefs,
When time shall serve, to show in articles;

80. **our audience:** i.e., the formal interview with the King that we sought

81. **unfold:** disclose, reveal

87. **instance:** i.e., urging

88. **ill-beseeming:** unsuitable, unbefitting

93. **gallèd:** i.e., injured

94. **suborned to grate on:** bribed to harass

97. **And . . . edge:** i.e., and sanctify the sword of insurrection

98–100. **My . . . particular:** Lines may be missing from this difficult passage. The Archbishop seems to be contrasting **general** and **particular** quarrels, brothers in **general** and natural brothers. (His own brother had been killed by the King.)

106. **unequal:** inequitable, unjust

109. **to their necessities:** i.e., according to what **the times** make necessary

"A loud trumpet and a point of war." (4.1.55)
From Hartmann Schopper, *Panoplia omnium . . .* (1568).

Which long ere this we offered to the King
And might by no suit gain our audience.   80
When we are wronged and would unfold our griefs,
We are denied access unto his person
Even by those men that most have done us wrong.)
The dangers of the days but newly gone,
Whose memory is written on the earth   85
With yet-appearing blood, and the examples
Of every minute's instance, present now,
Hath put us in these ill-beseeming arms,
Not to break peace or any branch of it,
But to establish here a peace indeed,   90
Concurring both in name and quality.

WESTMORELAND
Whenever yet was your appeal denied?
Wherein have you been gallèd by the King?
What peer hath been suborned to grate on you,
That you should seal this lawless bloody book   95
Of forged rebellion with a seal divine
[And consecrate commotion's bitter edge?]

ARCHBISHOP
My brother general, the commonwealth,
[To brother born an household cruelty,]
I make my quarrel in particular.   100

WESTMORELAND
There is no need of any such redress,
Or if there were, it not belongs to you.

MOWBRAY
Why not to him in part, and to us all
That feel the bruises of the days before
And suffer the condition of these times   105
To lay a heavy and unequal hand
Upon our honors?

WESTMORELAND   ⟨O, my good Lord Mowbray,
Construe the times to their necessities,

119. **breathed:** let breathe

120. **The King:** i.e., Richard II; **the state:** i.e., circumstances (For the story rehearsed here, see *Richard II* 1.3. See also the illustration on page 162.)

121. **force perforce:** i.e., against his will

123. **rousèd:** raised; **seats:** i.e., saddles

125. **armèd . . . charge:** i.e., steel-tipped lances in position for action; **beavers:** visors (See page 150.)

126. **sights:** slits in the visors

131. **did . . . down:** i.e., stopped the combat by throwing down the official staff

134. **dint of sword:** i.e., force of combat

135. **miscarried:** perished

137. **Earl of Hereford:** i.e., Henry Bolingbroke (now King Henry IV)

142. **ne'er . . . Coventry:** i.e., never would have carried the victory away from the field of combat

And you shall say indeed it is the time, 110
And not the King, that doth you injuries.
Yet for your part, it not appears to me
Either from the King or in the present time
That you should have an inch of any ground
To build a grief on. Were you not restored 115
To all the Duke of Norfolk's seigniories,
Your noble and right well remembered father's?

MOWBRAY
What thing, in honor, had my father lost
That need to be revived and breathed in me?
The King that loved him, as the state stood then, 120
Was ⌈force⌉ perforce compelled to banish him,
And then that Henry Bolingbroke and he,
Being mounted and both roused in their seats,
Their neighing coursers daring of the spur,
Their armèd staves in charge, their beavers down, 125
Their eyes of fire sparkling through sights of steel,
And the loud trumpet blowing them together,
Then, then, when there was nothing could have
    stayed
My father from the breast of Bolingbroke, 130
O, when the King did throw his warder down—
His own life hung upon the staff he threw—
Then threw he down himself and all their lives
That by indictment and by dint of sword
Have since miscarried under Bolingbroke. 135

WESTMORELAND
You speak, Lord Mowbray, now you know not what.
The Earl of Hereford was reputed then
In England the most valiant gentleman.
Who knows on whom fortune would then have
    smiled? 140
But if your father had been victor there,
He ne'er had borne it out of Coventry;

147–48. **the King:** i.e., Richard II

152. **wherein:** where

154. **set off:** excluded

157. **policy:** cunning, craftiness

158. **overween:** i.e., are arrogant, presumptuous

160. **a ken:** i.e., sight

163. **battle:** army; **names:** i.e., distinguished soldiers

166. **reason will:** i.e., it stands to reason that

168. **by my will:** i.e., **my will** is that

170. **A . . . handling:** This proverb, which means "it's a weak container that can't be handled," is here used to mean "it's an unsound argument that can't tolerate discussion" (playing on alternate meanings of **case** and **handling**).

172. **In . . . virtue:** i.e., with the full authority

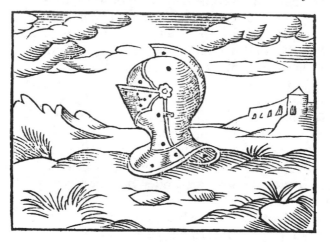

Helmet with beaver down. (4.1.125)
From Henry Peacham, *Minerua Britanna* (1612).

For all the country in a general voice
Cried hate upon him; and all their prayers and
    love   145
Were set on Hereford, whom they doted on
And blessed and graced, ⌜indeed⌝ more than the
    King.⟩
But this is mere digression from my purpose.
Here come I from our princely general   150
To know your griefs, to tell you from his Grace
That he will give you audience; and wherein
It shall appear that your demands are just,
You shall enjoy them, everything set off
That might so much as think you enemies.   155

MOWBRAY
But he hath forced us to compel this offer,
And it proceeds from policy, not love.

WESTMORELAND
Mowbray, you overween to take it so.
This offer comes from mercy, not from fear.
For, lo, within a ken our army lies,   160
Upon mine honor, all too confident
To give admittance to a thought of fear
Our battle is more full of names than yours,
Our men more perfect in the use of arms,
Our armor all as strong, our cause the best.   165
Then reason will our hearts should be as good.
Say you not then our offer is compelled.

MOWBRAY
Well, by my will, we shall admit no parley.

WESTMORELAND
That argues but the shame of your offense.
A rotten case abides no handling.   170

HASTINGS
Hath the Prince John a full commission,
In very ample virtue of his father,

173–74. **to . . . upon:** i.e., to decide about the **conditions** we shall insist on

175. **intended . . . name:** i.e., signified in **the General's** title

176. **muse . . . question:** i.e., wonder you raise doubts about something so obvious

179. **Each . . . redressed:** i.e., if **each** separate **article** included is **redressed**

180. **All:** i.e., if **all**

181. **insinewed:** i.e., joined as if by sinews

182. **Acquitted:** i.e., are **acquitted; true substantial form:** i.e., proper legal document

183. **wills:** demands

184. **To us . . . confined:** See longer note, page 254.

185. **awful:** respectful

188. **battles:** armies

189. **frame:** bring about

190. **place of difference:** i.e., battlefield

199. **our valuation:** i.e., the way we are valued

To hear and absolutely to determine
Of what conditions we shall stand upon?
WESTMORELAND
    That is intended in the General's name.   175
    I muse you make so slight a question.
ARCHBISHOP, ⌜*giving Westmoreland a paper*⌝
    Then take, my Lord of Westmoreland, this schedule,
    For this contains our general grievances.
    Each several article herein redressed,
    All members of our cause, both here and hence   180
    That are insinewed to this action,
    Acquitted by a true substantial form
    And present execution of our wills
    To us and ⟨to⟩ our purposes confined,
    We come within our awful banks again   185
    And knit our powers to the arm of peace.
WESTMORELAND
    This will I show the General. Please you, lords,
    In sight of both our battles we may meet,
    ⌜And⌝ either end in peace, which God so frame,
    Or to the place of difference call the swords   190
    Which must decide it.
ARCHBISHOP   My lord, we will do so.
                              Westmoreland exits.
MOWBRAY
    There is a thing within my bosom tells me
    That no conditions of our peace can stand.
HASTINGS
    Fear you not that. If we can make our peace   195
    Upon such large terms and so absolute
    As our conditions shall consist upon,
    Our peace shall stand as firm as rocky mountains.
MOWBRAY
    Yea, but our valuation shall be such
    That every slight and false-derivèd cause,   200

201. **nice:** petty; **wanton:** capricious

203. **That . . . love:** i.e., that, even if our allegiance to the King were as strong as martyrs' love of God

205. **corn:** i.e., wheat, grain

206. **partition:** separation

208. **dainty . . . picking:** i.e., **such** trifling

209. **doubt:** danger, risk

210. **heirs of life:** i.e., survivors

211. **tables:** writing tablet

213. **history:** recount, narrate

215. **precisely:** completely, absolutely

216. **misdoubts:** suspicions

217. **enrooted:** entangled root with root (See longer note, page 254.)

220. **an offensive wife:** a wife who has given offense

221. **him:** i.e., the wife's husband (but also **the King** [line 207])

223–24. **hangs . . . execution:** i.e., stops the blow in midair **resolved:** determined-upon

225. **wasted . . . rods:** i.e., used up all his whipping rods

226. **late:** recent

229. **offer:** i.e., threaten

231. **Lord Marshal:** i.e., Mowbray (See note to 1.3.0 SD.)

232. **atonement:** reconciliation

Yea, every idle, nice, and wanton reason,
Shall to the King taste of this action,
That, were our royal faiths martyrs in love,
We shall be winnowed with so rough a wind
That even our corn shall seem as light as chaff,   205
And good from bad find no partition.
ARCHBISHOP
No, no, my lord. Note this: the King is weary
Of dainty and such picking grievances,
For he hath found to end one doubt by death
Revives two greater in the heirs of life;   210
And therefore will he wipe his tables clean
And keep no telltale to his memory
That may repeat and history his loss
To new remembrance. For full well he knows
He cannot so precisely weed this land   215
As his misdoubts present occasion;
His foes are so enrooted with his friends
That, plucking to unfix an enemy,
He doth unfasten so and shake a friend;
So that this land, like an offensive wife   220
That hath enraged him on to offer strokes,
As he is striking holds his infant up
And hangs resolved correction in the arm
That was upreared to execution.
HASTINGS
Besides, the King hath wasted all his rods   225
On late offenders, that he now doth lack
The very instruments of chastisement,
So that his power, like to a fangless lion,
May offer but not hold.
ARCHBISHOP   'Tis very true,   230
And therefore be assured, my good Lord Marshal,
If we do now make our atonement well,
Our peace will, like a broken limb united,
Grow stronger for the breaking.

238. **just distance:** halfway

238 SD. **Enter:** Many editions mark a change of scene at this point.

241. **Before:** i.e., go before

242. **well encountered:** i.e., well met (a conventional greeting); **cousin:** a title given by princes to other princes and noblemen

244. **gentle:** noble

246. **it . . . you:** i.e., you looked better

247. **When that:** i.e., when

250. **iron man:** i.e., warrior in armor

255. **Would he:** i.e., if he should; **countenance:** favor

257. **In shadow of:** under the protection of

259. **even:** just

260. **How . . . God:** (1) how much you were in God's favor; (2) how theologically learned you were

Full armor for a warrior.
From Wilhelm Dilich, . . . *Krieges-Schule* . . . (1689).

MOWBRAY   Be it so.   235
Here is returned my Lord of Westmoreland.

Enter Westmoreland.

WESTMORELAND, ⌜*to the Archbishop*⌝
The Prince is here at hand. Pleaseth your Lordship
To meet his Grace just distance 'tween our armies.

Enter Prince John and his army.

MOWBRAY, ⌜*to the Archbishop*⌝
Your Grace of York, in God's name then set
    forward.   240
ARCHBISHOP
Before, and greet his Grace.—My lord, we come.
                            ⌜*All move forward.*⌝
JOHN OF LANCASTER
You are well encountered here, my cousin
    Mowbray.—
Good day to you, gentle Lord Archbishop,—
And so to you, Lord Hastings, and to all.—   245
My Lord of York, it better showed with you
When that your flock, assembled by the bell,
Encircled you to hear with reverence
Your exposition on the holy text
⟨Than⟩ now to see you here, an iron man talking,   250
Cheering a rout of rebels with your drum,
Turning the word to sword, and life to death.
That man that sits within a monarch's heart
And ripens in the sunshine of his favor,
Would he abuse the countenance of the King,   255
Alack, what mischiefs might he set abroach
In shadow of such greatness! With you, Lord
    Bishop,
It is even so. Who hath not heard it spoken
How deep you were within the books of God,   260

261. **the speaker . . . parliament:** i.e., the one who addressed God on behalf of humankind just as the **speaker** in **parliament** addresses the monarch on behalf of the Commons

263. **opener and intelligencer:** i.e., interpreter and messenger

265. **workings:** functions

268. **false:** treacherous

269. **ta'en up:** recruited, enlisted

273. **up-swarmed them:** perhaps, gathered them in swarms

278. **in common sense:** i.e., as is obvious

281. **parcels:** details; **grief:** formal grievance

284. **Hydra:** the mythological monster who grew two heads for each one cut off (See page 160.)

285. **eyes . . . asleep:** Hydra now seems to become Argus, the mythological giant with a hundred **eyes,** who was **charmed asleep** by the music of Mercury.

291. **though:** even if

292. **supplies:** reinforcements of troops; **second:** take the place of, succeed (as also in line 293)

294. **success of mischief:** i.e., a succession of trouble

To us the speaker in His parliament,
To us th' ⌜imagined⌝ voice of God Himself,
The very opener and intelligencer
Between the grace, the sanctities, of heaven,
And our dull workings? O, who shall believe   265
But you misuse the reverence of your place,
⟨Employ⟩ the countenance and grace of heaven
As a false favorite doth his prince's name,
In deeds dishonorable? You have ta'en up,
Under the counterfeited zeal of God,   270
The subjects of His substitute, my father,
And both against the peace of heaven and him
Have here up-swarmed them.
ARCHBISHOP   Good my Lord of
    Lancaster,   275
I am not here against your father's peace,
But, as I told my Lord of Westmoreland,
The time misordered doth, in common sense,
Crowd us and crush us to this monstrous form
To hold our safety up. I sent your Grace   280
The parcels and particulars of our grief,
The which hath been with scorn shoved from the
    court,
Whereon this Hydra son of war is born,
Whose dangerous eyes may well be charmed asleep   285
With grant of our most just and right desires,
And true obedience, of this madness cured,
Stoop tamely to the foot of majesty.
MOWBRAY
If not, we ready are to try our fortunes
To the last man.   290
HASTINGS   And though we here fall down,
We have supplies to second our attempt;
If they miscarry, theirs shall second them,
And so success of mischief shall be born,

295. **hold . . . up:** i.e., maintain this state of hostility

296. **generation:** offspring, progeny

301. **allow them:** approve of them

304. **lavishly:** loosely

318. **part:** depart

Hercules fighting the Hydra. (4.1.284)
From Guillaume de La Perrière, *Le théâtre
des bon engins* . . . [1539?].

And heir from heir shall hold his quarrel up   295
Whiles England shall have generation.
JOHN OF LANCASTER
You are too shallow, Hastings, much too shallow
To sound the bottom of the after-times.
WESTMORELAND
Pleaseth your Grace to answer them directly
How far forth you do like their articles.   300
JOHN OF LANCASTER
I like them all, and do allow them well,
And swear here by the honor of my blood
My father's purposes have been mistook,
And some about him have too lavishly
Wrested his meaning and authority.   305
⌐To the Archbishop.⌐ My lord, these griefs shall be
    with speed redressed;
Upon my soul, they shall. If this may please you,
Discharge your powers unto their several counties,
As we will ours, and here, between the armies,   310
Let's drink together friendly and embrace,
That all their eyes may bear those tokens home
Of our restorèd love and amity.
ARCHBISHOP
I take your princely word for these redresses.
⟨JOHN OF LANCASTER⟩
I give it you, and will maintain my word,   315
And thereupon I drink unto your Grace.
    ⌐The Leaders of both armies begin to drink together.⌐
⟨HASTINGS,⟩ ⌐to an Officer⌐
Go, captain, and deliver to the army
This news of peace. Let them have pay, and part.
I know it will well please them. Hie thee, captain.
                                    ⌐Officer ⟨exits.⟩⌐
ARCHBISHOP, ⌐toasting Westmoreland⌐
To you, my noble Lord of Westmoreland.   320
WESTMORELAND, ⌐returning the toast⌐

328. **in . . . season:** i.e., at an opportune moment

329. **on the sudden:** i.e., suddenly; **something:** i.e., somewhat

330. **Against ill chances:** i.e., just before disastrous events

331. **heaviness:** sadness, grief

335. **passing:** extremely

337. **rendered:** proclaimed

339. **had been:** i.e., would have been

Richard II.
From William Martyn, *The historie and lives of the kings of England . . .* (1638).

I pledge your Grace, and if you knew what pains
I have bestowed to breed this present peace,
You would drink freely. But my love to you
Shall show itself more openly hereafter.

ARCHBISHOP
I do not doubt you.   325

WESTMORELAND   I am glad of it.—
Health to my lord and gentle cousin, Mowbray.

MOWBRAY
You wish me health in very happy season,
For I am on the sudden something ill.

ARCHBISHOP
Against ill chances men are ever merry,   330
But heaviness foreruns the good event.

WESTMORELAND
Therefore be merry, coz, since sudden sorrow
Serves to say thus: "Some good thing comes
    tomorrow."

ARCHBISHOP
Believe me, I am passing light in spirit.   335

MOWBRAY
So much the worse if your own rule be true.
                                        Shout ⌜*within.*⌝

JOHN OF LANCASTER
The word of peace is rendered. Hark how they
    shout.

MOWBRAY
This had been cheerful after victory.

ARCHBISHOP
A peace is of the nature of a conquest,   340
For then both parties nobly are subdued,
And neither party loser.

JOHN OF LANCASTER, ⌜*to Westmoreland*⌝   Go, my lord,
And let our army be dischargèd too.
                          ⌜*Westmoreland ⟨exits.⟩*⌝

346. **trains:** i.e., troops

348. **coped withal:** i.e., fought with

353. **wherefore:** why

361. **sporting-place:** i.e., place of amusement or recreation

365. **capital treason:** treason punishable by death; **attach:** arrest

"The block of death." (4.1.379)
From [Richard Verstegen,] *Theatre des cruautez des hereticques* . . . (1607).

⌜*To the Archbishop.*⌝ And, good my lord, so please   345
    you, let our trains
March by us, that we may peruse the men
We should have coped withal.
ARCHBISHOP   Go, good Lord
    Hastings,   350
And ere they be dismissed, let them march by.
                                    ⌜*Hastings* ⟨*exits.*⟩⌝
JOHN OF LANCASTER
    I trust, lords, we shall lie tonight together.

                    Enter Westmoreland.

    Now, cousin, wherefore stands our army still?
WESTMORELAND
    The leaders, having charge from you to stand,
    Will not go off until they hear you speak.   355
JOHN OF LANCASTER   They know their duties.

                    Enter Hastings.

HASTINGS, ⌜*to the Archbishop*⌝
    My lord, our army is dispersed already.
    Like youthful steers unyoked, they take their
        courses
    East, west, north, south, or, like a school broke up,   360
    Each hurries toward his home and sporting-place.
WESTMORELAND
    Good tidings, my Lord Hastings, for the which
    I do arrest thee, traitor, of high treason.—
    And you, Lord Archbishop, and you, Lord Mowbray,
    Of capital treason I attach you both.   365
MOWBRAY
    Is this proceeding just and honorable?
WESTMORELAND   Is your assembly so?
ARCHBISHOP
    Will you thus break your faith?

369. **pawned:** pledged
373. **But for:** i.e., But as for
374. **Meet:** proper, fit
375. **arms:** active hostilities
376. **Fondly:** foolishly
377. **stray:** body of stragglers
379. **block of death:** i.e., wooden block for be-headings (See page 164.)

4.2 Falstaff meets a rebel knight, who surrenders to him. When Prince John reproaches Falstaff for his late arrival, Falstaff turns over his captive and requests permission to return to London by way of Gloucestershire.

---

0 SD. **Alarum:** a trumpet call to arms; **Excursions:** soldiers moving across the stage as if against the enemy
1. **condition:** social position, rank
6. **degree:** rank
9. **Dale:** wordplay on "dale" as a **deep** valley
13. **drops of thy lovers:** i.e., tears of your friends
15. **do observance:** i.e., pay your respects

JOHN OF LANCASTER   I pawned thee none.
  I promised you redress of these same grievances   370
  Whereof you did complain, which, by mine honor,
  I will perform with a most Christian care.
  But for you rebels, look to taste the due
  Meet for rebellion ⟨and such acts as yours.⟩
  Most shallowly did you these arms commence,   375
  Fondly brought here, and foolishly sent hence.
  Strike up our drums; pursue the scattered stray.
  God, and not we, hath safely fought today.—
  Some guard ⟨these traitors⟩ to the block of death,
  Treason's true bed and yielder-up of breath.   380
                            ⟨*They exit.*⟩

⌈Scene 2⌉

Alarum. Excursions. Enter Falstaff ⟨and Colevile.⟩

FALSTAFF   What's your name, sir? Of what condition are
  you, and of what place, ⟨I pray⟩?

COLEVILE   I am a knight, sir, and my name is Colevile of
  the Dale.

FALSTAFF   Well then, Colevile is your name, a knight is   5
  your degree, and your place the Dale. Colevile shall
  be still your name, a traitor your degree, and the
  dungeon your place, a place deep enough so shall
  you be still Colevile of the Dale.

COLEVILE   Are not you Sir John Falstaff?   10

FALSTAFF   As good a man as he, sir, whoe'er I am. Do
  you yield, sir, or shall I sweat for you? If I do sweat,
  they are the drops of thy lovers and they weep for
  thy death. Therefore rouse up fear and trembling,
  and do observance to my mercy.   15

COLEVILE   I think you are Sir John Falstaff, and in that
  thought yield me.

18–20. **I have . . . name:** i.e., my **belly** loudly proclaims who I am   **school:** i.e., multitude

20–21. **a belly . . . indifferency:** i.e., a **belly** of ordinary size

22. **womb:** belly; **undoes:** destroys

24. **heat:** i.e., urgency

25. **powers:** troops

30–31. **but . . . thus:** i.e., if it should be otherwise

31. **check:** reproach, reprimand

34. **expedition:** promptness

36. **foundered . . . posts:** i.e., made more than 180 post-horses lame

41. **hook-nosed . . . Rome:** i.e., Julius Caesar, whose boast "I came, I saw, I overcame" had become proverbial (See below.)

47–49. **I will . . . on 't:** Falstaff here describes a "broadside ballad," a narrative in doggerel printed on one side of a large sheet of paper and decorated with a woodcut.   **a particular ballad:** i.e., a ballad of my own   **else:** otherwise   **on 't:** i.e., of it

Julius Caesar (1.1.28; 4.2.41)
From Plutarch, *The liues of the noble Grecians and Romans . . .* (1579).

FALSTAFF I have a whole school of tongues in this belly
of mine, and not a tongue of them all speaks any
other word but my name. An I had but a belly of any   20
indifferency, I were simply the most active fellow in
Europe. My womb, my womb, my womb undoes
me. Here comes our general.

Enter John, Westmoreland, and the rest.

JOHN OF LANCASTER
The heat is past. Follow no further now.
Call in the powers, good cousin Westmoreland.   25
⌜*Westmoreland exits.*⌝ *Retreat* ⌜*is sounded.*⌝
Now, Falstaff, where have you been all this while?
When everything is ended, then you come.
These tardy tricks of yours will, on my life,
One time or other break some gallows' back.

FALSTAFF I would be sorry, my lord, but it should be   30
thus. I never knew yet but rebuke and check was the
reward of valor. Do you think me a swallow, an
arrow, or a bullet? Have I in my poor and old
motion the expedition of thought? I have speeded
hither with the very extremest inch of possibility. I   35
have foundered ninescore and odd posts, and here,
travel-tainted as I am, have in my pure and immacu-
late valor taken Sir John Colevile of the Dale, a most
furious knight and valorous enemy. But what of
that? He saw me and yielded, that I may justly say,   40
with the hook-nosed fellow of Rome, "There, cousin, I came, saw, and overcame."

JOHN OF LANCASTER It was more of his courtesy than
your deserving.

FALSTAFF I know not. Here he is, and here I yield him.   45
And I beseech your Grace let it be booked with the
rest of this day's deeds, or, by the Lord, I will have it
in a particular ballad else, with mine own picture
on the top on 't, Colevile kissing my foot; to the

50–51. **show . . . to me:** i.e., look like counterfeits in comparison **to me** **gilt twopences:** twopenny pieces painted in gilt to pass as half-crowns

53. **cinders of the element:** i.e., stars (See below.) **cinders:** embers, pieces of glowing coal

68. **dearer:** i.e., at more cost

73. **Retreat . . . stayed:** i.e., the pursuing forces have been recalled and the killing stopped

75. **present:** immediate

76. **sure:** securely

77. **dispatch:** hasten

78. **sore:** i.e., sorely, extremely

"The cinders of the element." (4.2.53)
From Jakob Rüff, *De conceptu et generatione hominis* . . . (1580).

which course if I be enforced, if you do not all show 50
like gilt twopences to me, and I in the clear sky of
fame o'ershine you as much as the full moon doth
the cinders of the element (which show like pins'
heads to her), believe not the word of the noble.
Therefore let me have right, and let desert mount. 55
JOHN OF LANCASTER Thine's too heavy to mount.
FALSTAFF Let it shine, then.
JOHN OF LANCASTER Thine's too thick to shine.
FALSTAFF Let it do something, my good lord, that may
  do me good, and call it what you will. 60
JOHN OF LANCASTER Is thy name Colevile?
COLEVILE It is, my lord.
JOHN OF LANCASTER A famous rebel art thou, Cole-
  vile.
FALSTAFF And a famous true subject took him. 65
COLEVILE
  I am, my lord, but as my betters are
  That led me hither. Had they been ruled by me,
  You should have won them dearer than you have.
FALSTAFF I know not how they sold themselves, but
  thou, like a kind fellow, gavest thyself away gratis, 70
  and I thank thee for thee

         Enter Westmoreland.

JOHN OF LANCASTER Now, have you left pursuit?
WESTMORELAND
  Retreat is made and execution stayed.
JOHN OF LANCASTER
  Send Colevile with his confederates
  To York, to present execution.— 75
  Blunt, lead him hence, and see you guard him sure.
        ⌜*Blunt ⟨exits with Colevile.⟩*⌝
  And now dispatch we toward the court, my lords.
  I hear the King my father is sore sick.

85. **stand:** i.e., act as

87. **in my condition:** i.e., as Duke of Lancaster

93. **never none:** i.e., never any

93–94. **demure:** sober, serious

94. **come . . . proof:** i.e., amount to anything; **thin drink:** i.e., beer

96. **green-sickness:** a form of anemia thought to affect girls at puberty

97. **get wenches:** beget girls

99. **inflammation:** i.e., inflaming the passions (with drink)

99–100. **sherris sack:** sherry (Falstaff uses the words **sherris** and **sack** to refer to this dry Spanish wine.)

100, 101. **ascends me, dries me:** i.e., ascends, dries

102. **crudy:** i.e., curdy, coagulated; **vapors:** unhealthy fumes

103. **apprehensive:** intelligent, discerning; **forgetive:** i.e., creative (a Shakespearean adjective, presumably created from the verb "to forge")

111. **inwards:** inner parts of the body; **extremes:** extremities

Our news shall go before us to his Majesty,
⌜*To Westmoreland.*⌝ Which, cousin, you shall bear   80
  to comfort him,
And we with sober speed will follow you.

FALSTAFF   My lord, I beseech you give me leave to go
  through Gloucestershire, and, when you come to
  court, stand my good lord, ⟨pray,⟩ in your good   85
  report.

JOHN OF LANCASTER
  Fare you well, Falstaff. I, in my condition,
  Shall better speak of you than you deserve.
                    ⌜*All but Falstaff* ⟨*exit.*⟩⌝

FALSTAFF   I would you had ⟨but⟩ the wit; 'twere better
  than your dukedom. Good faith, this same young   90
  sober-blooded boy doth not love me, nor a man
  cannot make him laugh. But that's no marvel; he
  drinks no wine. There's never none of these demure boys come to any proof, for thin drink doth so
  overcool their blood, and making many fish meals,   95
  that they fall into a kind of male green-sickness, and
  then, when they marry, they get wenches. They are
  generally fools and cowards, which some of us
  should be too, but for inflammation. A good sherris
  sack hath a two-fold operation in it. It ascends me   100
  into the brain, dries me there all the foolish and
  dull and crudy vapors which environ it, makes it
  apprehensive, quick, forgetive, full of nimble, fiery,
  and delectable shapes, which, delivered o'er to the
  voice, the tongue, which is the birth, becomes   105
  excellent wit. The second property of your excellent sherris is the warming of the blood, which,
  before cold and settled, left the liver white and pale,
  which is the badge of pusillanimity and cowardice.
  But the sherris warms it and makes it course from   110
  the inwards to the parts' extremes. It illumineth the

114. **vital . . . spirits:** i.e., the **spirits** carried by the blood   **inland:** interior

114–15. **muster me all to:** i.e., all gather around

119. **learning:** i.e., **learning** is

119–20. **kept by a devil:** i.e., guarded by an evil spirit

120–21. **commences . . . use:** i.e., empowers the use of the **hoard** of **learning** (wordplay on university "commencement," when the student is given authority to use his **learning**)

123. **lean:** poor

124. **husbanded:** cultivated

125. **good store:** great quantities

127. **human:** secular

134. **temp'ring:** softening (like the sealing wax alluded to in lines 135–36)

135. **seal:** reach a (profitable) agreement (with wordplay on **seal with him** as "use him to clinch the agreement by affixing him to the document")

face, which as a beacon gives warning to all the rest
of this little kingdom, man, to arm; and then the
vital commoners and inland petty spirits muster me
all to their captain, the heart, who, great and puffed   115
up with this retinue, doth any deed of courage, and
this valor comes of sherris. So that skill in the
weapon is nothing without sack, for that sets it
a-work; and learning a mere hoard of gold kept
by a devil till sack commences it and sets it in   120
act and use. Hereof comes it that Prince Harry is
valiant, for the cold blood he did naturally inherit
of his father he hath, like lean, sterile, and bare
land, manured, husbanded, and tilled with excellent endeavor of drinking good and good store   125
of fertile sherris, that he is become very hot and valiant. If I had a thousand sons, the first human prin-
ciple I would teach them should be to forswear
thin potations and to addict themselves to sack.

Enter Bardolph.

How now, Bardolph?   130
BARDOLPH The army is discharged all and gone.
FALSTAFF Let them go. I'll through Gloucestershire,
and there will I visit Master Robert Shallow,
Esquire. I have him already temp'ring between my
finger and my thumb, and shortly will I seal with   135
him. Come away.

(They exit.)

4.3 Just after receiving the good news about the defeat of all the rebel forces, Henry IV falls into a swoon. Prince Hal, sitting at the king's bedside, thinks him dead and takes the crown. The king berates him, Hal explains and apologizes, and peace is made between them. The king is taken into the Jerusalem Chamber to die.

---

2. **debate:** strife

3–4. **our . . . sanctified:** i.e., **lead** the armies only on a crusade (See note to 3.1.112 and picture, page 200.)

5. **addressed:** ready

6. **substitutes in absence:** i.e., deputies; **invested:** furnished with my power and authority

7. **lies level to:** is readily accessible to

8. **Only we want:** i.e., I only lack

13–14. **the Prince:** i.e., Prince Hal

19. **in presence:** in attendance (at the court)

20. **would:** i.e., wishes

⟨Scene ⌈3⌉⟩

Enter the King ⌈in a chair,⌉ Warwick, Thomas Duke of
Clarence, Humphrey ⌈Duke⌉ of Gloucester, ⌈and
Attendants.⌉

KING
  Now, lords, if God doth give successful end
  To this debate that bleedeth at our doors,
  We will our youth lead on to higher fields
  And draw no swords but what are sanctified.
  Our navy is addressed, our power collected,   5
  Our substitutes in absence well invested,
  And everything lies level to our wish.
  Only we want a little personal strength;
  And pause us till these rebels now afoot
  Come underneath the yoke of government.   10

WARWICK
  Both which we doubt not but your Majesty
  Shall soon enjoy.

KING
  Humphrey, my son of Gloucester, where is the
    Prince your brother?

HUMPHREY OF GLOUCESTER
  I think he's gone to hunt, my lord, at Windsor. 15

KING
  And how accompanied?

HUMPHREY OF GLOUCESTER   I do not know, my lord.

KING
  Is not his brother Thomas of Clarence with him?

HUMPHREY OF GLOUCESTER
  No, my good lord, he is in presence here.

THOMAS OF CLARENCE, ⌈*coming forward*⌉ What would   20
    my lord and father?

KING
  Nothing but well to thee, Thomas of Clarence.

28. **offices:** functions

31. **omit:** neglect

34. **gracious:** willing to be kind; **observed:** humored, treated with respect

36. **Open:** generous; **day:** daylight; **melting:** tender

38. **humorous:** capricious

39. **flaws . . . day:** i.e., flakes of snow turned to ice at daybreak (but with probable wordplay on **flaws** as outbursts of passion)

45. **Confound:** destroy, consume; **working:** exertion

47. **friends:** relatives

48–53. **A hoop . . . gunpowder:** In these lines Thomas is compared to a gold ring that encircles and secures the integrity of a chalice containing the blood of the royal family. **suggestion:** promptings to evil; or, perhaps, false charges **aconitum:** i.e., aconite, an extremely potent poison **rash:** quick-acting

54. **observe:** honor, court

55. **Windsor:** See longer note to 2.1.93, page 251.

How chance thou art not with the Prince thy
   brother?
He loves thee, and thou dost neglect him, Thomas.   25
Thou hast a better place in his affection
Than all thy brothers. Cherish it, my boy,
And noble offices thou mayst effect
Of mediation, after I am dead,
Between his greatness and thy other brethren.   30
Therefore omit him not, blunt not his love,
Nor lose the good advantage of his grace
By seeming cold or careless of his will.
For he is gracious if he be observed;
He hath a tear for pity, and a hand   35
Open as day for ⟨melting⟩ charity;
Yet notwithstanding, being incensed he is flint,
As humorous as winter, and as sudden
As flaws congealèd in the spring of day.
His temper therefore must be well observed.   40
Chide him for faults, and do it reverently,
When you perceive his blood inclined to mirth;
But, being moody, give him time and scope
Till that his passions, like a whale on ground,
Confound themselves with working. Learn this,   45
   Thomas,
And thou shalt prove a shelter to thy friends,
A hoop of gold to bind thy brothers in,
That the united vessel of their blood,
Mingled with venom of suggestion   50
(As, force perforce, the age will pour it in),
Shall never leak, though it do work as strong
As aconitum or rash gunpowder.

THOMAS OF CLARENCE
   I shall observe him with all care and love.
KING
   Why art thou not at Windsor with him, Thomas?   55

59. **Most . . . weeds:** proverbial   **fattest:** most fertile

69. **lavish:** impetuous, wild

70. **affections:** inclinations

71. **fronting peril:** dangers that face him; **opposed decay:** ruin opposing him

72. **look beyond:** i.e., misconstrue

74. **strange tongue:** foreign language

79. **gross terms:** i.e., **immodest** words (line 76)

83. **mete:** appraise, judge

An "angel." (1.2.168)
From Henry William Henfrey, *A guide to . . . English coins* (1885).

THOMAS OF CLARENCE
He is not there today; he dines in London.
KING
And how accompanied? ⟨Canst thou tell that?⟩
THOMAS OF CLARENCE
With Poins and other his continual followers.
KING
Most subject is the fattest soil to weeds,
And he, the noble image of my youth,   60
Is overspread with them; therefore my grief
Stretches itself beyond the hour of death.
The blood weeps from my heart when I do shape,
In forms imaginary, th' unguided days
And rotten times that you shall look upon   65
When I am sleeping with my ancestors.
For when his headstrong riot hath no curb,
When rage and hot blood are his counsellors,
When means and lavish manners meet together,
O, with what wings shall his affections fly   70
Towards fronting peril and opposed decay!
WARWICK
My gracious lord, you look beyond him quite.
The Prince but studies his companions
Like a strange tongue, wherein, to gain the
   language,   75
'Tis needful that the most immodest word
Be looked upon and learned; which, once attained,
Your Highness knows, comes to no further use
But to be known and hated. So, like gross terms,
The Prince will, in the perfectness of time,   80
Cast off his followers, and their memory
Shall as a pattern or a measure live,
By which his Grace must mete the lives of others,
Turning past evils to advantages.

85. **comb:** honeycomb (perhaps an allusion to the story of Samson finding the swarm of bees in their **comb** in the dead lion [Judges 14.8])

90. **doth . . . hand:** i.e., sends his respects to you

94. **olive:** olive branch, a symbol of peace and goodwill

97. **course:** phase or stage; or, perhaps, attack (**Course** was a technical term in both bearbaiting and hunting.); **in his particular:** i.e., in detail

99. **haunch:** i.e., latter end

100. **lifting up of day:** i.e., daybreak

107. **shrieve:** sheriff

109. **at large:** in full

Paíx.

Peace. (4.3.94)
From Gilles Corrozet, *Hecatongraphie* . . . (1543).

KING
　'Tis seldom when the bee doth leave her comb　　　　85
　In the dead carrion.

Enter Westmoreland.

　　　　　　　Who's here? Westmoreland?
WESTMORELAND
　Health to my sovereign, and new happiness
　Added to that that I am to deliver.
　Prince John your son doth kiss your Grace's hand.　　90
　Mowbray, the Bishop Scroop, Hastings, and all
　Are brought to the correction of your law.
　There is not now a rebel's sword unsheathed,
　But peace puts forth her olive everywhere.
　The manner how this action hath been borne　　　95
　Here at more leisure may your Highness read
　With every course in his particular.
　　　　　　　　⌈*He gives the King a paper.*⌉
KING
　O Westmoreland, thou art a summer bird,
　Which ever in the haunch of winter sings
　The lifting up of day.　　　　　　　　　　　100

Enter Harcourt.

　　　　　　　Look, here's more news.
HARCOURT
　From enemies heavens keep your Majesty,
　And when they stand against you, may they fall
　As those that I am come to tell you of.
　The Earl Northumberland and the Lord Bardolph,　　105
　With a great power of English and of Scots,
　Are by the shrieve of Yorkshire overthrown.
　The manner and true order of the fight
　This packet, please it you, contains at large.
　　　　　　　　⌈*He gives the King papers.*⌉

112. **Fortune:** the goddess Fortune, who personifies the operation of chance in one's life (See page 230.)

113. **still:** always

114. **a stomach:** i.e., an appetite

126. **straight:** i.e., straightway, immediately

128. **hold out:** i.e., endure

130. **wrought:** made, rendered; **mure:** wall

132. **fear me:** i.e., frighten me

133. **loathly:** hideous, disgusting

134. **as:** i.e., as if

138. **doting:** weakminded, senile

KING
  And wherefore should these good news make me   110
    sick?
  Will Fortune never come with both hands full,
  But ⟨write⟩ her fair words still in foulest ⟨letters⟩?
  She either gives a stomach and no food—
  Such are the poor, in health—or else a feast   115
  And takes away the stomach—such are the rich,
  That have abundance and enjoy it not.
  I should rejoice now at this happy news,
  And now my sight fails, and my brain is giddy.
  O, me! Come near me, now I am much ill.   120
HUMPHREY OF GLOUCESTER
  Comfort, your Majesty.
THOMAS OF CLARENCE   O, my royal father!
WESTMORELAND
  My sovereign lord, cheer up yourself, look up.
WARWICK
  Be patient, princes. You do know these fits
  Are with his Highness very ordinary.   125
  Stand from him, give him air. He'll straight be
    well.
THOMAS OF CLARENCE
  No, no, he cannot long hold out these pangs.
  Th' incessant care and labor of his mind
  Hath wrought the mure that should confine it in   130
  So thin that life looks through ⟨and will break out.⟩
HUMPHREY OF GLOUCESTER
  The people fear me, for they do observe
  Unfathered heirs and loathly births of nature.
  The seasons change their manners, as the year
  Had found some months asleep and leapt them   135
    over.
THOMAS OF CLARENCE
  The river hath thrice flowed, no ebb between,
  And the old folk, time's doting chronicles,

140. **Edward:** i.e., Edward III, grandfather of Henry IV (See below.) **sicked:** fell ill

142. **apoplexy:** paralysis

144. **Softly:** gently; **pray:** i.e., I beg you

144 SD. **The King . . . stage:** Many editions begin a new scene at this point.

146. **dull:** slow; **favorable:** well-disposed, kind

149. **Set me:** i.e., set, place

151. **Less noise:** perhaps in response to the **noise** of Prince Hal's approach

153. **heaviness:** sadness

154. **abroad:** out of doors

Edward III. (4.3.140)
From John Taylor, *All the workes of . . .* (1630).

Say it did so a little time before
That our great-grandsire, Edward, sicked and died.   140
WARWICK
Speak lower, princes, for the King recovers.
HUMPHREY OF GLOUCESTER
This apoplexy will certain be his end.
KING
I pray you take me up and bear me hence
Into some other chamber. ⟨Softly, pray.⟩
                    ⌜*The King is carried to a bed on another*
                                   part of the stage.⌝
Let there be no noise made, my gentle friends,   145
Unless some dull and favorable hand
Will whisper music to my weary spirit.
WARWICK, ⌜*to an Attendant*⌝
Call for the music in the other room.
KING
Set me the crown upon my pillow here.
                    ⌜*The crown is placed on the bed.*⌝
THOMAS OF CLARENCE, ⌜*aside to the others*⌝
His eye is hollow, and he changes much.   150
WARWICK
Less noise, less noise.

                    Enter ⟨Prince⟩ Harry.

PRINCE   Who saw the Duke of Clarence?
THOMAS OF CLARENCE, ⌜*weeping*⌝
I am here, brother, full of heaviness.
PRINCE
How now, rain within doors, and none abroad?
How doth the King?   155
HUMPHREY OF GLOUCESTER   Exceeding ill.
PRINCE
Heard he the good news yet? Tell it him.
HUMPHREY OF GLOUCESTER
He altered much upon the hearing it.

160. **physic:** medicine
169. **perturbation:** cause of disturbance
170. **ports:** gates
171. **watchful:** sleepless; **Sleep . . . now:** i.e., may you **sleep** despite its presence
172. **Yet not:** i.e., yet you will not sleep
173. **biggen:** nightcap
174. **watch of night:** i.e., all the watches of the night (The **night** was at one time divided into several intervals called "watches.")
175. **pinch:** torment
177. **with safety:** i.e., while providing **safety**
179. **suspire:** breathe
182. **rigol:** ring, circle
188. **as immediate from:** i.e., as next in succession to
189. **Derives itself:** i.e., passes by descent

PRINCE   If he be sick with joy, he'll recover without
    physic.   160
WARWICK
    Not so much noise, my lords.—Sweet prince, speak
    low.
    The King your father is disposed to sleep.
THOMAS OF CLARENCE
    Let us withdraw into the other room.
WARWICK
    Will 't please your Grace to go along with us?   165
PRINCE
    No, I will sit and watch here by the King.
                ⌜*All but Prince and King exit.*⌝
    Why doth the crown lie there upon his pillow,
    Being so troublesome a bedfellow?
    O polished perturbation, golden care,
    That keep'st the ports of slumber open wide   170
    To many a watchful night! Sleep with it now;
    Yet not so sound and half so deeply sweet
    As he whose brow with homely biggen bound
    Snores out the watch of night. O majesty,
    When thou dost pinch thy bearer, thou dost sit   175
    Like a rich armor worn in heat of day,
    That scald'st with safety. By his gates of breath
    There lies a downy feather which stirs not;
    Did he suspire, that light and weightless down
    Perforce must move. My gracious lord, my father,   180
    This sleep is sound indeed. This is a sleep
    That from this golden rigol hath divorced
    So many English kings. Thy due from me
    Is tears and heavy sorrows of the blood,
    Which nature, love, and filial tenderness   185
    Shall, O dear father, pay thee plenteously.
    My due from thee is this imperial crown,
    Which, as immediate from thy place and blood,
    Derives itself to me. ⌜*He puts on the crown.*⌝ Lo,
    where it sits,   190

214. **part:** action

"Why doth the crown lie there . . . ?" (4.3.167)
From Juan de Solorzano Pereira, . . . *Emblemata
regio politica* . . . (1653).

Which God shall guard. And, put the world's whole
     strength
Into one giant arm, it shall not force
This lineal honor from me. This from thee
Will I to mine leave, as 'tis left to me.   195
                    He exits ⌜*with the crown.*⌝
KING, ⌜*rising up in his bed*⌝   Warwick! Gloucester!
     Clarence!

Enter Warwick, Gloucester, Clarence, ⌜*and others.*⌝

THOMAS OF CLARENCE   Doth the King call?
WARWICK
What would your Majesty? ⟨How fares your Grace?⟩
KING
Why did you leave me here alone, my lords?   200
THOMAS OF CLARENCE
We left the Prince my brother here, my liege,
Who undertook to sit and watch by you.
KING
The Prince of Wales? Where is he? Let me see him.
[He is not here.]
WARWICK
This door is open. He is gone this way.   205
HUMPHREY OF GLOUCESTER
He came not through the chamber where we
     stayed.
KING
Where is the crown? Who took it from my pillow?
WARWICK
When we withdrew, my liege, we left it here.
KING
The Prince hath ta'en it hence. Go seek him out.   210
Is he so hasty that he doth suppose my sleep my
     death?
Find him, my Lord of Warwick. Chide him hither.
                    ⌜*Warwick exits.*⌝
This part of his conjoins with my disease

220. **thoughts:** i.e., worries, cares
221. **industry:** exertion, effort
222. **engrossèd:** collected, amassed
223. **cankered:** tarnished; **strange-achievèd:** amassed in foreign lands, or through extraordinary efforts
224. **thoughtful:** careful; **invest:** provide
226. **tolling:** i.e., taking as a toll
231–32. **This . . . father:** i.e., his acquisitions yield **this bitter taste** to the dying **father**
234. **determined:** terminated
236. **kindly:** natural, filial
237. **deep:** profoundly felt
240. **eyedrops:** tears
241. **wherefore:** why

And helps to end me. See, sons, what things you   215
   are,
How quickly nature falls into revolt
When gold becomes her object!
For this the foolish overcareful fathers
Have broke their sleep with thoughts,   220
Their brains with care, their bones with industry.
For this they have engrossèd and ⟨piled⟩ up
The cankered heaps of strange-achievèd gold.
For this they have been thoughtful to invest
Their sons with arts and martial exercises—   225
When, like the bee, tolling from every flower
⟨The virtuous sweets,⟩
Our ⟨thighs⟩ packed with wax, our mouths with
   honey,
We bring it to the hive and, like the bees,   230
Are murdered for our pains. This bitter taste
Yields his engrossments to the ending father.

Enter Warwick.

Now where is he that will not stay so long
Till his friend sickness ⟨hath⟩ determined me?
WARWICK
My lord, I found the Prince in the next room,   235
Washing with kindly tears his gentle cheeks,
With such a deep demeanor in great sorrow
That tyranny, which never quaffed but blood,
Would, by beholding him, have washed his knife
With gentle eyedrops. He is coming hither.   240
KING
But wherefore did he take away the crown?

Enter ⟨Prince⟩ Harry ⌜with the crown.⌝

Lo where he comes.—Come hither to me, Harry.—
Depart the chamber. Leave us here alone.
   ⌜*Gloucester, Clarence, Warwick, and others*⌝ *exit.*

248. **wilt needs:** must

252–54. **cloud . . . drop:** The image is of a cloud about to fall as rain because it is kept aloft only by a very weak wind (with wordplay on **wind** as respiration).

257. **sealed up my expectation:** ratified or confirmed my prediction

261. **Whom:** which

263. **forbear:** (1) put up with, tolerate; or, (2) spare

265–66. **bells . . . dead:** Bells would be tolled to announce the death of the king and later to celebrate the coronation of the new king.

267. **hearse:** a wooden structure used in royal funerals, covered and adorned with banners and lighted candles

268. **balm:** fragrant oil used for anointing a monarch in the coronation ceremony

272. **form:** proper behavior

273. **vanity:** This could mean, for example, "worthlessness," "futility," "triviality," and "folly," as well as "conceit and desire for admiration." All of these may be intended here.

277. **idleness:** foolishness

PRINCE
   I never thought to hear you speak again.
KING
   Thy wish was father, Harry, to that thought.   245
   I stay too long by thee; I weary thee.
   Dost thou so hunger for mine empty chair
   That thou wilt needs invest thee with my honors
   Before thy hour be ripe? O foolish youth,
   Thou seek'st the greatness that will overwhelm   250
      thee.
   Stay but a little, for my cloud of dignity
   Is held from falling with so weak a wind
   That it will quickly drop. My day is dim.
   Thou hast stol'n that which after some few hours   255
   Were thine without offense, and at my death
   Thou hast sealed up my expectation.
   Thy life did manifest thou loved'st me not,
   And thou wilt have me die assured of it.
   Thou hid'st a thousand daggers in thy thoughts,   260
   Whom thou hast whetted on thy stony heart
   To stab at half an hour of my life.
   What, canst thou not forbear me half an hour?
   Then get thee gone, and dig my grave thyself,
   And bid the merry bells ring to thine ear   265
   That thou art crownèd, not that I am dead.
   Let all the tears that should bedew my hearse
   Be drops of balm to sanctify thy head;
   Only compound me with forgotten dust.
   Give that which gave thee life unto the worms.   270
   Pluck down my officers, break my decrees,
   For now a time is come to mock at form.
   Harry the Fifth is crowned. Up, vanity,
   Down, royal state, all you sage councillors,
      hence,   275
   And to the English court assemble now,
   From every region, apes of idleness.

278. **confines:** regions
285. **curbed:** controlled as a dog is by a muzzle;
license: excess
287. **flesh his tooth on:** i.e., plunge his teeth into
288. **civil blows:** i.e., the **blows** of **civil** war
289. **care:** anxiety, attention, pains
290. **riot:** moral disorder, debauchery
295. **dear:** severe, dire
299. **affect:** want, desire
302. **obedience:** bow of submission
306. **course:** i.e., flowing

Now, neighbor confines, purge you of your scum.
Have you a ruffian that will swear, drink, dance,
Revel the night, rob, murder, and commit   280
The oldest sins the newest kind of ways?
Be happy, he will trouble you no more.
England shall double gild his treble guilt.
England shall give him office, honor, might,
For the fifth Harry from curbed license plucks   285
The muzzle of restraint, and the wild dog
Shall flesh his tooth on every innocent.
O my poor kingdom, sick with civil blows!
When that my care could not withhold thy riots,
What wilt thou do when riot is thy care?   290
O, thou wilt be a wilderness again,
Peopled with wolves, thy old inhabitants.
PRINCE, ⌜*placing the crown on the pillow*⌝
  O pardon me, my liege! But for my tears,
The moist impediments unto my speech,
I had forestalled this dear and deep rebuke   295
Ere you with grief had spoke and I had heard
The course of it so far. There is your crown,
And He that wears the crown immortally
Long guard it yours. ⌜*He kneels.*⌝ If I affect it
  more   300
Than as your honor and as your renown,
Let me no more from this obedience rise,
Which my most inward true and duteous spirit
Teacheth this prostrate and exterior bending.
God witness with me, when I here came in   305
And found no course of breath within your Majesty,
How cold it struck my heart! If I do feign,
O, let me in my present wildness die
And never live to show th' incredulous world
The noble change that I have purposèd.   310
Coming to look on you, thinking you dead,
And dead almost, my liege, to think you were,

313. **as having sense:** i.e., as if it had the **sense** of hearing

319. **med'cine potable:** i.e., *aurum potabile*, "drinkable gold," used as a medicine

321. **eat:** i.e., eaten (pronounced "et")

323. **try:** i.e., contest

327. **strain:** degree

329. **affection of:** tendency to

330. **the might of it:** i.e., the crown's power

339. **latest:** last, final

346. **opinion:** standing, reputation

The story of the Prodigal Son. (2.1.150–51)
From Guillaume Guéroult, Figures de la Bible . . . (1565–70).

I spake unto this crown as having sense,
And thus upbraided it: "The care on thee
   depending 315
Hath fed upon the body of my father;
Therefore thou best of gold art ⟨worst of⟩ gold.
Other, less fine in carat, ⟨is⟩ more precious,
Preserving life in med'cine potable;
But thou, most fine, most honored, most renowned, 320
Hast eat thy bearer up." Thus, my most royal liege,
Accusing it, I put it on my head
To try with it, as with an enemy
That had before my face murdered my father,
The quarrel of a true inheritor. 325
But if it did infect my blood with joy
Or swell my thoughts to any strain of pride,
If any rebel or vain spirit of mine
Did with the least affection of a welcome
Give entertainment to the might of it, 330
Let God forever keep it from my head
And make me as the poorest vassal is
That doth with awe and terror kneel to it.
KING ⟨O my son,⟩
God put ⟨it⟩ in thy mind to take it hence 335
That thou mightst win the more thy father's love,
Pleading so wisely in excuse of it.
Come hither, Harry, sit thou by my bed
And hear, I think, the very latest counsel
That ever I shall breathe. 340
       ⌜*The Prince rises from his knees and sits*
                      near the bed.⌝
            God knows, my son,
By what bypaths and indirect crook'd ways
I met this crown, and I myself know well
How troublesome it sat upon my head.
To thee it shall descend with better quiet, 345
Better opinion, better confirmation,

347. **soil of the achievement:** i.e., stain associated with how I got it

349. **boist'rous:** savage, violent

353. **fears:** i.e., things to be feared

354. **answerèd:** encountered, met in battle

356. **argument:** theme

358. **more fairer:** i.e., **fairer**

359. **garland:** crown; **successively:** by inheritance

361. **griefs are green:** i.e., grievances are fresh, or raw

368. **cut them off:** i.e., stopped them

370–71. **look . . . state:** i.e., examine my kingship too closely

373–74. **that action . . . out:** i.e., so that military action carried out elsewhere

375. **waste:** undermine the strength of, obliterate

376. **More would I:** i.e., I would say more

A map of the Holy Land. (3.1.112; 4.3.3–4, 399)
From the Geneva Bible (1562).

For all the soil of the achievement goes
With me into the earth. It seemed in me
But as an honor snatched with boist'rous hand,
And I had many living to upbraid   350
My gain of it by their assistances,
Which daily grew to quarrel and to bloodshed,
Wounding supposèd peace. All these bold fears
Thou seest with peril I have answerèd,
For all my reign hath been but as a scene   355
Acting that argument. And now my death
Changes the mood, for what in me was purchased
Falls upon thee in a more fairer sort.
So thou the garland wear'st successively.
Yet though thou stand'st more sure than I could do,   360
Thou art not firm enough, since griefs are green,
And all ⌐my⌐ friends, which thou must make thy
    friends,
Have but their stings and teeth newly ta'en out,
By whose fell working I was first advanced   365
And by whose power I well might lodge a fear
To be again displaced; which to avoid,
I cut them off and had a purpose now
To lead out many to the Holy Land,
Lest rest and lying still might make them look   370
Too near unto my state. Therefore, my Harry,
Be it thy course to busy giddy minds
With foreign quarrels, that action, hence borne
    out,
May waste the memory of the former days.   375
More would I, but my lungs are wasted so
That strength of speech is utterly denied me.
How I came by the crown, O God forgive,
And grant it may with thee in true peace live.
PRINCE ⟨My gracious liege,⟩   380
    You won it, wore it, kept it, gave it me.

383. **pain:** effort
389. **Upon thy sight:** i.e., upon seeing you
390. **My . . . period:** i.e., my life reaches its end
394. **lodging:** bedroom
398. **but:** except
399. **vainly:** foolishly

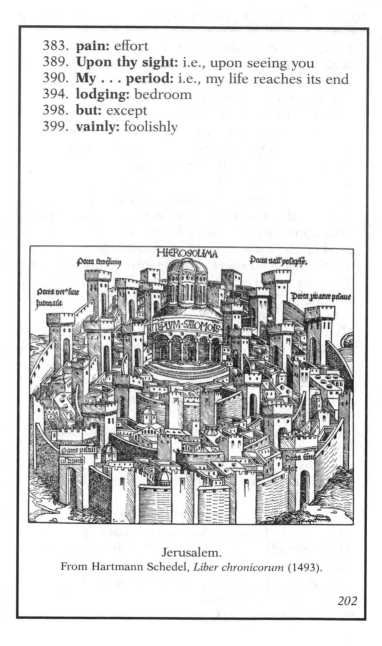

Jerusalem.
From Hartmann Schedel, *Liber chronicorum* (1493).

Then plain and right must my possession be,
Which I with more than with a common pain
'Gainst all the world will rightfully maintain.

Enter ⟨John of⟩ Lancaster ⌜*and others.*⌝

KING
Look, look, here comes my John of Lancaster.   385
JOHN OF LANCASTER
Health, peace, and happiness to my royal father.
KING
Thou bring'st me happiness and peace, son John,
But health, alack, with youthful wings is flown
From this bare withered trunk. Upon thy sight
My worldly business makes a period.   390
Where is my Lord of Warwick?
PRINCE   My Lord of Warwick.

⌜*Enter ⟨Warwick.⟩*⌝

KING
Doth any name particular belong
Unto the lodging where I first did swoon?
WARWICK
'Tis called Jerusalem, my noble lord.   395
KING
Laud be to God! Even there my life must end.
It hath been prophesied to me many years,
I should not die but in Jerusalem,
Which vainly I supposed the Holy Land.
But bear me to that chamber; there I'll lie.   400
In that Jerusalem shall Harry die.

                           ⟨*They exit.*⟩

HENRY IV
Part 2

ACT 5

5.1 Falstaff observes Shallow and his servants in order to be ready to entertain Prince Hal with amusing stories.

---

1. **By . . . pie:** a mild oath (i.e., "by God and the church ordinal")
2. **What:** an interjection introducing an exclamation
10. **marry:** a mild oath (originally an oath on the name of the Virgin Mary); **cook:** i.e., the **cook**
13. **precepts:** writs, summonses
14. **again:** further, moreover; **hade land:** strip of unplowed land
16. **red wheat:** a variety of common wheat
18. **note:** bill, account
20. **cast:** calculated
22. **link:** chain; **bucket:** yoke (or perhaps pail)

⟨ACT 5⟩

⟨Scene 1⟩
Enter Shallow, Falstaff, ⟨Page,⟩ and Bardolph.

SHALLOW By cock and pie, sir, you shall not away
    tonight.—What, Davy, I say!
FALSTAFF You must excuse me, Master Robert Shallow.
SHALLOW I will not excuse you. You shall not be
    excused. Excuses shall not be admitted. There is no   5
    excuse shall serve. You shall not be excused.—
    Why, Davy!

⌜*Enter ⟨Davy.⟩*⌝

DAVY Here, sir.
SHALLOW Davy, Davy, Davy, Davy, let me see, Davy, let
    me see, Davy, let me see. Yea, marry, William cook,   10
    bid him come hither.—Sir John, you shall not be
    excused.
DAVY Marry, sir, thus: those precepts cannot be served.
    And again, sir: shall we sow the hade land with
    wheat?   15
SHALLOW With red wheat, Davy. But for William cook,
    are there no young pigeons?
DAVY Yes, sir. Here is now the smith's note for shoeing
    and plow irons.   ⌜*He gives Shallow a paper.*⌝
SHALLOW Let it be cast and paid.—Sir John, you shall   20
    not be excused.
DAVY Now, sir, a new link to the bucket must needs be

207

25. **Hinckley:** a market town near Coventry

28. **kickshaws:** i.e., fancy dishes (French *quelques choses*)

34. **back-bitten:** i.e., bitten by vermin

35. **marvelous:** i.e., marvelously

36. **Well-conceited:** i.e., very clever; **About:** i.e., go about

38. **countenance:** favor

48–49. **bear out:** support

53–54. **Look about:** i.e., be alert

Agamemnon. (2.4.222)
From Geoffrey Whitney, *A choice of emblemes . . .* (1586).

had. And, sir, do you mean to stop any of William's
wages about the sack he lost ⟨the other day⟩ at
⟨Hinckley⟩ Fair?   25

SHALLOW He shall answer it. Some pigeons, Davy, a
couple of short-legged hens, a joint of mutton, and
any pretty little tiny kickshaws, tell William cook.
⌜*Shallow and Davy walk aside.*⌝

DAVY Doth the man of war stay all night, sir?

SHALLOW Yea, Davy, I will use him well. A friend i' th'   30
court is better than a penny in purse. Use his men
well, Davy, for they are arrant knaves and will
backbite.

DAVY No worse than they are back-bitten, sir, for they
have marvelous foul linen.   35

SHALLOW Well-conceited, Davy. About thy business,
Davy.

DAVY I beseech you, sir, to countenance William Visor
of Woncot against Clement Perkes o' th' hill.

SHALLOW There is many complaints, Davy, against that   40
Visor. That Visor is an arrant knave, on my knowledge.

DAVY I grant your Worship that he is a knave, sir, but
yet, God forbid, sir, but a knave should have some
countenance at his friend's request. An honest   45
man, sir, is able to speak for himself when a knave is
not. I have served your Worship truly, sir, this eight
years; an I cannot once or twice in a quarter bear
out a knave against an honest man, I have ⟨but a
very⟩ little credit with your Worship. The knave is   50
mine honest friend, sir; therefore I beseech you let
him be countenanced.

SHALLOW Go to, I say, he shall have no wrong. Look
about, Davy. ⌜*Davy exits.*⌝ Where are you, Sir John?
Come, come, come, off with your boots.—Give me   55
your hand, Master Bardolph.

59. **tall:** brave (with wordplay on the page's small stature)

63. **quantities:** small pieces

66. **semblable coherence:** i.e., complete similarity

66–67. **his men's . . . his:** i.e., the dispositions of his men and himself

68. **conversing:** associating

70. **married in conjunction:** i.e., closely joined

70–71. **with . . . society:** i.e., through their close association

72. **consent:** consensus, agreement

73–74. **with . . . near:** i.e., by implying I was a close friend of

75. **curry with:** i.e., flatter

76–78. **It . . . another:** Proverbial: "He that walketh with the wise shall be wise; but a companion of fools shall be afflicted." **carriage:** behavior **take:** catch

81–83. **the wearing . . . intervallums:** i.e., a whole year without intermission **terms:** i.e., the **four terms** that make up the legal year **actions:** legal processes, suits **intervallums:** intervals (i.e., between the **terms**)

85. **sad:** serious

87. **like . . . up:** i.e., all wrinkled **ill laid up:** improperly put away

BARDOLPH   I am glad to see your Worship.

SHALLOW   I thank thee with ⟨all⟩ my heart, kind Master
Bardolph, (⌜*to   Page*⌝) and   welcome,   my   tall
fellow.—Come, Sir John.   60

FALSTAFF   I'll follow you, good Master Robert Shallow.
⌜*Shallow exits.*⌝ Bardolph, look to our horses. ⌜*Bardolph and Page exit.*⌝ If I were sawed into quantities,
I should make four dozen of such bearded hermits'
staves as Master Shallow. It is a wonderful thing to   65
see the semblable coherence of his men's spirits
and his. They, by observing ⟨of⟩ him, do bear
themselves like foolish justices; he, by conversing
with them, is turned into a justice-like servingman.
Their spirits are so married in conjunction with the   70
participation of society that they flock together in
consent like so many wild geese. If I had a suit to
Master Shallow, I would humor his men with the
imputation of being near their master; if to his men,
I would curry with Master Shallow that no man   75
could better command his servants. It is certain
that either wise bearing or ignorant carriage is
caught, as men take diseases, one of another. Therefore let men take heed of their company. I will
devise matter enough out of this Shallow to keep   80
Prince Harry in continual laughter the wearing out
of six fashions, which is four terms, or two actions,
and he shall laugh without intervallums. O, it is
much that a lie with a slight oath and a jest with a
sad brow will do with a fellow that never had the   85
ache in his shoulders. O, you shall see him laugh till
his face be like a wet cloak ill laid up.

SHALLOW, ⌜*within*⌝   Sir John.

FALSTAFF   I come, Master Shallow, I come, Master
Shallow.   90

                                              ⌜*He exits.*⌝

5.2 Prince Hal reassures an anxious Lord Chief Justice.

---

3. **well:** Proverbial: "He is **well,** since he is in Heaven."
7. **would:** wish
8. **truly:** loyally
15. **heavy issue:** i.e., sorrowful sons
17. **he the worst:** i.e., whichever is least worthy
19. **strike sail:** i.e., submit (literally, to lower the topsail as a salute or sign of surrender)

⟨Scene 2⟩

Enter Warwick ⌜and⌝ Lord Chief Justice.

WARWICK
How now, my Lord Chief Justice, whither away?
CHIEF JUSTICE   How doth the King?
WARWICK
Exceeding well. His cares are now all ended.
CHIEF JUSTICE
I hope, not dead.
WARWICK   He's walked the way of nature,   5
And to our purposes he lives no more.
CHIEF JUSTICE
I would his Majesty had called me with him.
The service that I truly did his life
Hath left me open to all injuries.
WARWICK
Indeed, I think the young king loves you not.   10
CHIEF JUSTICE
I know he doth not, and do arm myself
To welcome the condition of the time,
Which cannot look more hideously upon me
Than I have drawn it in my fantasy.

Enter John, Thomas, and Humphrey.

WARWICK
Here come the heavy issue of dead Harry.   15
O, that the living Harry had the temper
Of he the worst of these three gentlemen!
How many nobles then should hold their places
That must strike sail to spirits of vile sort!
CHIEF JUSTICE
O God, I fear all will be overturned.   20
JOHN OF LANCASTER
Good morrow, cousin Warwick, good morrow.

23. **forgot:** i.e., forgotten how
24. **argument:** theme, subject
31. **grace:** fortune, destiny
32. **coldest:** least friendly, gloomiest; most discouraging
34. **speak . . . fair:** address . . . kindly
35. **swims . . . quality:** i.e., goes against your nature
39. **A ragged . . . remission:** i.e., a worthless pardon that has already been withdrawn before it is given

HUMPHREY OF GLOUCESTER, THOMAS OF
   CLARENCE   Good morrow, cousin.
JOHN OF LANCASTER
  We meet like men that had forgot to speak.
WARWICK
  We do remember, but our argument
  Is all too heavy to admit much talk.   25
JOHN OF LANCASTER
  Well, peace be with him that hath made us heavy.
CHIEF JUSTICE
  Peace be with us, lest we be heavier.
HUMPHREY OF GLOUCESTER
  O, good my lord, you have lost a friend indeed,
  And I dare swear you borrow not that face
  Of seeming sorrow; it is sure your own.   30
JOHN OF LANCASTER, ⌜*to the Chief Justice*⌝
  Though no man be assured what grace to find,
  You stand in coldest expectation.
  I am the sorrier; would 'twere otherwise.
THOMAS OF CLARENCE
  Well, you must now speak Sir John Falstaff fair,
  Which swims against your stream of quality.   35
CHIEF JUSTICE
  Sweet princes, what I did I did in honor,
  Led by th' impartial conduct of my soul;
  And never shall you see that I will beg
  A ragged and forestalled remission.
  If truth and upright innocency fail me,   40
  I'll to the king my master that is dead
  And tell him who hath sent me after him.

    Enter the Prince, ⌜as Henry V,⌝ and Blunt.

WARWICK   Here comes the Prince.
CHIEF JUSTICE
  Good morrow, and God save your Majesty.

49. **Amurath:** the name of a Turkish sultan who secured the throne by having his brothers killed

53. **deeply:** solemnly

55. **entertain:** i.e., take upon yourselves

57. **For:** as for

59. **Let me but:** i.e., if you will only let me

71. **rate:** reprove, scold

72. **easy:** insignificant

73. **Lethe:** in Greek mythology, the river of forgetfulness

74. **use the person of:** i.e., act on behalf of, represent

Jove as a bull, abducting Europa. (2.2.174–75)
From Gabriele Simeoni, *La vita . . . d'Ouidio . . .* (1559).

PRINCE
  This new and gorgeous garment majesty   45
  Sits not so easy on me as you think.—
  Brothers, you ⟨mix⟩ your sadness with some fear.
  This is the English, not the Turkish court;
  Not Amurath an Amurath succeeds,
  But Harry Harry. Yet be sad, good brothers,   50
  For, by my faith, it very well becomes you.
  Sorrow so royally in you appears
  That I will deeply put the fashion on
  And wear it in my heart. Why then, be sad.
  But entertain no more of it, good brothers,   55
  Than a joint burden laid upon us all.
  For me, by heaven, I bid you be assured,
  I'll be your father and your brother too.
  Let me but bear your love, I'll bear your cares.
  Yet weep that Harry's dead, and so will I,   60
  But Harry lives that shall convert those tears
  By number into hours of happiness.
BROTHERS
  We hope no otherwise from your Majesty.
PRINCE
  You all look strangely on me. ⌜*To the Chief Justice.*⌝
    And you most.   65
  You are, I think, assured I love you not.
CHIEF JUSTICE
  I am assured, if I be measured rightly,
  Your Majesty hath no just cause to hate me.
PRINCE
  No? How might a prince of my great hopes forget
  So great indignities you laid upon me?   70
  What, rate, rebuke, and roughly send to prison
  Th' immediate heir of England? Was this easy?
  May this be washed in Lethe and forgotten?
CHIEF JUSTICE
  I then did use the person of your father;

80. **presented:** represented

82. **as an offender:** i.e., **as** you were **an offender**

84. **commit you:** i.e., sentence you to prison (See longer note to 1.2.56–58, **committed**, page 249.) **ill:** blameworthy

85. **Be you:** i.e., would you be

87. **awful:** awe-inspiring

88. **trip . . . law:** i.e., pervert justice (The image is of tripping a runner.)

90. **spurn at:** trample

91. **second body:** i.e., deputy

93. **propose:** imagine

98. **soft:** gently

99. **cold:** deliberate; **considerance:** reflection

104. **balance:** i.e., the balance scales, which, together with the **sword,** emblematize justice (See below, and page 144.)

Justice with her scales and sword. (5.2.103–4)
From Thomas Peyton, *The glasse of time . . .* (1620).

The image of his power lay then in me.   75
And in th' administration of his law,
Whiles I was busy for the commonwealth,
Your Highness pleasèd to forget my place,
The majesty and power of law and justice,
The image of the King whom I presented,   80
And struck me in my very seat of judgment,
Whereon, as an offender to your father,
I gave bold way to my authority
And did commit you. If the deed were ill,
Be you contented, wearing now the garland,   85
To have a son set your decrees at nought?
To pluck down justice from your awful bench?
To trip the course of law and blunt the sword
That guards the peace and safety of your person?
Nay more, to spurn at your most royal image   90
And mock your workings in a second body?
Question your royal thoughts, make the case yours;
Be now the father and propose a son,
Hear your own dignity so much profaned,
See your most dreadful laws so loosely slighted,   95
Behold yourself so by a son disdained,
And then imagine me taking your part
And in your power soft silencing your son.
After this cold considerance, sentence me,
And, as you are a king, speak in your state   100
What I have done that misbecame my place,
My person, or my liege's sovereignty.
PRINCE
You are right, justice, and you weigh this well.
Therefore still bear the balance and the sword.
And I do wish your honors may increase   105
Till you do live to see a son of mine
Offend you and obey you as I did.
So shall I live to speak my father's words:

110. **do justice on:** punish; **proper:** own

115. **have used to bear:** i.e., are accustomed to carrying

116. **remembrance:** reminder

117. **like:** same

124. **is gone wild:** i.e., has carried my wildness with him

125. **affections:** passions

126. **sadly:** i.e., as a serious person

129. **who:** i.e., which

130. **After my seeming:** i.e., according to the way I've appeared; **blood:** passion

133. **state:** majestic dignity; **floods:** i.e., the ocean

136. **limbs:** i.e., members (but treated literally in line 137 where the **state** is a **great body** and where **go** means "walk")

"Happy am I that have a man so bold
That dares do justice on my proper son;   110
And not less happy, having such a son
That would deliver up his greatness so
Into the hands of justice." You did commit me,
For which I do commit into your hand
Th' unstainèd sword that you have used to bear,   115
With this remembrance: that you use the same
With the like bold, just, and impartial spirit
As you have done 'gainst me. There is my hand.
                          ⌜*They clasp hands.*⌝
You shall be as a father to my youth,
My voice shall sound as you do prompt mine ear,   120
And I will stoop and humble my intents
To your well-practiced wise directions.—
And, princes all, believe me, I beseech you:
My father is gone wild into his grave,
For in his tomb lie my affections,   125
And with his spirits sadly I survive
To mock the expectation of the world,
To frustrate prophecies, and to raze out
Rotten opinion, who hath writ me down
After my seeming. The tide of blood in me   130
Hath proudly flowed in vanity till now.
Now doth it turn and ebb back to the sea,
Where it shall mingle with the state of floods
And flow henceforth in formal majesty.
Now call we our high court of parliament,   135
And let us choose such limbs of noble counsel
That the great body of our state may go
In equal rank with the best-governed nation;
That war, or peace, or both at once, may be
As things acquainted and familiar to us,   140
⌜*To the Chief Justice.*⌝ In which you, father, shall
    have foremost hand.

143. **accite:** summon
144. **remembered:** mentioned; **state:** i.e., nobles
145. **consigning:** subscribing

5.3 On the news of Henry IV's death, Falstaff and Shallow set off joyfully for London.

---

1. **orchard:** garden (See page 10.)
2. **pippin:** apple
3. **graffing:** i.e., grafting; **caraways:** i.e., caraway seeds; or, sweets made with caraway seeds
8. **Spread:** i.e., lay the table
9. **Well said:** i.e., well done
11. **husband:** household manager, steward
12. **varlet:** servant
22. **ever among:** all the while
24. **give you a health:** i.e., drink a toast to you; **anon:** right away

Grafting "last year's pippin." (5.3.2–3)
From Marco Bussato, *Giardino de agricoltura* . . . (1599).

Our coronation done, we will accite,
As I before remembered, all our state.
And, God consigning to my good intents,   145
No prince nor peer shall have just cause to say
God shorten Harry's happy life one day.
                                            ⟨*They exit.*⟩

⟨Scene 3⟩
Enter Sir John ⟨Falstaff,⟩ Shallow, Silence, Davy,
Bardolph, ⌜*and*⌝ *Page.*

SHALLOW Nay, you shall see my orchard, where, in an
  arbor, we will eat a last year's pippin of mine own
  graffing, with a dish of caraways, and so forth.—
  Come, cousin Silence.—And then to bed.
FALSTAFF Fore God, you have here ⟨a⟩ goodly dwelling,   5
  and ⟨a⟩ rich.
SHALLOW Barren, barren, barren, beggars all, beggars
  all, Sir John. Marry, good air.—Spread, Davy,
  spread, Davy. Well said, Davy.
FALSTAFF This Davy serves you for good uses. He is   10
  your servingman and your husband.
SHALLOW A good varlet, a good varlet, a very good
  varlet, Sir John. By the Mass, I have drunk too
  much sack at supper. A good varlet. Now sit down,
  now sit down.—Come, cousin.   15
SILENCE Ah, sirrah, quoth he, we shall
  ⌜*Sings.*⌝*Do nothing but eat and make good cheer,*
       And praise God for the merry year,
       When flesh is cheap and females dear,
       And lusty lads roam here and there   20
                        So merrily,
       And ever among so merrily.
FALSTAFF There's a merry heart!—Good Master Silence, I'll give you a health for that anon.

28. **Proface:** a welcome given at a meal; **want:** lack; **meat:** food

29. **bear:** put up with

34. **beards wags all:** i.e., all the men's beards wag (in talking and laughing)

35. **Shrovetide:** the days before Lent and a time of feasting and drinking

39. **merry:** This word could mean "tipsy, happily drunk."

41. **leather-coats:** russet apples

44. **straight:** straightway, immediately

47. **leman:** mistress

54. **I'll . . . bottom:** i.e., I'll drink to the **bottom** of the cup in toasting you, even if it is **a mile** deep

A bearherd. (1.2.172–73)
From Jacobus a. Bruck, *Emblemata moralia & bellica* . . . (1615).

SHALLOW   Give Master Bardolph some wine, Davy.   25
DAVY, ⌜*to the guests*⌝ Sweet sir, sit. I'll be with you
anon. Most sweet sir, sit. Master page, good master
page, sit. Proface. What you want in meat, we'll
have in drink, but you must bear. The heart's all.
⌜*He exits.*⌝

SHALLOW   Be merry, Master Bardolph.—And, my little   30
soldier there, be merry.
SILENCE ⌜*sings*⌝
Be merry, be merry, my wife has all,
For women are shrews, both short and tall.
'Tis merry in hall when beards wags all,
And welcome merry Shrovetide.   35
Be merry, be merry.

FALSTAFF   I did not think Master Silence had been a
man of this mettle.
SILENCE   Who, I? I have been merry twice and once ere
now.   40

Enter Davy.

DAVY, ⌜*to the guests*⌝ There's a dish of leather-coats for
you.
SHALLOW   Davy!
DAVY   Your Worship, I'll be with you straight.—A cup
of wine, sir.   45
SILENCE ⌜*sings*⌝
A cup of wine that's brisk and fine,
And drink unto thee, leman mine,
And a merry heart lives long-a.

FALSTAFF   Well said, Master Silence.
SILENCE   And we shall be merry; now comes in the   50
sweet o' th' night.
FALSTAFF   Health and long life to you, Master Silence.
SILENCE ⌜*sings*⌝
Fill the cup, and let it come,
I'll pledge you a mile to th' bottom.

56. **beshrew:** i.e., a plague on
59. **cabileros:** soldiers, gallants
60. **once:** one day
62. **crack:** i.e., empty
64. **pottle-pot:** two-quart tankard
65. **liggens:** a word not recorded elsewhere and as yet undefined
67. **out:** i.e., pass out; or, perhaps, drop out, leave you
72. **done me right:** i.e., kept up with me in drinking
73–75. **Do . . . Samingo:** part of a popular drinking song "Monsieur Mingo" (The Latin verb *mingo* means "I urinate.")
79. **somewhat:** something

The Muses. (5.3.104)
From Natale Conti, *Natalis Comitis Mythologiae . . .* (1616).

SHALLOW   Honest Bardolph, welcome. If thou want'st   55
   anything and wilt not call, beshrew thy heart.—
   Welcome, my little tiny thief, and welcome indeed
   too. I'll drink to Master Bardolph, and to all the
   cabileros about London.

DAVY   I hope to see London once ere I die.   60

BARDOLPH   An I might see you there, Davy!

SHALLOW   By the Mass, you'll crack a quart together,
   ha, will you not, Master Bardolph?

BARDOLPH   Yea, sir, in a pottle-pot.

SHALLOW   By God's liggens, I thank thee. The knave   65
   will stick by thee, I can assure thee that. He will not
   out, he. 'Tis true bred!

BARDOLPH   And I'll stick by him, sir.

SHALLOW   Why, there spoke a king. Lack nothing, be
   merry. (*One knocks at door.*) Look who's at door   70
   there, ho. Who knocks?   ⌜*Davy exits.*⌝

FALSTAFF   Why, now you have done me right.

SILENCE ⌜*sings*⌝

> *Do me right,*
> *And dub me knight,*
> *Samingo.*   75

Is 't not so?

FALSTAFF   'Tis so.

SILENCE   Is 't so? Why then, say an old man can do
   somewhat.

⌜*Enter Davy.*⌝

DAVY   An 't please your Worship, there's one Pistol   80
   come from the court with news.

FALSTAFF   From the court? Let him come in.

Enter Pistol.

How now, Pistol?

PISTOL   Sir John, God save you.

85–86. **What . . . good:** Lines 85 and 86 are both proverbs.

89. **but Goodman Puff:** i.e., except for yeoman **Puff** (Silence takes **greatest** to mean "biggest.")

91. **Puff:** swagger, speak insolently

96. **price:** value, excellence

97. **them:** i.e., the **news** (regarded as plural)

97–98. **man . . . world:** i.e., ordinary mortal

99. **foutre:** a French word (meaning "fornicate") used in English phrases of contempt

100. **Africa:** associated with gold (especially in Marlowe's *Tamburlaine*) For Pistol's quoting of old plays, see note to 2.4.158–59.

101–2. **O . . . thereof:** Falstaff imitates Pistol's style. Assyrians were associated with brigands. **King Cophetua** was the hero of a ballad referred to more than once in Shakespeare's plays.

104. **Helicons:** Mount Helicon was sacred to the Muses of Greek mythology. (See page 226.)

105. **baffled:** subjected to public disgrace

106. **Furies' lap:** i.e., the **lap** of the Erinyes, mythological beings who punished those who broke natural or moral laws (See page 236 and note to 5.5.35–36.)

109. **therefor:** for that

114. **besonian:** knave, beggar (from the Italian *bisogno*, meaning "need, want")

FALSTAFF   What wind blew you hither, Pistol?   85
PISTOL   Not the ill wind which blows no man to good.
   Sweet knight, thou art now one of the greatest men
   in this realm.
SILENCE   By 'r Lady, I think he be, but Goodman Puff of
   Barson.   90
PISTOL   Puff?
   Puff ⟨in⟩ thy teeth, most recreant coward base!—
   Sir John, I am thy Pistol and thy friend,
   And helter-skelter have I rode to thee,
   And tidings do I bring, and lucky joys,   95
   And golden times, and happy news of price.
FALSTAFF   I pray thee now, deliver them like a man of
   this world.
PISTOL
   A foutre for the world and worldlings base!
   I speak of Africa and golden joys.   100
FALSTAFF
   O base Assyrian knight, what is thy news?
   Let King Cophetua know the truth thereof.
SILENCE ⌜*sings*⌝
       And Robin Hood, Scarlet, and John.
PISTOL
   Shall dunghill curs confront the Helicons,
   And shall good news be baffled?   105
   Then, Pistol, lay thy head in Furies' lap.
SHALLOW   Honest   gentleman,   I   know   not   your
   breeding.
PISTOL   Why then, lament therefor.
SHALLOW   Give me pardon, sir. If, sir, you come with 110
   news from the court, I take it there's but two ways,
   either to utter them, or ⟨to⟩ conceal them. I am, sir,
   under the King in some authority.
PISTOL
   Under which king, besonian? Speak or die.

121. **fig me:** The "fig of Spain" was a contemptuous gesture that consisted of thrusting the thumb between two clinched fingers or into the mouth.

127–28. **double-charge:** i.e., fill you twice over (with wordplay on Pistol's name)

136. **withal:** in addition

137. **Boot:** i.e., put on your boots

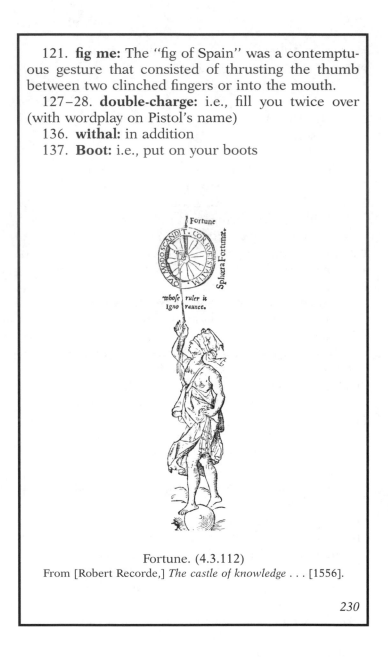

Fortune. (4.3.112)
From [Robert Recorde,] *The castle of knowledge . . .* [1556].

SHALLOW
 Under King Harry.   115
PISTOL   Harry the Fourth, or Fifth?
SHALLOW
 Harry the Fourth.
PISTOL   A foutre for thine office!—
 Sir John, thy tender lambkin now is king.
 Harry the Fifth's the man. I speak the truth. 120
 When Pistol lies, do this and fig me, like
 The bragging Spaniard.   ⌜*Pistol makes a fig.*⌝
FALSTAFF   What, is the old king dead?
PISTOL
 As nail in door. The things I speak are just
FALSTAFF Away, Bardolph.—Saddle my horse.— 125
 Master Robert Shallow, choose what office thou
 wilt in the land, 'tis thine.—Pistol, I will double-
 charge thee with dignities.
BARDOLPH O joyful day! I would not take a ⟨knight-
 hood⟩ for my fortune.   130
PISTOL What, I do bring good news!
FALSTAFF Carry Master Silence to bed.—Master Shal-
 low, my Lord Shallow, be what thou wilt. I am
 Fortune's steward. Get on thy boots. We'll ride all
 night.—O sweet Pistol!—Away, Bardolph!—Come, 135
 Pistol, utter more to me, and withal devise something to do thyself good.—Boot, boot, Master Shallow. I know the young king is sick for me. Let us
 take any man's horses. The laws of England are at
 my commandment. Blessed are they that have been 140
 my friends, and woe to my Lord Chief Justice!
PISTOL
 Let vultures vile seize on his lungs also!
 "Where is the life that late I led?" say they.
 Why, here it is. Welcome these pleasant days.
              ⟨*They exit.*⟩

5.4 Doll Tearsheet is arrested.

---

0 SD. **Beadles:** sheriff's officers, under-bailiffs

4. **delivered . . . me:** i.e., given Doll to me to punish

5. **whipping cheer:** i.e., flogging (the standard punishment for whores) **cheer:** hospitality, entertainment

7. **about her:** in her company; or, because of her

8. **Nut-hook:** a hooked stick used to pull down tree branches when gathering nuts; here an allusion to the beadle's thinness or to the weapon he carries

9. **tripe-visaged:** sallow-faced (The insult is repeated in line 11 with **paper-faced.**)

16–17. **If . . . now:** The beadle accuses Doll of faking pregnancy.

20. **thin . . . censer:** i.e., figure embossed on an incense burner (Allusions to his thinness are repeated in **famished correctioner** [22], **starved bloodhound** [28], **Goodman Bones** [29], and **atomy** [30], the Hostess's mistake for "anatomy" or skeleton.)

21. **swinged:** thrashed; **bluebottle:** a reference to the beadle's blue coat

23. **forswear half-kirtles:** i.e., give up wearing skirts

24. **she-knight-errant:** presumably a pun on "night" and on "errant" as (1) walking around and (2) sinning (A **knight-errant** was a medieval knight who wandered in search of adventure.)

25–26. **that . . . might:** The proverb actually reads "Might overcomes right."

26. **sufferance:** i.e., suffering

31. **rascal:** lean deer

⟨Scene 4⟩

⟨*Enter Hostess Quickly, Doll Tearsheet, and Beadles.*⟩

HOSTESS No, thou arrant knave. I would to God that I might die, that I might have thee hanged. Thou hast drawn my shoulder out of joint.

BEADLE The Constables have delivered her over to me, and she shall have whipping cheer ⟨enough,⟩ I 5 warrant her. There hath been a man or two ⟨lately⟩ killed about her.

DOLL Nut-hook, nut-hook, you lie! Come on, I'll tell thee what, thou damned tripe-visaged rascal: an the child I ⟨now⟩ go with do miscarry, thou wert better 10 thou hadst struck thy mother, thou paper-faced villain.

HOSTESS O the Lord, that Sir John were come! I would make this a bloody day to somebody. But I pray God the fruit of her womb ⟨might⟩ miscarry. 15

BEADLE If it do, you shall have a dozen of cushions again; you have but eleven now. Come, I charge you both go with me, for the man is dead that you and Pistol beat amongst you.

DOLL I'll tell you what, you thin man in a censer, I will 20 have you as soundly swinged for this, you bluebottle rogue, you filthy famished correctioner. If you be not swinged, I'll forswear half-kirtles.

BEADLE Come, come, you she-knight-errant, come.

HOSTESS O God, that right should thus overcome 25 might! Well, of sufferance comes ease.

DOLL Come, you rogue, come, bring me to a justice.

HOSTESS Ay, come, you starved bloodhound.

DOLL Goodman Death, Goodman Bones!

HOSTESS Thou atomy, thou! 30

DOLL Come, you thin thing, come, you rascal.

BEADLE Very well.

⟨*They exit.*⟩

5.5   The newly crowned King Henry V keeps his word to the Lord Chief Justice.

———————

0 SD. **Grooms:** servingmen
1. **rushes:** coverings for the path of the royal procession
4. **Dispatch:** hurry
6. **do you grace:** i.e., honor you; **leer upon:** i.e., look meaningfully at
11. **have . . . liveries:** i.e., have had **new liveries** made
12. **bestowed:** spent
13. **you:** i.e., Justice Shallow
14. **infer:** show, imply
22. **shift me:** change clothes

King Henry V.
From John Taylor, *All the workes of . . .* (1630).

⟨Scene 5⟩
⟨*Enter two Grooms.*⟩

⟨FIRST GROOM⟩   More rushes, more rushes.
⟨SECOND GROOM⟩   The trumpets have sounded twice.
⟨FIRST GROOM⟩   'Twill be two o'clock ere they come
    from the coronation. Dispatch, dispatch.

⟨*Grooms exit.*⟩

Trumpets sound, and the King and his train pass over
the stage. After them enter Falstaff, Shallow, Pistol,
Bardolph, and the ⟨Page.⟩

FALSTAFF   Stand here by me, Master ⟨Robert⟩ Shallow. I   5
    will make the King do you grace. I will leer upon
    him as he comes by, and do but mark the counte-
    nance that he will give me.
PISTOL   God bless thy lungs, good knight!
FALSTAFF   Come here, Pistol, stand behind me.—O, if I   10
    had had time to have made new liveries, I would
    have bestowed the thousand pound I borrowed of
    you. But 'tis no matter. This poor show doth better.
    This doth infer the zeal I had to see him.
⟨SHALLOW⟩   It doth so.   15
FALSTAFF   It shows my earnestness of affection—
⌈SHALLOW⌉   It doth so.
FALSTAFF   My devotion—
⌈SHALLOW⌉   It doth, it doth, it doth.
FALSTAFF   As it were, to ride day and night, and not to   20
    deliberate, not to remember, not to have patience
    to shift me—
SHALLOW   It is best, certain.
⟨FALSTAFF⟩   But to stand stained with travel and sweat-
    ing with desire to see him, thinking of nothing else,   25
    putting all affairs else in oblivion, as if there were
    nothing else to be done but to see him.

28. **semper idem:** a Latin motto meaning "ever the same"; **obsque . . . est:** "apart from this there is nothing" (*obsque* is a mistake for *absque*)

28–29. **'tis . . . part:** The proverb "all in all and all in every part" described absolute perfection.

31. **liver:** seat of violent passion

32–33. **Helen . . . thoughts:** i.e., your own **Helen** of Troy

33. **contagious:** foul, noxious

34. **mechanical:** mean, base

35–36. **Alecto's snake:** Alecto was one of the Furies, pictured with snakes twined in their hair. (See note to 5.3.106 and picture below.)

41. **imp:** offshoot, child

43. **vain:** foolish

48. **ill:** badly; **becomes:** i.e., are suitable for

52. **hence:** henceforth

The Furies. (5.3.106; 5.5.35–36)
From Vincenzo Cartari, *Le vere e noue imagini de gli dei delli antichi . . .* (1615).

PISTOL   'Tis *semper idem,* for *obsque hoc nihil est;* 'tis
⟨all⟩ in every part.

SHALLOW   'Tis so indeed.   30

PISTOL   My knight, I will inflame thy noble liver, and
make thee rage. Thy Doll and Helen of thy noble
thoughts is in base durance and contagious prison,
haled thither by most mechanical and dirty hand.
Rouse up revenge from ebon den with fell Alecto's   35
snake, for Doll is in. Pistol speaks nought but truth.

FALSTAFF   I will deliver her.
                    ⌜*Shouts within.* ⟨*The trumpets sound.*⟩⌝

PISTOL.
There roared the sea, and trumpet-clangor sounds.

Enter the King and his train.

FALSTAFF
God save thy Grace, King Hal, my royal Hal.

PISTOL
The heavens thee guard and keep, most royal   40
imp of fame!

FALSTAFF   God save thee, my sweet boy!

KING
My Lord Chief Justice, speak to that vain man.

CHIEF JUSTICE, ⌜*to Falstaff*⌝
Have you your wits? Know you what 'tis you
speak?   45

FALSTAFF, ⌜*to the King*⌝
My king, my Jove, I speak to thee, my heart!

KING
I know thee not, old man. Fall to thy prayers.
How ill white hairs becomes a fool and jester.
I have long dreamt of such a kind of man,
So surfeit-swelled, so old, and so profane;   50
But being awaked, I do despise my dream.
Make less thy body hence, and more thy grace;

58. **turned away:** dismissed

66. **For . . . you:** i.e., I will give you enough money to sustain life

80. **Fear not:** i.e., don't worry about

87. **color:** pretext, pretense (Shallow's response puns on **color** as "collar," the hangman's noose, and on **die** as "dye." See "Historical Background," pages 299–300, for a discussion of the execution of Sir John Oldcastle.)

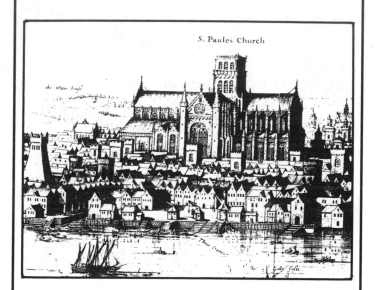

St. Paul's Cathedral. (1.2.53)
From Claes Jansz Visscher, *Londinum florentissima Britanniae urbs . . .* [c. 1625].

Leave gormandizing. Know the grave doth gape
For thee thrice wider than for other men.
Reply not to me with a fool-born jest.   55
Presume not that I am the thing I was,
For God doth know—so shall the world perceive—
That I have turned away my former self.
So will I those that kept me company.
When thou dost hear I am as I have been,   60
Approach me, and thou shalt be as thou wast,
The tutor and the feeder of my riots.
Till then I banish thee, on pain of death,
As I have done the rest of my misleaders,
Not to come near our person by ten mile.   65
For competence of life I will allow you,
That lack of means enforce you not to evils.
And, as we hear you do reform yourselves,
We will, according to your strengths and qualities,
Give you advancement. ⌐ *To the Lord Chief Justice.* ⌐   70
     Be it your charge, my lord,
To see performed the tenor of my word. —
Set on.
                              ⟨*King* ⌐ *and his train* ⌐ *exit.*⟩

FALSTAFF   Master Shallow, I owe you a thousand pound.
SHALLOW   Yea, marry, Sir John, which I beseech you to   75
    let me have home with me.
FALSTAFF   That can hardly be, Master Shallow. Do not
    you grieve at this. I shall be sent for in private to
    him. Look you, he must seem thus to the world.
    Fear not your advancements. I will be the man yet   80
    that shall make you great.
SHALLOW   I cannot ⟨well⟩ perceive how, unless you
    ⟨should⟩ give me your doublet and stuff me out with
    straw. I beseech you, good Sir John, let me have five
    hundred of my thousand.   85
FALSTAFF   Sir, I will be as good as my word. This that
    you heard was but a color.

89. **Fear no colors:** i.e., have no fear (proverbial)
92. **the Fleet:** a famous London prison
97. **Si . . . contenta:** See note to 2.4.181–82.
101. **conversations:** behavior
107. **civil swords:** i.e., swords used in civil war
108. **I . . . sing:** proverbial

King Henry V.
From John Taylor, *All the workes of* . . . (1630).

SHALLOW   A color that I fear you will die in, Sir John.
FALSTAFF   Fear no colors. Go with me to dinner.—
    Come, Lieutenant Pistol.—Come, Bardolph.—I   90
    shall be sent for soon at night.

Enter ⌜the Lord Chief⌝ Justice and Prince John, ⌜with
Officers.⌝

CHIEF JUSTICE
    Go, carry Sir John Falstaff to the Fleet.
    Take all his company along with him.
FALSTAFF   My lord, my lord—
CHIEF JUSTICE
    I cannot now speak. I will hear you soon.—   95
    Take them away.
PISTOL   *Si fortuna me tormenta, spero ⟨me⟩ contenta.*
                       ⌜*All but John of*⌝ ⟨*Lancaster and*
                                    Chief Justice⟩ *exit.*

JOHN OF LANCASTER
    I like this fair proceeding of the King's.
    He hath intent his wonted followers
    Shall all be very well provided for,   100
    But all are banished till their conversations
    Appear more wise and modest to the world.
CHIEF JUSTICE   And so they are.
JOHN OF LANCASTER
    The King hath called his parliament, my lord.
CHIEF JUSTICE   He hath.   105
JOHN OF LANCASTER
    I will lay odds that, ere this year expire,
    We bear our civil swords and native fire
    As far as France. I heard a bird so sing,
    Whose music, to my thinking, pleased the King.
    Come, will you hence?   110
                                    ⟨*They exit.*⟩

Epilogue. The speaker apologizes for the play and promises another play with Falstaff in it.

---

1. **curtsy:** bow
5, 6. **making, marring:** Proverbial: "make or mar."
6. **doubt:** fear
7. **to the purpose:** to the matter at hand; **to the venture:** i.e., I'll risk it
8–9. **in the end:** i.e., at the conclusion
11. **ill venture:** i.e., unlucky voyage
12. **break:** fail, become bankrupt; or, **break my promise** (line 10)
14–15. **Bate me some:** i.e., forgive some part of my debt

EPILOGUE

First my fear, then my curtsy, last my speech. My
fear is your displeasure, my curtsy my duty, and my
speech, to beg your pardons. If you look for a good
speech now, you undo me, for what I have to say is
of mine own making, and what indeed I should say   5
will, I doubt, prove mine own marring.

But to the purpose, and so to the venture. Be it
known to you, as it is very well, I was lately here in
the end of a displeasing play to pray your patience
for it and to promise you a better. I meant indeed to   10
pay you with this, which, if like an ill venture it
come unluckily home, I break, and you, my gentle
creditors, lose. Here I promised you I would be,
and here I commit my body to your mercies. Bate
me some, and I will pay you some, and, as most   15
debtors do, promise you infinitely. And so I kneel
down before you, but, indeed, to pray for the
Queen.

If my tongue cannot entreat you to acquit me,
will you command me to use my legs? And yet that   20
were but light payment, to dance out of your debt.
But a good conscience will make any possible
satisfaction, and so would I. All the gentlewomen
here have forgiven me; if the gentlemen will not,
then the gentlemen do not agree with the gentle-   25

32. of a sweat: (1) from exertion; (2) from the sweating-sickness, an epidemic disease characterized by fever and sweating; (3) from venereal disease, a treatment for which was sweating in a tub of hot water (See below.)

34. Oldcastle: See "Historical Background," page 295.

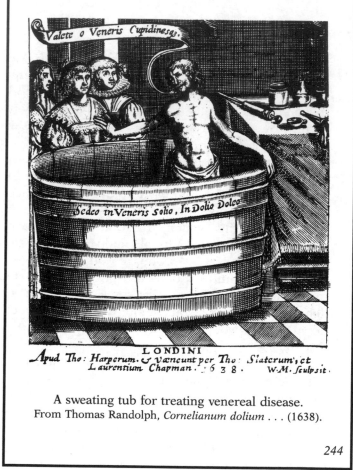

A sweating tub for treating venereal disease.
From Thomas Randolph, *Cornelianum dolium . . .* (1638).

women, which was never seen ⟨before⟩ in such an assembly.

Onc word more, I beseech you: if you be not too much cloyed with fat meat, our humble author will continue the story, with Sir John in it, and make 30
you merry with fair Katherine of France, where, for anything I know, Falstaff shall die of a sweat, unless already he be killed with your hard opinions; for Oldcastle died ⟨a⟩ martyr, and this is not the man. My tongue is weary; when my legs are too, I will bid 35
you good night.

Longer Notes

1.1.40 Sir John Umfrevile: Many editors believe that this refers to Lord Bardolph and that the name Umfrevile, later discarded, remains in the play by accident. Others believe that Umfrevile instead refers to the gentleman "of good name" mentioned at line 32.

1.1.125–38. spirit . . . field: These lines employ a complex of images to describe the effect of Hotspur's death on his troops. His **spirit** is first pictured as a **fire** that turned the **mettle**/metal of his men into well-tempered steel. Then his spirit is itself pictured as metal/**mettle** that **steeled** his men (i.e., strengthened them so that they became like unbending steel). When he died, his metal/**mettle** was blunted, and the troops became instead like **dull and heavy lead.** Their very heaviness (i.e., sadness) made them fly the **swifter** from the battlefield. (Lines 132–33 suggest that they became like lead bullets. See, for comparison, *Love's Labor's Lost* 3.1.58–64, where a character uses the phrase "as swift as lead." He is answered, "Is not lead a metal heavy, dull, and slow?" to which he responds, "Is that lead slow which is fired from a gun?")

1.2.37 yea-forsooth: This adjective means, literally, "addicted to saying 'yea forsooth' in the way of superficial assent" (*Oxford English Dictionary*, or *OED*). Here, as invective against Master Dommelton, it may be used to accuse the tradesman of saying "yes" when he does not mean it, or it may refer to the lower class's use of mild oaths (attacked in *Henry IV, Part 1*, 3.1.256–65) or to the Puritans' substitution of words like "forsooth" in

247

the place of oaths. The word **smoothy-pates** (line 39) may continue the allusion to Puritans or to lower-class merchants (members of both groups wore their hair cropped short).

　　1.2.46–50. **he may sleep . . . light him:** Falstaff's attack on the tradesman here is based on multiple puns. **Security** takes on the meaning of "false security, complacency"; **horn** refers simultaneously to (1) a cornucopia (both as a **horn** overflowing with fruit, a sign of prosperity, and as a term for the tradesman's own material **abundance**), (2) the cuckold's **horn** (which was supposed to grow on the forehead of a man whose wife is unfaithful), and (3) the material used in making lanterns (hence the frequent spelling "lanthorn"); **lightness** means both "radiance, illumination" and "wantonness, promiscuousness," both of which meanings affect how we hear the word **light**.

　　We print the phrase "Where's Bardolph" as it is placed in the Folio. In the earlier Quarto printing, the final sentence of the speech reads: "well he may sleepe in security, for he hath the horne of aboundance, and the lightnesse of his wife shines through it: wheres Bardolf, & yet can not he see though he haue his owne lanthorne to light him."

　　In modern punctuation it would read as follows: "Well, he may sleep in security, for he hath the horn of abundance, and the lightness of his wife shines through it—Where's Bardolph?—yet cannot he see though he have his own lantern to light him." In this version Falstaff suddenly interrupts his description of the merchant's wife's shining lightness with the question "Where's Bardolph?" Falstaff's swerve toward Bardolph may be triggered by his recollection of the fiery brightness of Bardolph's drink-reddened face. The Folio's placement of "Where's Bardolph?" at the end of Falstaff's speech has the obvious and distinct advantage of making the dialogue more readily intelligible, but the Folio does not have Falstaff make the association with the lightning quickness that may be evident in the Quarto version; nor does the Folio have Falstaff recover after his self-interruption in order to conclude his mockery of the merchant.

1.2.56–58. **committed:** The reference to **"the nobleman that committed the Prince for striking him about Bardolph"** is to an incident recounted in the chronicles (though not dramatized by Shakespeare in *Henry IV, Part 1*) in which Hal, enraged because his servant has been imprisoned for felony, attacks the Lord Chief Justice and is himself sent to prison. The incident assumes importance near the end of *Henry IV, Part 2*, when, in 5.2, the Lord Chief Justice is confronted by Hal, now the newly crowned king.

1.2.168. **Your ill angel is light:** This is, on one level, an allusion to Lucifer, brightest of the angels, who was cast from heaven for rebelling against God. (Saint Paul, in 2 Corinthians 11.14, remarks that "Satan himself is transformed into an Angel of light.") On this level, **ill** means "evil." On a second level, it refers to the coin known as an **angel**, which is called **"light"** when it is clipped of some of its metal and therefore weighs less. (See page 180.) Here, **ill** means "defective." There is also the obvious pun on **light** as "not heavy." The surface meaning of the line is "I can't be his evil angel because I'm too heavy." **Your,** here, is not a personal pronoun; the phrase "your ill angel is" means simply "ill angels are."

1.2.178–79. **livers, galls:** Falstaff's contrast of the **heat of our livers** with **the bitterness of your galls** is, on one level, a physical comparison: the **liver** was considered the source of love and violent passion and the **gall,** or gallbladder, was associated with the bitter bile that it stores. On the figurative level, the heat of the liver was also the love or passion that arose in the liver, while the word "gall" itself meant "rancor, ill temper, the spirit to resent an insult."

1.3.28. **cause:** Editors have generally followed the Folio reading, "case," rather than the Quarto reading, "cause." We print "cause" because we follow the Quarto whenever it can be made intelligible. One of the many definitions of "cause" provided by the *OED* for the period of this play is "the case as it concerns any one"; furthermore, the *OED* cross-references this meaning of "cause" with a particular meaning of "case": "a thing that happens to any one." Thus the line now in question, "It was young Hotspur's cause at Shrewsbury," could well have meant "It was what happened to Hotspur at Shrewsbury." The *OED* also assigns the same meaning for "cause" to one appearance of the word in Shakespeare's poem *The Rape of Lucrece:* "The cause craves haste" (line 1295).

1.3.30. **Eating the air and promise of supply:** The phrase **air and promise** may be a hendiadys (i.e., a joining of two words by "and" rather than having one modify the other). If so, it means "airy promise." The Folio reading, "Eating the air on promise of supply," is generally preferred by editors. It means, "Living on false hopes of reinforcement." The phrase "to eat the air" was proverbial for feeding on false hopes. Hamlet says of his hopes of becoming king: "I eat the air,

promise-crammed. You cannot feed capons so"
(3.2.99–101).

1.3.43–64. When we mean to build . . . winter's tyranny: These lines expand Luke 14.28–30, which read, in the Geneva Bible: "For which of you minding to build a tower, sitteth not down before, and counteth the cost, whether he have sufficient to perform it, Lest that after he hath laid the foundation, and is not able to perform it, all that behold it, begin to mock him, Saying, This man began to build, and was not able to make an end?" (Spelling modernized.)

1.3.93 94. An habitation giddy and unsure . . . heart: These lines may allude to Luke 6.49, which describes "a man that built an house upon the earth without foundation . . . against which the flood did beat, and it fell by and by, and the fall of that house was great."

2.1.25. continuantly: We print the Folio reading here because we accept the traditional editorial argument that the Folio's "continuantly" seems too appropriate to the Hostess's habitual and comic misuse of language to have been the result of accident. That is, it hardly seems to be a copyist's or a compositor's error for the Quarto's "continually." By contrast, a careless or an officious agent might misread or "correct" the Folio's "continuantly" to the Quarto's comparatively ordinary reading "continually."

2.1.93. singing-man of Windsor: There has been much debate about why a comparison of Hal's father to a "singing-man of Windsor" caused Hal to break Falstaff's head. Most editors cite various disparagements of professional singers, and specifically of choristers of the royal chapel. **Windsor,** of course, refers to the royal castle of that name.

2.2.11. **creature:** In 1 Timothy 4, when Paul writes that "every **creature** of God is good," it is in the context of condemning those who would command church members to "abstain from meats [i.e., food] which God hath created . . . For every **creature** of God is good, and nothing ought to be refused, if it be received with thanksgiving" (4.3–4). In *Othello,* wine is called "a good familiar **creature**" (2.3.328–29).

2.2.21–24. **the rest . . . kingdom:** These lines are so thick with wordplay that any paraphrase merely hints at the possibilities of meaning. **The low countries** means "the Netherlands," but also probably alludes to the lower parts of the body and/or to the brothel district; **made a shift to** means "tried all means," with wordplay on "shift" as "shirt" and perhaps as "change of clothing"; **holland** refers to a kind of linen, while punning on Holland as the Netherlands; **those that bawl out the ruins of thy linen** may refer to babies "bawling," perhaps swaddled in the **ruins** of Poins's shirts. The phrase **shall inherit His kingdom** also points in more than one direction. It may reinforce the allusion to children by echoing Mark 10.14: "Suffer the little children to come unto me and forbid them not; for of such is the kingdom of God," and Matthew 18.3: "except ye be converted and become as little children, ye shall not enter into the kingdom of heaven." At the same time, it echoes even more clearly Matthew 25.34–36: "Then shall the King say to them on his right hand, Come ye blessed of my Father: **inherit** ye the **kingdom** prepared for you from the foundations of the world. For I was . . . naked, and ye clothed me."

2.4.165. **humors:** In early usage, "humor" referred to the bodily fluids of blood, phlegm, black bile, and yellow bile; later, the term referred to the dispositions, character traits, or moods thought to be caused by these fluids, and then to moods or whims in general. Here, the term is extremely vague.

2.4.168. **Caesars, cannibals:** While "Caesar" was the name taken by all rulers of the Roman Empire from 30 B.C. to A.D. 138, it originated with Julius Caesar, the great Roman military leader who conquered, among other territories, France and England (102?–44 B.C.). (See Shakespeare's play *Julius Caesar* for a dramatization of his death and its aftermath.) The appearance of Pistol's word **cannibals** in such close conjunction to things Roman suggests that it may be read as his confusion for the name "Hannibal," which belonged to the great Carthaginian general (247–182? B.C.) who very nearly succeeded in conquering the Romans.

2.4.346. **for that:** Falstaff's joke seems to accuse the Hostess of usury—i.e., lending money in order to make interest at the expense of the borrower—a practice against traditional Christian teaching, but the play gives no other indication that she charges Falstaff interest.

3.2.25. **bona robas:** John Florio's *Worlde of Wordes* (1598) defines *buonarobba* as "as we say, good stuffe, a good wholesome plum-cheeked wench." Editors' reductions of "bona roba" to "prostitute" may anachronistically impose a later social category on early modern London culture.

3.2.324. **invincible:** Many editors emend this word to "invisible." We allow the Quarto's "invincible" to stand because Falstaff's speech may use the figure of speech called catachresis (the Greek word for "misuse"), which is the deliberate misuse of a word—i.e., the deliberate use of the wrong word—for effect.

4.1.184. To us and to our purposes confined: If this line refers back to **wills,** it may mean "these demands relating only to ourselves and our grievances"; if, as many editors argue, it relates instead to **We** (in line 185), it may mean "restricting ourselves to our own affairs." In the second reading, the word **confined** would look forward to the metaphor of the river flowing within its **banks.**

4.1.217. enrooted: The image in lines 217–19 of destroying both friends and enemies draws on the parable of the wheat and the tares at Matthew 13.24–30, especially 13.29: "Nay, lest while ye go about to gather the tares, ye pluck up also with them the wheat."

Textual Notes

The reading of the present text appears to the left of the
square bracket. Unless otherwise noted, the reading to
the left of the bracket is from **Q**, the First Quarto text
(upon which this edition is based). Q survives in two
states, identified as Qa and Qb. Qa contains the first
printed version of 2.4.347–400 and 3.2.0–108. Qb contains the second printed version of these two passages
and the first printed version of the scene (3.1) between
them. Qb's version of the twice-printed text may be
based on the Qa printing of it. Therefore our edition
follows Qa for the twice-printed passages. We list only
the Qb variants that affect meaning. The earliest sources
of readings not in **Q** are indicated as follows: **F** is the
First Folio of 1623; **F2** is the Second Folio of 1632; **F3** is
the Third Folio of 1663–64; **F4** is the Fourth Folio of
1685; **Ed.** is an earlier editor of Shakespeare, beginning
with Rowe in 1709. No sources are given for emendations of punctuation or for corrections of obvious typographical errors, like turned letters that produce no
known word. **SD** means stage direction; **SP** means
speech prefix; ***uncorr.*** means the first or uncorrected
state of Q or F; ***corr.*** means the second or corrected
state of Q or F; ~ stands in place of a word already
quoted before the square bracket; ∧ indicates the omission of a punctuation mark.

In.   INDUCTION] F *only, where it is preceded by "Actus*
Primus. Scœna Prima."
        0. SD *Enter . . . tongues*] Q; *Enter Ru-*
          mour F
        5. earth.] ~, Q

255

6. tongues] Q; Tongue F
8. men] Q; them F
8. reports.] ~, Q
13. grief] Q; griefes F
16. jealousies, conjectures] ~∧~ Q
21. ∧My . . . body∧] (~ . . . ~) Q
21. anatomize] Q (anothomize); Ana-
   thomize F
27. rebels'] rebels Q, F
34. that] Q; the F
35. hold] Ed.; hole Q, F
36. Where] F; When Q
42. SD *Rumor*] *Rumours* Q; *not in* F

1.1 Act 1 Scene 1] *not in* Q, *which is not divided into
   acts or scenes; Scena Secunda* F

0. SD *Enter . . . door*] Q; *Enter Lord
   Bardolfe, and the Porter* F
1 *and hereafter (except at line 4).* SP
   LORD BARDOLPH] F (*L. Bar.*); *Bard.*
   Q
4. SP LORD BARDOLPH] Ed.; *Bard.* Q, F
8. SD *the Earl*] Q *only*
10 *and hereafter in this scene.* SP NORTH-
   UMBERLAND] F; *Earle* Q
17. God] Q; heauen F
31. lord] Q; L. F
33. SD *2 lines earlier in* Q; *2 lines later in*
   F
34. who] Q; whom F
39. with] Q; from F
42. hard] Q; head F
47. bad] Q; ill F
50. armèd] Q; able F
55. Again:] F; ~, Q
63. that] Q; the F

68. Spoke at a venture] Q; Speake at
    aduenture F
68. SD *1/2 line later in* Q *and* F
72. strand] Q (strond)
72. whereon] Q; when F
94. son—] ~: Q; ~. F
101. an] Q; thy F
109. slain, say so] F; slaine Q
110. tongue] tongne Q
116. tolling] Q; knolling F
118. SP MORTON] *Monr.* Q
119. God] Q; heauen F
122. Harry] Q; Henrie F
129. mettle] Q (mettal)
139. So] Q; Too F
150. these] Q; this F
156. keeper's] keepers Q, F
171. this] Q; the F
177. SP LORD BARDOLPH] Ed.; *Vmfr.* Q;
    line 177 not in F
178. SP MORTON] Ed.; *Bard.* Q; *L. Bar.* F
179. The] *Mour.* The Q, F
180. Lean . . . your] F; Leaue . . . you Q
182–97. F *only*
196. did] Ed.; hath F; *not in* Q
200. 'twas] Q; was F
201. ventured, . . . proposed∧] ~∧ . . . ~,
    Q, F
206. dare] Q; do F
207–29. F *only*
235. and] Q; nor F

1.2   Scene 2] Ed.; *Scena Tertia* F
        0. SD *Enter . . . buckler.] Enter sir Iohn
           alone, with his page bearing his
           sword and buckler.* Q; *Enter Fal-
           staffe, and Page.* F

1 *and hereafter in this scene (except at
lines 74, 95, 110, 114, 118, 129–68
(where* Q *reads "Falst."), and 123
(where* Q *reads "Old.").* SP FAL-
STAFF] F; *Iohn, sir Iohn* Q

7. foolish-compounded clay, man] ~∧
   ~ ~.~ Q, F

8. intends] Q; tends F

14. judgment.] F; ~∧ Q

16. heels.] F; ~∧ Q

17. inset] Q; sette F

21. fledge] Q; fledg'd F

22. off] Q; on F

23. and yet] Q; yet F

24. God] Q; Heauen F

31. my slops] Q; Slops F

32 *and hereafter.* SP PAGE] F; *Boy* Q

35–36. Pray God] Q; may F

37. rascally] F; rascall Q

39. smoothy] Q; smooth F

42. lief] F; Q (liue)

45. a true] Q; true F

48–50. it, and . . . him. Where's Bardolph?]
   F; it: wheres Bardolf, & . . . him.
   Q

51. in] Q; into F

54. Smithfield.] F; ~, Q

54. An] Q (and); If F

54. me but] Q; mee F

55. SD *Enter . . . Servant.*] Ed.; *Enter
   Lord chiefe Iustice.* Q; *Enter Chiefe
   Iustice, and Seruant.* F

60 *and hereafter in this scene.* SP CHIEF
   JUSTICE] F (*at this line only*);
   Iustice, Iust. Q, F *elsewhere in this
   scene*

74. begging] Q; beg F
76. King] Q; K. F
76. need] Q; want F
76. soldiers?] F; ~, Q
82. man?] F; ~, Q
89. me so?] F; ~, ~∧ Q
90. me?] F; ~, Q
95. God] Q; *omit* F
96. the day] F; day Q
99–100. have . . . an ague] Q; hath . . . age F
101. in you] Q; *omit* F
104. for] Q; *omit* F
106. An 't] Q; If it F
106. Lordship] lorship Q
112. God] Q; hcaucn F
112. pray you] Q; pray F
114. apoplexy, as . . . it, is a kind] Q (~∧
    ~ . . . ~? ~ ~ ~); Apoplexie is
    (as . . . it) a kind F
115–16. lethargy, an 't . . . Lordship, a kind
    of sleeping in] Q; Lethargie, a
    sleeping of F
117. it?] F; ~, Q
123. SP FALSTAFF] F; *Old.* Q
127–28. do become] Q; be F
141. himself] Q; him F
143–44. means are . . . waste is great] Q;
    Meanes is . . . wast great F
146. waist] Q (waste)
146. slender] Q; slenderer F
158. to smell] F; smell Q
163. in] Q; on F
167. ill] Q; euill F
172. times] Q; *omit* F
172–73. bearherd] Q (Berod); F (Beare-
    heard)

173. and hath his] F; and his Q
175. appurtenant] Q (appertinent)
175. this] F; his Q
176. them, are] F; the one Q
178. do] Q; *omit* F
181 *and hereafter in this scene.* SP CHIEF
        JUSTICE] Ed.; *Lo., Lord* Q; *Iust.* F
186. your chin double] Q; *omit* F
190–91. about . . . afternoon] Q *only*
192. belly.] F; ~, Q
197. him.] F; ~∧ Q
198. ear] F; yeere Q
203, 205, 227. God] Q; heauen F
207–8. you and Prince Harry] F; you Q
211. Yea] Q; Yes F
213–14. for . . . Lord] Q; for if F
216. and] Q; if F
216. a] Q; my F
216. bottle, I would] bottle, would F; bot-
        tle. I would Q
219–26. But . . . motion] Q *only*
219. always] Q (alway)
249. of] Q; on F
256. SD *He exits*] *omit* Q; *Exeunt* F

1.3 Scene 3] Ed.; *Scena Quarta* F
0. SD *Enter . . . Hastings, and Lord Bar-
        dolph.*] Ed.; *Enter . . . Hastings,
        Fauconbridge, and Bardolfe* Q; *En-
        ter Archbishop, Hastings, Mowbray,
        and Lord Bardolfe* F
1 *and hereafter in this scene.* SP ARCH-
        BISHOP] F; *Bishop, Bish.* Q
1. cause] Q; causes F
1. known] Q; kno F
6. SP MOWBRAY] F; *Marsh.* Q
20. Yea] Q; I F

23–26. F *only*
28. cause] Q; case F
30. and] Q; on F
31. in] Q; with F
38–57. F *only*
59. instead] Q (in steed), F
60. one] Q (on), F
61. through] Q (thorough)
68. a] F; so Q
73. Are] F; And Q
80. to be] Q; be F
82. He . . . Welsh] F; French and Welch
ho leaues his | back vnarmde,
they Q
87. against] Q; 'gainst F
89–114. F *only*
115. SP MOWBRAY] F; *Bish.* Q
116. SD *They exit.*] Q (*ex.*); *omit* F
2.1 Act 2 Scene 1] F (*Actus Secundus. Scœna Prima*)
0. SD *of the tavern*] Q; *not in* F
0. SD *with two Officers, Fang and Snare*]
F; *and an Officer or two* Q
6. O Lord] Q; I F
6. Master] Q; M. F
9. Yea] Q; I F
9. Master] Q; M. F
11. for] Q; *omit* F
14. and that] F *only*
14–15. in good faith] Q *only*
15–16. does. . . . out,] ~, . . . ~, Q; ~, . . .
~. F
20. An . . . an] Q; If . . . if F
21. view—] ~. Q; Vice. F
22. by] Q; with F
22. you] Q; *omit* F

22–25. going. . . . score. . . . sure. . . .
    'scape.]   ~, . . . ~, . . . ~, . . . ~,
    Q; ~: . . . ~. . . . ~: . . . ~, F

23, 24. Master] Q; M. F

25. continuantly] F; continually Q

28. Master] Q; M. F

33–34. been . . . off from] Q; bin fub'd off,
    and fub'd-off, from F

38. knave] Q *only*

40. Master] Q; M. F (*twice*)

41. SD *Enter . . . Page*] Ed.; *Enter sir
    Iohn, and Bardolfe, and the boy* Q;
    Enter Falstaffe and Bardolfe.* F, 4
    lines earlier*

44. Sir John] F *only*

44–45. Mistress Quickly] Q *corr.* (mistres
    Quickly); mistris, quickly Q
    uncorr.; Mist. *Quickly* F

49–50. thee in the channel] Q; thee there F

51, 53. Ah] Q; O F

56. SP OFFICERS] Q (*Offic.*); *Fang.* F

57–58. or two . . . wot ta] Q; Thou wilt not?
    thou wilt not? F

60. SP PAGE] F; *Boy* Q

60. scullion] Q (scullian), F

60–61. fustilarian!] ~, Q; ~: F

61. tickle] Q; tucke F

61. SD *Enter . . . Men.*] Q; *Enter. Ch.
    Iustice.* F

62 *and hereafter except at lines 65, 74,
    82, 139, 175 to end of scene (where
    F has "Ch. Iust.").* CHIEF JUSTICE]
    Ed.; *Iust.* F; *Lord, Lo.* Q

62. What is] Q; What's F

69. thou] Q *only*

75. all] Q; all: all F

79. o'] Q (a), F
82. Fie] F *only*
82. what] Q; what a F
91. upon] Q; on F
92. Wheeson] Q; Whitson F
93. liking his father] Q; lik'ning him F
101. thou not] Q; not thou F
103. so familiarity] Q; familiar F
105–6. thirty shillings] Q; 30.s F
108. mad] Q (made), F
119–20. You have . . . practiced] Q; I know
   you ha' practis'd F
121–22. and made . . . person] Q *only*
123. Yea] Q; Yes F
123. truth] Q; troth F
124. Pray thee] Q; Prethee F
125. with] Q *only*
130. make] Q *only*
131. my humble] Q; your humble F
133. do] Q *only*
138. SD *Enter . . . Gower*] Ed.; *enter a*
   messenger Q (*1 line later*); *Enter M.*
   Gower F
140. Harry] Q; *Henrie* F
143. Faith] Q; Nay F
152. hangers] Q; hangings F
153. tapestries] F; tapestrie Q
153. ten pound] Q (x. £); tenne pound F
154. an] Q; if F
156. the action] Q; thy action F
157. me? . . . come. I] Q (~, . . . ~, ~);
   me, come, I F
159. Pray thee] Q; Prethee F
160. nobles.] ~, Q
160. I' faith, I am] Q; I F
160–61. so God save me] Q; in good earnest F

164. though] Q; although F
165. gown.] F; ~, Q
171. SD *Hostess . . . exit.*] Ed.; *exit host-esse and sergeant* Q, *3 lines earlier; not in* F
172. better] Q; bitter F
173. good] F *only*
176. tonight] Q; last night F
177, 181. SP GOWER] Ed.; *Mes.* Q, F
177. Basingstoke] F; Billingsgate Q
184. lord] Q; L. F
186. Master] Q; M. F
194. counties] Q; Countries F
202. SD *They . . . exit.*] F *only*

2.2 Scene 2] F (*Scena Secunda*)
0. SD *Enter . . . Poins*] Ed.; *Enter the Prince, Poynes, sir Iohn Russel, with other.* Q; *Enter Prince Henry, Pointz, Bardolfe, and Page.* F
1. Before God] Q; Trust me F
4. Faith] Q *only*
10. by my] Q; in F
15. with] Q; Viz. F
16. ones] F; once Q
18. another] Q; one other F
20. keepest] Q; kept'st F
22. the] Q; thy F
22. have made a shift to eat] F; haue eate Q
23–27. and God . . . strengthened] Q *only*
23. bawl] Q (bal)
30. being] Q; lying F
31. as . . . is] Q; as yours is F
33. faith] Q *only*
38. Marry] Q; Why F
43. By this hand] Q *only*

62. SP POINS] *Poyne* Q
62. By this light] Q; Nay F
62. spoke on] Q; spoken of F
66. By the Mass] Q; Looke, looke F
67. SD *Page*] Ed.; *boy* Q; *Enter Bardolfe* F
69. look] Q; see F
71. God] Q *only*
73. virtuous] Q; pernitious F
78. calls] Q; call'd F
78. e'en now] enow Q; euen now F
81. ale-wife's] Q (ale wiues)
81. new] F *only*
82. so] Q *only*
84–85. rabbit] F (Rabbet); rabble Q
88. Althea] Q (Althear)
92. good] F *only*
94. An] Q; If F
94. be hanged] F; hangd Q
95. have wrong] Q; be wrong'd F
97. good] F *only*
105. how] Q *only*
113. conceive.] ~∧ Q; ~? F
113. borrower's] Ed.; borowed Q, F
115. or] Q; but F
116. to the letter] F; the letter Q
123. He sure] Q; Sure he F
124. SP PRINCE] Ed.; *not in* Q, F
131. familiars] F; family Q
132. sisters] Q; *Sister* F
139. God . . . no] Q; May the Wench haue no F
144. Yea] Q; Yes F
152. Mistress Doll] Q; M. *Doll* F
161. come to] Q; in F
168. Saint] Q, F (S.)
172. leathern] Q; Leather F

173. as] Q; like F
174. descension] Q; declension F
175. case.] F; ~, Q
175. prince] F; pince Q
176. everything] enery thing Q

2.3   Scene 3] F (*Scena Tertia*)
0. SD *Enter . . . Percy.*] Q *Enter Northumberland, his Ladie, and Harrie
Percies Ladie.* F
1. pray thee] Q; prethee F
2. even] Q; an euen F
5 *and hereafter in this scene.* SP LADY
NORTHUMBERLAND] Ed.; *Wife* Q, F
9 *and hereafter in this scene.* SP LADY
PERCY] Ed.; *La.*, *Lady* F; *Kate* Q
9. God's] Q; heauens F
10. that] Q; when F
11. endeared] F; endeere Q
17. the God of heaven] Q; may heauenly
glory F
23–45. F *only*
32. wondrous∧ him!] ~! ~, F

2.4   Scene 4] F (*Scæna Quarta*)
0. SD *Enter . . . Drawer.*] Ed.; *Enter a
Drawer or two.* Q; *Enter two Drawers* F
1 *and hereafter.* SP FRANCIS] Q; I.
Drawer. F
1. the devil] Q *only*
4. SP SECOND DRAWER] F (2. *Draw.*);
Draw. Q
4. Mass] Q *only*
12. hear] Q; haue F
12. Dispatch] Ed.; *Dra. Dispatch* Q
12–14. Dispatch . . . straight] Q *only*
14. SD Q *only, 4 lines later*

15. SP WILL] Ed.; *Francis* Q; 2 *Draw.* F
19. SP SECOND DRAWER] *Draw.* Q; I. *Draw.* F
19. By the Mass] Q; Then F
19. old] Q *corr.,* F; oll Q *uncorr.*
21. SP FRANCIS] Q; 2. *Draw.* F
21. SD *Enter . . . Tearsheet.*] Ed.; *Enter mistris Quickly, and Doll Teresheet.* Q; *Enter Hostesse, and Dol* F
22, 31. SP HOSTESS] F; *Quickly, Qui,* Q
22. I' faith] Q *only*
25–26. in . . . i' faith] Q; But F
28. one] Q; wee F
30, 40, 43. SP DOLL] F; *Tere.* Q
31. that's] Q; that was F
32. Lo] Q; Looke F
32. SD *Enter . . . Falstaff.*] Ed.; *enter sir Iohn.* Q; *Enter Falstaffe.* F
33. SP FALSTAFF] F; *sir Iohn* Q
37. faith] Q; sooth F
38. An] Q; if F
40. A pox damn you] Q *only*
40. rascal.] ~, Q
43. them] F; *omit* Q
45. help to] Q *only*
47. you.] ~∧ Q
49. Yea, joy] Q; I marry F
55. DOLL Hang . . . yourself!] Q *only*
56. By my troth] Q; Why F
58. truth] Q; troth F
60. good-year!] ~∧ Q; ~? F
63. SP DOLL] F; *Dorothy* Q
74–75. No, by my faith] Q *only*
75. among] Q; amongst F
84. And] Q *only*
86. debuty] Q; Deputie F
87–88. Wednesday] wedsday Q

88. i' good faith] Q *only*
91. said] Q; sayth F
98–99. i' faith.] ~, Q; hee F
105. swaggering.] ~ ∧ Q
105. By my troth] Q *only*
108. SP DOLL] F; *Teresh.* Q
109. an] Q; if F
110. SD *Enter . . . Page.*] Ed.; *Enter
       antient Pistol, and Bardolfes boy* Q;
       *Enter Pistol, and Bardolph and his
       Boy.* F
111. God] Q *only*
117. not] Q *only*
124, 129, 141. SP DOLL] F; *Doro.* Q
131. an] Q; if F
133. God's light] Q; what F
135. God . . . but] Q *only*
137–38. FALSTAFF . . . Pistol] Q *only* (SP: *sir
        Iohn*)
142. An] Q; If F
149. God's light] Q *only*
149–51. as odious . . . sorted] Q; Captaine
        odious F
156. of] Q; on F
159. by this hand] Q *only*
159. with] Q; where F
161. Fates] F; faters Q
164. i' faith] Q *only*
167. mile] Q; miles F
168. Caesars] Q; *Caesar* F
171. captain] Q *corr.* (captaine), F; cap-
     tane Q *uncorr.*
175. Die] F; *omit* Q
175. dogs!] ~∧ Q
177. O'] Q (A); On F
179. For God's sake] Q; I pray F
181. give 's] Q (giues); giue me F

182. *contento*] Q; *contente* F
183. sweetheart, lie] Q *corr.* (sweet hart,
    lie), F; sweet hartlie Q *uncorr.*
185. etceteras] Q (& cæteraes)
185. nothings] Q (no things); nothing F
189. For God's sake] Q *only*
193. Quoit] Q (Quaite), F
194. an] Q; if F
200. grievous] grieuons Q
202. goodly] Q; good F
207. afore] Q; before F
211. valiant] vliaunt Q
215. Yea] Q; Yes F
220. i' faith] Q *only*
226. an . . . An] Q; if . . . if F
227. SD *1 line later in* Q, *where* "Musi-
    cians" *reads* "musicke" *as in* F
232. I' faith] Q *only*
232. church.] ~, Q
234. a- . . . a-] Q; on . . . on F
236. SD *disguised*] F *only*
253. boots] Q; Boot F
258. the] F *only*
259. avoirdupois] Q (haber de poiz)
263. whe'er] Q (where); if F
271. master's] F; master Q
274. By my troth] Q; Nay truely F
279. thou] F *only*
280. thou] F *only*
280, 319. o'] Q (a); on F
283. By my troth] Q *only*
283. an] Q; if F
285. a' th'] Q; the F
289. Poins his] Q; ~, ~ F
296. good] F *only*
296–97. By my troth] Q *only*

297. the Lord] Q; Heauen F
298. O Jesu] Q; what F
301. light flesh] F; ~, ~ Q
307. even] F *only*
309. of] Q; on F
312. Yea] Q; Yes F
321. chipper] Q; chopper F
327. thee] Q; him F
330. faith] Q *only*
334. thy boy] Q; the Boy F
342. blinds] Q; out-bids F
347–400. *This edition follows* Qa.
353. vitlars] Q; Victuallers F
358. SD *Peto knocks at door*] Q *only*
360. SD *Enter Peto*] F *only*
362. Westminster] Qa, F; Weminster Qb
370. south∧] Ed.; ~. Qa; ~, Qb
374. SD *Prince . . . exit.*] Q; *Exit.* F
390. SD *He exits*] This ed.; *exit* Qb, F; *omit* Qa
399–400. Come.—She . . . come,   Doll?]   Q *only*

3.1   *This edition follows* Qb, *this scene being absent from* Qa
Act 3 Scene 1] F (*Actus Tertius. Scena Prima*)
0. SD *Enter . . . Page.*] Ed.; *Enter the King in his night-gowne alone* Q; *Enter the King, with a Page.* F
1. Warwick] Q (War.)
3. SD *Page exits*] Ed.; *Exit.* F; *omit* Q
10. pallets] Q; Pallads F
11. night-flies] Q; Night, flyes F
14. sound] Q; sounds F
18. mast] F; masse Q
22. billows] F; pillowes Q

24. deafing] Q; deaff'ning F
24. clamor] Q; Clamors F
24. slippery] Q; slipp'ry F
26. thy] F; them Q
27. sea-boy] F; season Q
31. SD *Enter . . . Blunt*] Q; *Enter War-*
 wicke and Surrey F
36. letter] Q; Letters F
45, 73. God] Q; Heauen F
46. times∧] F; ~, Q
53–56. O, if . . . die] Q *only*
59. years] F; yeare Q
82. natures] Q; nature F
85. who] Q; which F
86. beginning] Q; beginnings F
102. soul] Q; Life F

3.2 Scene 2] F (*Scena Secunda*)
0. SD *Enter . . . Silence*] Q; *Enter Shal-*
 low and Silence: with Mouldie,
 Shadow, Wart, Feeble, Bull-calfe F
0–108. *Enter . . . young*] *This edition follows*
 Qa.
1. on. Give] Qa, F; on sir, giue Qb
8. ousel] Q (woosel); F (Ouzell)
9. no] Q; nay F
9. sir.] Ed.; ~, Qa, F; ~: Qb
13, 23. o'] Q (a); of F
18. By the Mass] Q *only*
21. Barnes] Q; *Bare* F
22. Cotswold] Q (Cotsole)
25. robas] Q (robes), F
29. This Sir John, cousin] Qa, F; Coosin,
 this sir Iohn Qb
31. Sir John,] Qa, F; (sir Iohn) Qb
31. see] Q; saw F

35. Jesu, Jesu] Q; Oh F
40. as . . . saith] Q *only*
41. Stamford] F; Samforth Q
43. cousin] F *only*
47. Jesu, Jesu] Q; Dead? See, see F
48. o'] Q (a); of F
58. SD *Enter . . . him.*] Q; *Enter Bar-
    dolph and his Boy.* F, *2 lines earlier*
59. SP SHALLOW] F; Good Qa *corr.; Bar-
    dolfe* Good Qa *uncorr.*
63. good pleasure] Qa, F; pleasure Qb
65–66. by heaven] Q *only*
70–71. accommodated] F; accommodate Q
72. in faith] Q *only*
74–75. ever were] Q; euery where F
77–78. Pardon . . . day] Qa, F; Pardon
    me . . . good day Qb
81. by heaven] Q *only*
83. may be] Q *only*
84. SD *Enter Falstaff.*] Qa, F; *Enter sir
    Iohn Falstaffe* Qb
85. SP SHALLOW] F; *Iust.* Q
86–87. good   hand . . . good   hand]   Q;
    hand . . . good hand F
87. By my troth] Q; Trust me F
87. like] Q; looke F
89, 93. Master] Q, F (M.)
90. Sure-card] F; Soccard Q
92. commission] Qb, F; commssion Qa
97. dozen] Q; dozen of F
101. Let me see] Qa, F; *omit* Qb
101–2. So, so, so, so, so. So, so] Q; so, so,
    so, so F
103–4. do∧ . . . do∧] Qb, F; ~, . . . ~, Qa
106, 110, 116. an] Q; if F
112. i' faith] Q *only*

113–14. in faith] Q *only*
115. FALSTAFF Prick him.] F; *John prickes him.* Q
127. Yea] Q; I F
135. much] Q; not F
139. to] F *only*
147. down] F *only*
148. his] F *only*
158. ha'] Q (a); haue F
165. mouse.—] Q *corr.* (~,); ~∧ Q *uncorr.*; ~. F
166–67. tailor well, Master . . . Master] tailer: wel∧ M. . . . M. Q
174. sir] Q *only*
176. the] F *only*
180. Fore God] Q; Trust me F
180. prick me] F; pricke Q
182, 185. Lord] Q *only*
188. caught] cought Q
190. Come, . . . go] Q *corr.*, F; Come∧ . . . goe Q *uncorr.*
194. Here] Q; There F
197. SP FALSTAFF] Fa. Q *corr.*; Fal. Q *uncorr.*, F
198. dinner.] F; ~: Q *corr.*; ~, Q *uncorr.*
198. by my] Q; in good F
201. Saint] Q; F (S.)
202 3. good Master Shallow, no more of that] F; master Shallow Q
206, 209. Master] Q; F (M.)
210. By the Mass] Q *only*
210. could] conld Q
216. Clement's Inn] Q *corr.* (Clements inne), F; Clemham Q *uncorr.*
217. year] Q; yeeres F
218–19. that that] Q *corr.*; ~, ~ Q *uncorr.*

219. John,] Q *corr.*, F; ~∧ Q *uncorr.*
220. well] Q *corr.*; wel Q *uncorr.*
221–22, 236, 269, 298, 299. Master] Q (M.)
223–24. SHALLOW . . . have. In faith] Q *corr.*;
~ . . . ~∧ ~ ~Q *uncorr.*; *Shal.*
That wee haue, that wee haue; in
faith F
226. Jesus] Q; Oh F
226. SD *Shallow . . . exit.*] Q *only* (*They
exit.*)
230. lief] Q (liue), F
236. Master] Q *uncorr.* (master), F; M. Q
corr.
237. old] Q *corr.*, F; *omit* Q *uncorr.*
242. By my troth] Q *only*
243. God] Q *only*
244. destiny] destny Q
244. an] Q; if F (*twice*)
249. Faith] Q; Nay F
249. SD Q *only*
258. Shadow] Sadow Q
269. Here's] Q; Where's F
282. Thas . . . thas] Q; thus, thus, thus F
286. i' faith] Q *only*
298. will] Q (wooll), F
299. God keep you] Q; Farewell F
303. the Lord] Q; Heauen F
303. God prosper] Q; and F
304. God] Q; and F
304. peace.] F; ~∧ Q
304. At your] Q; As you F
305. our] Q; my F
307. Fore God] Q; I F
307–8. Master Shallow] F *only*
309. God keep you] Q; Fare you well F

311. On] F; *Shal.* On Q
313. Lord, Lord] Q *only*
318. duer] Q (dewer)
321. radish] Q (reddish)
325. genius] Q *corr.*, F; gemies Q *uncorr.*
325–26. yet . . . mandrake] Q *only*
327. ever] F; ouer Q
327–30. and sung . . . good-nights] Q *only*
329. swore] Q (sware)
332, 336. o'] Q (a)
337. thrust] Q; truss'd F
338. eel-skin] Q *corr.* (eele), F; eele-shin Q *uncorr.*
338. hautboy] Q (hoboy)
340. be] Q *corr.*, F; he Q *uncorr.*
342. me.] ~, Q
344. him. Let] Q *uncorr.* (him: let), F; him, till Q *corr.*
345. SD *He exits.*] *omit* Q; *Exeunt.* F
4.1 Act 4 Scene 1] F (*Actus Quartus. Scena Prima*)
0. SD *Enter . . . Gaultree.*] Q; *Enter the Arch-bishop, Mowbray, Hastings, Westmerland, Coleuile* F
1. SP ARCHBISHOP] Ed.; *Bish., Bishop* Q, F
2. Gaultree] Q; Gualtree F
13. could] Q *corr.*, F; would Q *uncorr.*
18. him∧] Q *uncorr.*; ~, Q *corr.*, F
19. SD *Messenger*] Q; *A Messenger* F
26. SD *1 line later in* Q
33–34. WESTMORELAND Then, my lord, | Unto] Q *corr.* (*We.* Then my L. vnto), F; *West.* Vnto Q *uncorr.*
33. lord] Q (L.), F
34. do] Q *corr.*; doe Q *uncorr.*, F
38. countenanced] Q *corr.*

(countenaunst), F; counteenaunst Q *uncorr.*

39. appeared] Ed.; appeare Q, F
45. see] Q (Sea)
48. figure] Q *corr.*, F; figures Q *uncorr.*
57. end:] F; ~∧ Q
58–83. F *only*
97. Q *uncorr. only* (commotions)
99. Q *uncorr. only* (borne, houshold)
108–48. F *only*
121. force] Ed.; forc'd F
147. indeed] Ed.; and did F
178–79. grievances. . . . redressed,]   ~, . . .
       ~. Q; ~: . . . ~, F
184. to] F *only*
187. General.] ~, Q; ~. F
189. And] Ed.; At Q, F
189. God] Q; Heauen F
192. SD Q *only, 1 line earlier*
195. not∧ that.] ~, ~∧ Q, F
199. Yea] Q; I F
237. hand.] ~, Q; ~: F
238. SD *Enter . . . army.*] Q; *Enter Prince Iohn* F, *3 lines later*
239. God's] Q; heauen's F
239. set] Q *only*
242 *and hereafter.* SP JOHN OF LANCAS-TER] Ed.; *Iohn* Q, F
250. Than] F; That Q
250. talking] Q *only*
260, 262, 270, 378. God] Q; Heauen F
262. imagined] Ed.; imagine Q, F
267. Employ] F; Imply Q
269. dishonorable?] F; ~∧ Q
269. ta'en] Q; taken F

271. His] Q; Heauens F
284. Hydra son] ~, ~ Q; ~-~ F
295. his] Q; this F
297 *and hereafter in this scene.* SP JOHN
OF LANCASTER] F; *Prince* Q
308. soul] Q; Life F
308. shall.] F; ~, Q
315. SP JOHN OF LANCASTER] F; *omit* Q
317. SP HASTINGS] F; *Prince* Q
319. SD F *only*
336. SD Q *only*
344. SD F *only, 3 lines later*
351. SD F *only*
352. SD *1 line earlier in* Q
357. My lord] Q *only*
357. already] Q *only*
358. take] Q; tooke F
359. courses] Q; course F
374. and such acts as yours] F *only*
378. hath] Q; haue F
379. these traitors] F; this traitour Q
380. SD F *only*

4.2   Scene 2] Ed.; *omit* F
0. SD *Alarum . . . Colevile*] *Alarum
Enter Falstaffe   excursions* Q;
Enter Falstaffe and Colleuile F
2. I pray] F *only*
7. be still] Q; still be F
16–17. COLEVILE I . . . thought] Q *corr.*
(*Colle.* I . . . thought), F; *Colle.*
I . . . thoght Q *uncorr.*
18. FALSTAFF I . . . school . . . tongues]
Q *corr.*, F; I . . . schoole . . . tongs
Q *uncorr.*
20. name.] ~, Q
23. SD *Enter . . . rest.*] *Enter Iohn West-*

merland, and the rest. Retraite Q;
Enter Prince Iohn, and Westmer-
land. F
24. further] Q; farther F
41–42. There, cousin,] Q *only*
43. courtesy] Q *corr.* (curtesie), F;
cnrtesie Q *uncorr.*
47. by the Lord] Q; I sweare F
48. else] Q *only*
49. on 't] Q; of it F
56 *and hereafter in this scene.* SP JOHN
OF LANCASTER] F; *Prince* Q
70. gratis] Q *only*
72. Now] Q *only*
76. SD *Blunt exits with Colevile] Exit with*
Colleuile F; *omit* Q
85. pray] F *only* ('pray)
88. SD *All . . . exit.] Exit.* F; *omit* Q
89. but] F *only*
91–92. love me, nor . . . cannot] Q *corr.*
(loue me, nor . . . cānot), F;
loueme, nor . . . canot Q *uncorr.*
93. none] Q; any F
102. crudy] Q; cruddie F
111. illumineth] Q; illuminateth F
116. this] Q; his F
119. hoard] Q (whoord), F
127. human] Q (humane), *omit* F
129. SD *1 line later in* Q
133. Master] Q (M.)
136. SD F *only*
4.3   Scene 3] *Scena Secunda* F
0. SD *Warwike, Kent, Thomas* Q; *Enter*
King, Warwicke, Clarence, Glouces-
ter. F
1. God] Q; Heauen F

15 *and hereafter except at lines 121, 132, 142, 156, 158, 206, 5.2.28, where* Q *reads "Hum."* SP HUMPHREY OF GLOUCESTER] Ed.; *Glo.* Q, F

20 *and hereafter except at lines 56, 58.* THOMAS OF CLARENCE] Ed.; *Clar.* Q, F

36. melting] F; meeting Q

37. he is] Q; hee's F

43. time] Q; Line F

56, 58. SP THOMAS OF CLARENCE] F; *Tho.* Q

57. Canst thou tell that?] F *only*

75. language.] F; ~: Q

76. needful] needfnll Q

78. further] Q; farther F

83. others] Q (other)

86, 100. SD *1 line later in* Q

91. Bishop∧ Scroop] ~, ~ Q, F

100. SD *Harcourt*] Q (*Harcor.*), F

102. heavens] Q; Heauen F

107. shrieve] Q; Sherife F

112. full,] ~. Q

113. write] F; wet Q

113. letters] F; termes Q

119. And] Aud Q

131. through and will break out] F; through Q

144. Softly, pray] F *only* ('pray)

151. SD *Enter Prince Harry.*] *Enter Harry* Q; *Enter Prince Henry.* F

152 *and hereafter until line 244.* PRINCE] Q; *P. Hen.* F

158. altered] Q *corr.* (altred), F; vttred Q *uncorr.*

165. Will 't] Q (Wilt); F (Wil't)

178. downy] Q (dowlny)

179. down] Q (dowlne)
180. move.] ~∧ Q
190. where] Q; heere F
191. God] Q; Heauen F
197. SD *Enter . . . Clarence*]. Q *and F, 2
　　　lines earlier*
199. How fares your Grace?] F *only*
204. He . . . here] Q *only*
220. sleep] Q; sleepes F
222. piled] F; pilld Q
226. tolling] Q; culling F
227. The virtuous sweets] F *only*
228. thighs] F; thigh Q
232. SD *2 lines later in* Q
234. hath] F; hands Q
241. SD *Enter Prince Harry*] *Enter Harry*
　　　Q, *1 line earlier; Enter Prince Henry*
　　　F
243. SD *Gloucester . . . exit.*] Ed.; *exeunt*
　　　Q; *Exit* F
244. SP PRINCE] F (*P. Hen.*); *Harry* Q
245. thought.] ~∧ Q; ~: F
259. die∧ . . . it.] ~, . . . ~, Q
261. Whom] Q; Which F
269. compound] compouud Q
273. Harry] Q; Henry F
273, 285. Fifth] Q (fift)
279. will] Q; swill F
283. gild] Q; gill'd F
287. on] Q; in F
294. moist] Q; most F
303. inward true and] Q; true, and in-
　　　ward F
304–5. bending. . . . me,] F; ~, . . . ~. Q
305, 331. God] Q; Heauen F
313. this] Q; the F
317. worst of] F; worse then Q

318. is more] F; more Q
321. thy] Q; the F
321. most] Q *only*
334. O my son] F *only*
335. God] Q; Heauen F
335. it in] F; in Q
336. win] Q; ioyne F
341, 378, 396. God] Q; Heauen F
342. crook'd] Q (crookt)
344. sat] Q (sate)
362. my] Ed.; thy Q, F
380. My gracious liege] F *only*
384. SD *Enter . . . others.*] *enter Lancaster,* Q; *Enter Lord Iohn of Lancaster, and Warwicke.* F
386. SP JOHN OF LANCASTER] F; *Lanc.* Q
394. swoon] Q (swound)
401. SD F *only*
5.1 Act 5 Scene 1] F (*Actus Quintus. Scœna Prima*)
0. SD *Enter . . . Bardolph.*] *Enter Shallow, Falstaffe, and Bardolfe.* Q; *Enter Shallow, Silence, Falstaffe, Bardolfe, Page, and Dauie.* F
1. sir] Q *only*
9–10. SHALLOW Davy . . . William] Q; *Shal. Dauy, Dauy, Dauy,* let me see (*Dauy*) let me see: *William* F
14. hade land] Q; head-land F
22. Now] Q *only*
24. the other day] F *only*
25. Hinckley] F; Hunkly Q
28. tiny] Q; tine F
30. Yea] Q; Yes F
34. back-bitten] Q; bitten F
35. marvelous] Q (maruailes)
39. o'] Q (a'); of F

40. is] Q; are F
44. God] Q; heauen F
47. this] Q; these F
48. an] Q; and if F
49–50. but a very] F *only*
51. you] Q; your Worship F
55. Come, come, come] Q; Come F
56. Master] Q, F (M.)
58. all my] F; my Q
67. observing of] F; obseruing Q
83. without] Q; with F
90. SD *He exits.*] *omit* Q; *Exeunt* F

5.2   Scene 2] F (*Scena Secunda*)

0. SD *Enter . . . Justice.*] Ed.; *Enter Warwike, duke Humphrey, L. chiefe Iustice, Thomas Clarence, Prince, Iohn Westmerland.* Q *uncorr.*; *Enter . . . Prince Iohn Westmerland* Q *corr.*; *Enter the Earle of Warwicke, and the Lord Chiefe Iustice.* F
2 *and hereafter.* SP CHIEF JUSTICE] F; *Iust.* Q
14. SD *Enter . . . Humphrey.*] *Enter Iohn of Lancaster, Gloucester, and Clarence.* F
17. he] Q; him F
20. O God] Q; Alas F
22. SP   HUMPHREY . . . CLARENCE]   F; *Prin. ambo* Q
37. impartial] Q; Imperiall F
39. remission.] F; ~, Q
40. truth] Q; Troth F
40. me,] F; ~. Q
42. SD *Enter Prince Henrie* F, *1 line later*

44, 145, 147. God] Q; heauen F
  47. mix] F; mixt Q
  51. by my faith] Q; to speake truth F
  60. Yet] Q; But F
  63. SP BROTHERS] Q; *Iohn,&c.* F
  63. otherwise] Q; other F
  97. your] Q; you F
 111. not] Q; no F
 113. justice.] F; ~∧ Q
 128. raze] Q *and* F (race)
 130. seeming.] F; ~, Q
 141. you] Q *corr.*, F; your Q *uncorr.*
 147. SD *They exit.*] F (*Exeunt.*); *exit.* Q

5.3 Scene 3] F (*Scena Tertia*)
   0. SD *Enter . . . Page.*] *Enter sir Iohn,*
    Shallow, Scilens, Dauy, Bardolfe,
    page. Q; *Enter Falstaffe, Shallow,*
    Silence, Bardolfe, Page, and Pistoll.
    F
   5. Fore God] Q *only*
  5–6. a goodly . . . a rich] F; goodly . . .
    rich Q
 13, 62. By the Mass] Q *only*
  18. God] Q; heauen F
  23. SP FALSTAFF] F; *Sir Iohn* Q
  23. Master] Q *and* F (M.)
  25. Give Master Bardolph∧] Q; Good M.
    Bardolfe: F
  27. good master] Q; good M. F
  29. must] Q *only*
30, 37, 49, 52, 58, 63. Master] Q; M. F
  34. *wags*] Q; wagge F
  40. SD Q *only*
  47. *thee*] Q *and* F (the)
  50. And] Q; If F

51. o'] Q (a'); of F
57. tiny] Q; tyne F
61. An] Q; If F
64. Yea] Q; Yes F
65. By God's liggens] Q *only*
66. that.] F; ∼∧ Q
67. he.] a∧ Q
67. 'Tis] Q; is F
70. SD Q *only, 2 lines earlier*
80. An 't] Q (And 't); If F
82. SD *1 line earlier in* Q
84. God] Q *only*
84. you] Q; you sir F
86. no man] Q; none F
88. this] Q; the F
89. By 'r Lady] Q; Indeed F
92. in] F; ith Q
94. And] Q *only*
102. Cophetua] Q (Couetua); *Couitha* F
112. to conceal] F; conceal Q
116, 120. Fifth] Q (fift)
126. Master] Q (M.)
129–30. knighthood] F; Knight Q
140. Blessed . . . that]   Q;   Happie . . .
which F
141. to] Q; vnto F
144. these] Q; those F
144. SD *They exit.*] F; *exit.* Q

5.4   Scene 4] F (*Scena Quarta*)
0. SD   *Enter . . . Beadles.*]   F;   *Enter*
Sincklo and three or foure officers.
Q
1. to God that] Q *only*
4 *and   hereafter.* SP   BEADLE]   Ed.;
Sincklo Q; *Off., Officer.* F
5. cheer enough] F; cheere Q

6. lately] F *only*

8 *and hereafter.* DOLL] F; *Whoore* Q

9. an] Q; if F

10. now] F *only*

10. wert] Q; had'st F

13. the Lord] Q *only*

13. I] Q; hee F

14. pray God] Q; would F

15. might] F *only*

19. amongst] Q; among F

20. you . . . you] Q; thee . . . thou F

21. bluebottle] Q; blew-Bottel'd F

25. God] Q *only*

28. Ay] Q (I); Yes F

30. atomy] Q; Anatomy F

32. SD F *only*

5.5 Scene 5] F (*Scena Quinta*)

0. SD *Enter two Grooms*] F; *Enter strewers of rushes* Q

1. SP FIRST GROOM] F; 1 Q

2. SP SECOND GROOM] F; 2 Q

3. SP FIRST GROOM] F; 3 Q

3. o'] Q (a); of the F

4. Dispatch, dispatch] Q *only*

4. SD *Grooms exit.*] F only (*Exit Groo.*)

4. SD *Page*] F; *Boy* Q; *Enter Falstaffe, Shallow, Pistoll, Bardolfe, and Page* F

5. Master] Q; M. F

5. Robert] F *only*

9. God] Q *only*

15. SP SHALLOW] F; *Pist.* Q

16. of] Q; in F

17, 19. SP SHALLOW] Ed.; *Pist.* Q, F

23. best,] ~∧ Q; most∧ F

24. SP FALSTAFF] F *only*

24. travel] Q (trauaile)
29. all] F *only*
36. truth] Q; troth F
37. SD *Shouts . . . sound.*] *The Trumpets sound. Enter King Henrie the Fift, Brothers, Lord Chiefe Iustice.* F
39, 42. God] Q *only*
48. becomes] Q; become F
51. awaked] Q; awake F
57. God] Q; heauen F
67. evils] Q; euill F
69. strengths] Q; strength F
72. my] Q; our F
73. SD *King . . . exit.*] *Exit King.* F; *omit* Q
74 *and hereafter (except at line 94).* SP FALSTAFF] F; *Iohn* Q
75. Yea] Q; I F
77. Master] Q; M. F
80. advancements] Q; aduancement F
82. well] F *only*
83. should] F *only*
88. that I fear you] Q; I feare, that you F
91. SD Q *only*
97. *me contenta*] *contenta* Q; *me contento* F
97. SD *All . . . exit.*] *exeunt.* Q, *1 line earlier; Exit. Manet Lancaster and Chiefe Iustice.* F
108. heard] Q; heare F
110. SD *They exit.*] F *only (Exeunt)*

Ep.
10. meant] Q; did meane F
16–18. And so I . . . Queen.] Q; *at the end of the Epilogue, omitting "I"* F
23. would] Q; will F
26. before] F *only*
34. a] F *only*

Textual Problems in
Henry IV, Part 2
The Folio-only Passages: Cuts from the Quarto or Authorial Revisions in the Folio?

Since the early eighteenth century editors have discussed how the major differences between Q and F may have arisen. According to Alexander Pope, writing in the early 1720s, the eight F-only passages were added to the play by Shakespeare's own revising hand. Samuel Johnson, writing in the 1760s, thought instead that the F-only passages had been cut from the Q text by actors abridging the play for performance. Although there has recently been an unpersuasive attempt to revive and modify Pope's theory of Shakespearean revision, Johnson's view has generally prevailed. Close attention to the contexts of the F-only passages indicates that their omission from Q always renders Q's dialogue discontinuous. Such discontinuity strongly suggests that the F-only passages were once part of the Q text as well. Surviving dramatic manuscripts from Shakespeare's time that show signs of their use in the theater are marked with cuts that resemble the omissions from Q in their quantity and in the discontinuity they produce in dialogue.

Yet some of those discontinuities are so jarring that scholars have speculated that these cuts may not have been made by actors but by a censor for the crown, perhaps on the occasion of Q's publication. Take, for example, 1.1.207–29, 1.3.89–114, and 4.1.58–83. The topics of all three speeches, these scholars contend, may have caused anxiety among royal officials. The first argues for the power that churchmen may exert in

287

sponsoring rebellion, the second deals with the fickleness of subjects' loyalty, and the third is a justification of armed rebellion. However, the royal censors apparently allowed stage representations of successful rebellions against the crown in other plays. Thus, while it is clear that passages have been cut from Q, it is not clear who may have cut them or for what reason.

Censorship and Scribal Transmission of the Folio Text

It is certain that F has been subjected to a kind of censorship—not political censorship, but censorship of profanity and oaths. Yet uncertainty arises concerning who carried out this censorship. Editors have noted the many times that the various names of the deity—present in Q as "God," "God's light," "the Lord," "Jesus," and "Jesu"—are expurgated from F, which in some cases offers substitutes (e.g., "heaven") and in other cases does not. In trying to explain this expurgation, editors have pointed to a 1606 Act to Restrain Abuses of Players that forbade actors to use the names of God onstage. Its enforcement was the responsibility of the Master of the Revels, who censored acting companies' manuscripts. Therefore editors have concluded from the expurgation of the names of God in F that it must derive ultimately from a manuscript kept in the theater.

This conclusion overlooks two facts about F. First, "God" has not completely disappeared from F. Still present are the Hostess's reference to "God's officers" (2.1.52), the Chief Justice's prayer for Falstaff "the Lord lighten thee" (2.1.201), and the Hostess's prayer for Prince Hal "the Lord preserve thy good Grace" (2.4.296). These references to "God" and "the Lord" are important differences between F and surviving dramatic manuscripts from the period after 1606 that contain signs of having passed through the hands of the Master of the Revels. Second, F sporadically censors such mild oaths from Q as "by my troth" or "i' faith," oaths that were not necessarily censored by the Master of the Revels before the 1620s. It would seem that some other agent may have censored F, and therefore F may be based on something other than a theatrical manuscript.

The person who censored F may have been a scribe, for we know that scribes sometimes did censor dramatic manuscripts according to their own lights; moreover, we have good reason to believe that a scribe was responsible for the manuscript that underlies F. Signs of scribal transcription are to be found in the style of the prose passages of F. Comparing F to Q, editors have observed the many times that F prints formal language instead of Q's colloquial speech. Over and over, where Q prints "there's," F prints "there is"; where O prints "Ile" (i.e., I'll), F prints "I will"; where Q prints " 'tis," F prints "it is." These are only a few of the many examples available. Close study of the Folio typesetters' work on other plays (like the stylistically similar *Henry IV, Part 1*) indicates that they very seldom formalized language in this way. Such changes therefore must have their origin elsewhere than the printing shop.

If these minor stylistic changes were the only differences between Q and F, such scribal intervention would be of little importance, since these changes have no impact on the text's meaning. However, discovery of a scribal hand in the F text raises the possibility that some significant differences between Q and F may be his responsibility too. Perhaps he was the one who fixed the grammar of King Henry's accusation against Prince Hal. In Q the accusation reads "Thou hid'st a thousand daggers in thy thoughts, / *Whom* thou hast whetted on thy stony heart," but in F "Which" has replaced "Whom" (4.3.260–61). Even though "Whom" is not incorrect in sixteenth-century usage, "which" would have been the more correct form in the early seventeenth century. Perhaps the scribe was also responsible for modifying Falstaff's colloquial phrasing in Q by adding to it a word (here printed in italics) in order to make the phrasing perfectly balanced: "To wake a wolf is as bad as *to* smell a fox" (1.2.158). Or perhaps the scribe transformed Shallow's peculiar expression "I thank thee with my heart" as it reads in Q, into the more customary version printed in F: "I thank thee with *all* my heart" (5.1.58). In *The Merry Wives of Windsor*, the only other Shakespeare play in which he appears, Shallow is given (in the Folio version) the expression as printed in Q *Henry IV, Part 2*. Finally, the scribe may even have introduced into the F text entire half-lines in order to make its verse, as well as its language, more regular and more conventional. Some half-lines unique to F seem to do no more than complete a verse line. An example is the one printed here in italics: "But for you rebels, look to taste the due / Meet for rebellion *and such acts as yours*" (4.1.373–74). The discovery of a scribe in the F text thus calls into question many F readings that vary from Q. Nonetheless, it is impossible *in the case of any specific reading* to know that it originates with the scribe. Therefore F's readings cannot simply be dismissed as merely scribal.

The Printing of the Quarto and the Folio

Not only may a scribe have intervened decisively in the F text, but printers also significantly affected both the Q and F texts. While printers make some difference in the case of every Shakespeare play (since none exists in manuscript), *Henry IV, Part 2* offers editors the opportunity to observe that difference in more specific terms.

As far as Q is concerned, we have already called attention in the Introduction to This Text to its existence in two different states, Qa and Qb, which contain independently printed versions of the same 165 or so lines from the end of 2.4 and the beginning of 3.2. When Qa's and Qb's versions of these lines are minutely compared to each other letter for letter and punctuation mark for punctuation mark (through a process called collation), there turn out to be well over a hundred differences between Qa and Qb. No more than fifteen of these differences (all those listed in our Textual Notes) can possibly affect meaning; and only nine of these involve the form, the addition, the deletion, or the transposition of words. However, all fifteen differences must have been introduced by the printer; and although not all are serious, no fewer than a dozen must be classified as printer's errors.

Occasionally, it is clear that Qa is right, as when it prints "Westminster" and Qb erroneously prints "Weminster"; similarly the reverse is sometimes true, as when Qb twice prints "do so" and Qa prints "do, so." Peculiar circumstances surrounding the printing of the last reprinted page in Qb also cast doubt on some Qb variants from Qa. It is obvious that the printer was forced to waste a good deal of space on this page. Thus when we find scattered about here no fewer than four words that do not appear in Qa, we must be suspicious that the printer may have added these words in an attempt to fill up the page. But we cannot be certain that these four words are printer's additions; it remains just possible that they derive from the printer's manuscript and were left out in the printing of Qa. In most other cases, it is not at all clear which of Qa and Qb is right, even though one presumably reproduces what was in the printer's manuscript and the other presumably does not. Twelve errors in a little over 300 lines of Q (150 lines in Qa and 150 in Qb) is an alarming number, testimony to the irreducible difference that it makes to put a text into print.

The typesetters of the F text of *Henry IV, Part 2* appear to have worked under even more trying circumstances than those faced by their counterparts who printed Q. During the printing of the First Folio, both *Henry IV, Part 1* and *Henry IV, Part 2* were set aside until plays immediately following them in the Folio had been set into type and printed. But the Folio printer evidently made a serious miscalculation when he counted the number of pages he should keep blank for the later printing of the two parts of *Henry IV*. His mistake made little difference to the Folio printing of *Henry IV, Part 1*, but it had a striking effect on *Part 2*. Some of the early pages of *Henry IV, Part 2* are the most crowded ones in the entire First Folio. Such obvious last-minute adjustments make it hard to throw off the suspicion that the typesetter may sometimes also have altered the dialogue in order to make it fit the space he could give it. There are a number of words printed in the Q version of these pages' dialogue that fail to appear in F, and a number of F readings are shortened versions of what appears in Q. For example, in F the Hostess says only "I warrant," while in Q she says "I warrant you." A few lines later the F expression "I pra'ye" takes the place of Q's "I pray you." Then only a few more lines further down the Folio page, the Hostess complains that she has "bin fub'd off, and fub'd-off" by Falstaff, but in Q she says "fubd off" three times, not twice. Finally, in F she identifies Bardolph as "that arrant Malmesey-Nose," although Q has "that arrant malmsie-nose *knaue*." These omissions and changes *may* be the typesetter's.

The problem of setting F into type had changed when the workmen turned to the concluding scenes of *Henry IV, Part 2* because the printer had by then added several more pages to those originally allotted to the play; indeed, as is evident from the lavish white space in the pages of the closing scenes, the printer had added an excess of pages, and the typesetter had to find ways to waste space. Now the possibility arises that the typesetter may have added words to the F text as one way to fill up an all too empty page. For example, in F one speaker issues the threat of "shee shall haue Whipping cheere enough," and then observes that "There hath beene a man or two (lately) kill'd." Neither "enough" nor "lately" is printed in the Q version of this speech. An editor cannot altogether dismiss the possibility that these words and a number of others—including even some F-only half-lines—may have been introduced into F by the typesetter; but an editor cannot confirm this possibility either. All in all, however, the severe difficulties besetting the typesetters of F, as well as the evidence of scribal interference in the transmission of the F text, make Q the text to be preferred.

Historical Background: Sir John Falstaff and Sir John Oldcastle

The Epilogue to *Henry IV, Part 2* draws an absolute distinction between the play's character Sir John Falstaff and the Protestant martyr Oldcastle. The reason for the explicit differentiation is that the character Falstaff was first created under the name Sir John Oldcastle. Evidence that Falstaff was once Oldcastle can be found in early printed texts of *Parts 1* and *2* of *Henry IV* and in letters and documents from the early seventeenth century (see, for example, the entry for 1.2.1 in our Textual Notes, which records that once the speech prefix for "Falstaff" in the 1600 Quarto of *Henry IV, Part 2* read "*Old.*"). It has long been believed—and there seems little reason to doubt it now—that one of Sir John's descendants, a powerful nobleman in Elizabeth's court, forced the company to rename Hal's companion. This evidence of censorship, along with questions about whether or not Shakespeare was deliberately satirizing Sir John's late-sixteenth-century descendant, has until recently kept scholarly attention focused on the name change rather than on the significance of Shakespeare's having created a comic character bearing the name of a famous proto-Protestant martyr.

Knowledge about the historical Sir John Oldcastle (known also as Lord Cobham) adds a remarkable complexity to Shakespeare's *Henry IV, Part 2*—a complexity certainly present for Shakespeare's original audience. Oldcastle was a knight who served Henry IV in battles in France and Wales, who was famous for his courage in battle, and who was known to have once been held in high esteem by Prince Hal. At the time Shakespeare was writing his *Henry IV, Part 2,* Sir John's reputation was being hotly debated.[1] Everyone knew that Oldcastle had been put to death in a particularly gruesome manner early in Hal's reign as King Henry V; what was at issue was whether Oldcastle died a martyr to Catholic persecution or whether he was a heretic/traitor whose death was richly deserved.

The story of Hal and Sir John—as told in Holinshed's *Chronicles,* Shakespeare's major source for his English history plays—begins in the *Chronicles'* account of the first year of Hal's kingship as Henry V.[2] In that year Sir John was accused of heresy against the Roman Catholic church. We know from other records that Oldcastle believed that the Bible should be made available in English for lay people to read, that he did not grant allegiance to the pope, and that he held other religious views that would in later centuries be called "Protestant." At the time, he was called a "Lollard" and a heretic.

When Oldcastle was accused of heresy, the archbishop of Canterbury, knowing Oldcastle "to be highly in the king's favor, declared to his highness the whole accusation. The king, first having compassion" on Oldcastle, told the archbishop that Oldcastle could better be returned to the fold of the church through gentleness rather than harshness. The king then sent for Oldcastle "and right earnestly exhorted him, and lovingly admonished him to reconcile himself to God and to his laws."

> The lord Cobham [i.e., Oldcastle] not only thanked him [i.e., the king] for his most favorable clemency, but also declared first to him by mouth and afterwards by writing, the foundation of his faith and the ground of his belief, affirming his Grace to be his

supreme head and competent judge, and none other person. . . .

Henry V at this point sent Oldcastle to the Tower of London—as the *Chronicles* puts it, the king understood and was "persuaded by his council that, by order of the laws of his realm, such accusations touching matters of faith ought to be tried by his spiritual prelates." Soon after, in "solemn sessions" in St. Paul's Cathedral and "in the hall of the Black friers in London," Oldcastle "was examined . . . and fully heard." He was denounced as a heretic by the archbishop of Canterbury and was sent "back again to the Tower of London," from which he escaped.

A few months later Henry V was warned that a large assembly of armed men was seeking his life under the captaincy of Lord Cobham. Henry

by proclamation promised a thousand marks to [anyone] that could bring [Oldcastle] forth, with great liberties to the cities or towns that would discover [i.e., reveal] where he was. By this it may appear how greatly he [i.e., Oldcastle] was beloved, that there could not one be found that for so great a reward would bring him to light.

Oldcastle was not captured at this time, but many others were; they were convicted of heresy and treason and put to death by hanging, quartering, and burning. According to the *Chronicles,*

Some say the occasion of their death was only for the conveying of the Lord Cobham out of prison. Others write that it was both for treason and heresy. . . . Certain affirm that it was for feigned causes surmised by the spirituality [i.e., church officials], more upon displeasure than truth, and that they were assembled [not to kill the king, but] to hear their preacher . . . in that place there, out of the way from resort [i.e., gathering] of people, sith [i.e., since] they might not come together openly . . . without danger to be apprehended; as the manner is, and hath been ever of the persecuted flock when they are prohibited publicly the exercise of their religion. But howsoever the matter went with these men, apprehended they were, and divers of them executed. . . .

The Hal/Oldcastle story picks up in the *Chronicles* three years later (in 1417), when Oldcastle and his men are sought by five thousand armed men protecting the lord of Abergavenny against a supposed attack from Oldcastle. Oldcastle's hiding place was discovered and some of his most trusted men captured. Found among his possessions were some religious books,

written in English, and some of those books in times past had been trimly gilt, limned, and beautified with images, the heads whereof had been scraped off, and in the Litany they had blotted forth the name of Our Lady [i.e., the Virgin Mary] and of other saints. . . . Divers writings were found there also, in derogation of such honor as then was thought due Our Lady. The Abbot of Saint Albans sent the book so disfigured with scrapings and blottings out, with other such writings as there were found, unto the King,

who sent the book to the archbishop of Canterbury for the archbishop to exhibit "in his sermons at Paul's Cross in London" so that "the citizens and other people of the realm might understand the purposes of those that then were called Lollards, to bring them further into discredit with the people."

Later in that same year Oldcastle himself was badly wounded and captured; he was charged with heresy and high treason. At that time an assembly was under way in London "for the levying of money to furnish the king's great charges . . . [for] the maintenance of his wars in France."

It was therefore determined that the said Sir John Oldcastle should be brought and put to his trial [before] the assembly brake up. [He was] brought to London in a litter, wounded as he was. Herewith, being first laid fast in the Tower, shortly after he was brought before the duke of Bedford, regent of the realm, and the other estates, where in the end he was condemned; and finally was drawn from the Tower unto saint Giles field, and there hanged in a chain by the middle, and after consumed with fire, the gallows and all.

Some editors have argued that Shakespeare chose the name of Oldcastle without thought, taking it from an earlier play about Prince Hal called *The Famous Victories of Henry V*. (In that play Oldcastle, Hal's companion, serves some of the functions of Falstaff in *Henry IV, Part 2*, though he has a much less important role.) But given current awareness of the prominence in Shakespeare's day of the debate about Oldcastle's martyrdom/treachery, it seems unlikely to editors today that Oldcastle was introduced by Shakespeare into the *Henry IV* plays casually or that the name was chosen carelessly.

While it is impossible to know why Shakespeare, in his *Henry IV* plays, chose to portray Oldcastle as a comic figure,[3] it is clear that the plays have a deeper resonance when one knows Oldcastle's history. This is most true, perhaps, of the conclusion of *Henry IV, Part 2*, a scene which is often called "the banishment of Falstaff." The newly crowned King Henry V certainly banishes Falstaff (and all his former tavern friends) from the royal presence, and does so in harsh language: "I know thee not, old man. Fall to thy prayers" (5.5.47). While in the conclusion to this speech the new king shows some compassion, offering Falstaff subsistence and suggesting that the old knight's "reform" may in the future win him some "advancement" or promotion, the events that conclude the play seem seriously to threaten Falstaff, especially when one is aware of his historical prototype's fate. Shallow can be understood to allude to Oldcastle's grisly death when he predicts for Falstaff "A color [with wordplay on "collar" or hangman's noose] that I fear you will die in" (line 88). Officers then arrive to take Falstaff off to prison. If these moments were present in the Oldcastle version of the play, those in Shakespeare's audience convinced that Oldcastle was a traitor to Christianity and to the king would have found in these moments a special kind of pleasure; for those in the audience who agreed with John Foxe's *Book of Martyrs* that Oldcastle died a courageous if terrible death at his former friend's hand, the moments would have carried instead a somber undertone. Audiences today tend to divide in their responses to Henry V and to Falstaff: some see Falstaff as a threat to the kingdom and approve Henry V's harsh treatment of the drunken knight in *Henry IV, Part 2* and in *Henry V* (see, e.g., Kenneth Branagh's film of *Henry V*); others find Falstaff human and sympathetic and see Henry V as cold and self-serving (see, e.g., the film *My Own Private Idaho*). Awareness of the historical reality of the Henry V/Oldcastle relationship can no doubt be used to support either view.

In addition, awareness of the religious beliefs for which Oldcastle died makes us listen to the language of *Henry IV, Part 2* with new ears. The character we now know as Falstaff is given language heavily dependent on the Bible. For example, his first substantial speech in the play alludes to the Book of Genesis (2.7 and 3.19) in characterizing "man" as "foolish-compounded clay" (1.2.7). He then attacks the satin merchant Master Dommelton by calling him "Achitophel" (1.2.36), the name of the traitor who conspires against King David in 2 Samuel 15–17. (For further biblical allusions in Falstaff's dialogue, in his letter [read by Prince Hal], and in references to him, see 2.1.150–51; 2.2.129, 149.) Again, while it is impossible to know how Shakespeare expected his audience to respond if such language issued from the mouth of a character named Sir John Oldcastle, it seems unlikely that the character would have been given so much biblical language by mere coincidence. At the very least, the language reminds us that swirling around the seemingly timeless comic figure of Falstaff are Reformation controversies still powerfully present in Shakespeare's day.

---

1. See Peter Corbin and Douglas Sedge, eds., *The Oldcastle Controversy* (Manchester: Manchester University Press, 1991), pp. 1–33.

2. The quotations from the *Chronicles* are taken from Raphael Holinshed, *The Third Volume of Chronicles* (1586), pp. 544, 560, 561. (These passages are also reprinted in *The Oldcastle Controversy*, pp. 216–22.)

3. Whatever the changes that may have accompanied the alteration of the name Oldcastle to Falstaff, it seems clear that the Oldcastle character was, in fact, designed to be comic, "a buffoon." In a letter written by Richard James in 1625 and attached to his manuscript edition of

The Legend and defence of ye noble Knight and Martyr Sir Jhon Oldcastle, we read "in Shakespeare's first show of Harry the fifth [i.e., *Henry IV, Part 1*], the person with which he undertook to play a buffoon was not Falstaff, but Sir John Oldcastle . . ." (printed in *The Oldcastle Controversy,* p. 10; we have modernized the spelling).

Henry IV, Part 2:
A Modern Perspective

A. R. Braunmuller

As inventor, or part-inventor, of the English history play, William Shakespeare sought to dramatize the historical information he found in texts chronicling England's past. Amid a welter of detail, doubts over precise causality, and factual contradictions, the chroniclers Shakespeare read sometimes tried to give their narratives a moral or political shape. The most celebrated of their shapings appears in the lengthy title of Edward Hall's 1548 *The Union of the two noble and illustre famelies of Lancastre & Yorke, beeyng long in continual discension for the croune of this noble realme . . . beginnyng at the tyme of kyng Henry the fowerth, the first aucthor of this devision, and so successively proceadyng to the reigne of . . . kyng Henry the eight, the undubitate flower and very heire of both the sayd linages.* For Hall, the long span of events from Henry IV's deposition of Richard II in 1399 to Henry VIII's accession in 1509 represented a movement from "division" to "union," from wrong and civil war to right and peace, and from uncertain title to undoubtable ("undubitate") authority. Even if Shakespeare had adopted wholesale Hall's proposed historical pattern (and he did not), the question of how to *dramatize* that pattern or any other remains.[1]

One large dramatic structure Shakespeare did choose—it is particularly visible in *Henry IV, Part 2*—is a dynamic of anticipation and fulfillment. Such a dynamic is theatrically and dramatically appropriate in plays about events already known to their audiences: Richard II will always be deposed, Richard III always dies at Bosworth Field (1485), Prince Hal will always become Henry V (1413), and so forth to the end of English (and all) history. These fulfillments, however, must be treated in such a way as to arouse expectation rather than boredom, or the players will have no audiences. Making an analogy between card tricks and the dramatization of times already past, already known, a character in John Arden's play about nineteenth-century history, *Serjeant Musgrave's Dance,* succinctly defines Shakespeare's task and his achievement: "That's what I call life—it all turns up in the expected order, but not when you expect it."[2]

Following classical Greek and Roman playwrights who dramatized mythical and legendary subjects whose outlines and outcomes were similarly familiar, Shakespeare uses devices that make the unexpected expected: prophecy and curse, prediction and omen, repetition and quotation, rise and fall. Thus, Queen Margaret's curses and their fulfillments in *Richard III* summarize the events of *Henry VI, Parts 1, 2,* and *3;* they recall those events for the audience of the first tetralogy's culminating play, and they give a question-and-answer shape to *Richard III* itself.[3] Likewise, the bishop of Carlisle's prophecy of "woefullest division" if Richard II is deposed (*Richard II* 4.1) is regularly recalled in the second tetralogy's subsequent plays even as it becomes, or is becoming, "true." In that same scene, Richard II excoriates his enemy Northumberland and predicts he will be no more loyal to Bolingbroke (later Henry IV) than he has proved to Richard. Sure enough, and testifying to anticipation now fulfilled, Henry IV virtually quotes Richard II, who

> Did speak these words, now proved a prophecy[:]
> "Northumberland, thou ladder by the which
> My cousin Bolingbroke ascends my throne"—
> . . . .

"The time shall come," thus did he follow it,
"The time will come that foul sin, gathering head,
Shall break into corruption"—so went on,
Foretelling this same time's condition
And the division of our amity.

(Henry IV, Part 2, 3.1.70–80)

Anticipating Henry IV's death and worrying over what kind of king Hal will be, Gloucester and Clarence make gloomy deductions from various omens:

HUMPHREY OF GLOUCESTER
The people fear [i.e., scare] me, for they do observe
Unfathered heirs and loathly births of nature.
The seasons change their manners, as [if] the year
Had found some months asleep and leapt them
    over.
THOMAS OF CLARENCE
The river [Thames] hath thrice flowed, no ebb
    between,
And the old folk, time's doting chronicles,
Say it did so a little time before
That our great grandsire, Edward, sicked and died.

(4.3.132–40)

Clarence's speech is a good example of Shakespeare's imposition of an omen's fulfillment, this time anachronistically backward instead of forward; Raphael Holinshed's *Chronicles* (1587) records the River Thames' odd behavior in 1412 (not 1413, the year of Henry IV's death, as imagined in *Henry IV, Part 2*),[4] but it is Shakespeare who adds the detail of Edward III's death being similarly preceded or predicted. Thus an omen's fulfillment is retroactively—and dramatically—created.

The dynamic of anticipation and fulfillment has some special features in *Henry IV, Part 2*, distinguishing this play from Shakespeare's other history plays and in the process making it his fullest reflection on the nature of history. This special treatment produces a spectrum of responses—in both characters and audiences—that range from morose determinism to a desperate whistling-past-the-graveyard attempt at spontaneity.

Theatrically, one of the most pertinent aspects of the dynamic is the relation between *Henry IV, Part 2* and its elder-brother-play, *Henry IV, Part 1*. As G. K. Hunter first showed, the two plays have numerous parallel episodes; the parallels diminish as the second play goes forward, and by the last act of *Henry IV, Part 2* there are few or none.[5] For instance, *Part 1* contains a splendid episode in which Hal and Poins plan (2.2) and then play (2.4) a trick forcing Falstaff to defend his flight from the abortive Gadshill's robbery; Hal and Poins similarly disguise themselves in order to lure Falstaff into defending his ridicule of Hal in *Part 2* (planning, 2.2; execution, 2.4). Or consider the way each play seems to be leading to a climactic confrontation between disputed authority (Henry IV) and arguably honorable opposition (Northumberland et al.). The results? In *Henry IV, Part 1*, the Battle of Shrewsbury, mixing royal deceit (the numerous fake King Henry IVs) with feudal single combat (Hotspur and Hal) and with Falstaff's cunning, temporarily successful, bid to gain the glory of Hotspur's defeat; in *Henry IV, Part 2*, the Gaultree episode, not a battle, where Prince John deceives his opponents into ignominious defeat and instant execution and Falstaff captures Colevile of the Dale without even the effort it took to stab dead Hotspur's thigh.

These "parallels," too, exemplify a pattern of anticipation and fulfillment, this time within and between the two plays; they are also not really parallels so much as they are echoes with difference. The Gadshill episode requires ingenuity and risk in its planning and execution and some truly hilarious fast-talking when Falstaff's initial heroic explanation is mortally wounded, forcing him to shift to another instantaneously. Its echo in *Part 2* is a sad little matter of Poins and Hal eavesdropping in disguise and then revealing themselves as a punishment for Falstaff's trivial insults. To keep the joke (and the threat of physical violence) alive, Hal claims Falstaff had seen through their disguises and deliberately insulted the Prince of Wales; thus he forces Falstaff to attack Doll Tearsheet, Mistress Quickly, and other tavern habitués to exculpate himself:

> See now whether pure fear and entire cowardice doth not make thee wrong this virtuous gentlewoman to close with [i.e., pacify] us. Is she [Doll] of the wicked, is thine hostess here of the wicked, or is thy boy of the wicked, or honest Bardolph, whose zeal burns in his nose, of the wicked?
>
> (2.4.331–36)

The small-minded nastiness of this riposte lies in Hal's own occasional contempt for Quickly, Doll, and their companions, illustrated by his treatment of Poins himself, Falstaff's "boy," and the two women— "parish heifers [i.e., prostitutes] . . . to the town bull" (2.2.156–57)—in act 2, scene 2. The contrast between Shrewsbury in *Part 1* and Gaultree in *Part 2* is similarly sharp and similarly distasteful: heroism and a contrary pragmatism that deserves a hearing in the first; a cheat, realpolitik, and the immoral arrogance of deadly choplogic in the second.

In *Henry IV, Parts 1* and *2*, Prince Hal is a hypocrite, a

peculiarly subtle version of anticipation and fulfillment
played out on a personal level, for—in plays if not in
life—the discrepancy between ulterior design and appearance leads us always to anticipate a revelatory
moment when design and appearance publicly coincide
for good or ill. Yet how different is the princely hypocrisy of *Part 1* from that in *Part 2*. In *Part 1*, Hal continually
invites the audience to note the crafted difference
between the way he appears and the way he will appear,
advantageously for him and disadvantageously for others. In *Part 2*, Hal's actions make him a prisoner of his
own sham:

> thou [Poins] thinkest me as far in the devil's book as
> thou and Falstaff for obduracy and persistency. Let
> the end try the man. But I tell thee, my heart bleeds
> inwardly that my father is so sick; and keeping such
> vile company as thou art hath in reason taken from
> me all ostentation of sorrow.
> POINS   The reason?
> PRINCE   What wouldst thou think of me if I should
> weep?
> POINS   I would think thee a most princely hypocrite.
> (2.2.43–52)

There is no advantage in being hypocritical if one does
not or cannot keep the hypocrisy secret. Further, the
reputation of hypocrisy makes expressing genuine feel-
ing (the inwardly bleeding heart that leads to "ostentation of sorrow") impossible, as Henry IV's response to
Hal's premature mourning and removal of the sleeping
king's crown makes clear:

> Thy wish was father, Harry, to that thought.
> I stay too long by thee; I weary thee.

Dost thou so hunger for mine empty chair
That thou wilt needs invest thee with my honors
Before thy hour be ripe?

(4.3.245–49)

Hypocritical behavior may or may not be justifiable, and Hal's in *Part 1* has been defended as a necessary form of self-sacrifice to the greater need of the commonwealth. When hypocrisy freezes into self-loathing, however, it is both ineffective and unattractive.

Each of these repetitions that are not quite parallel shows *Henry IV, Part 2* to be a more stunted and unforgiving dramatic environment than that of its predecessor: the comic tricks become more malicious, requiring Falstaff to be actively cruel rather than self-deprecatingly and self-justifyingly grandiloquent; the laudable aim of political and social peace loses any pretence to justice; and the price of healing the divisions his father caused is still exacted from Hal, but the reward is only a weary contempt for his companions and his father's sick disbelief.[6]

A dynamic of anticipation and fulfillment describes not only a pattern in Shakespeare's English history plays, especially in *Henry IV, Part 2*, but also a pattern in the experience of every spectator who sees the same play more than once. We can learn more about the special nature of *Henry IV, Part 2* if we ask what distinguishes the ways it repeats *Part 1* from the way any single performance of *Henry IV, Part 1* repeats another.

Why, for instance, does repeating a joke on Falstaff seem stale and bitter when it crosses between the two plays, yet ever-fresh when we see it happen again and again in performances of *Part 1*? First, we see Falstaff and Hal together much less frequently and at much less length in *Part 2* than in *Part 1*. Falstaff therefore appears in circumstances where the personal and political stakes do not have much opportunity to impress us. The victories are more trivial, the deceits needed to achieve them shabbier. Second, a sense of tolerance and forbearance evident among the Eastcheap gang in *Part 1* has vanished in *Part 2*, a forbearance that marked more than the temporary suspension of the inevitable and long-predicted showdown between Falstaff and Hal that hangs over both parts. Mere swagger and bravado among the men in *Part 1* are now real blows, real wounds. Pistol, not present in *Part 1* and humbled to a bawd's role in *Henry V* (5.1), here speaks *Henry IV, Part 2*'s recapitulation of many earlier plays and appears nearly crazed with masculine, military violence. Mistress Quickly has evidently given up hope—her first act in *Part 2* is to attempt to have Falstaff arrested—and though he soon enough bamboozles her again, he succeeds only through the paradoxical and morally repugnant argument that to expect him to be honest is to be in a "humor" and someone else's dupe: "Come, thou must not be in this humor with me. Dost not know me? Come, come. I know thou wast set on to this" (2.1.156–58). Like another of Falstaff's perpetually deceived women, "old Mistress Ursula, whom I have weekly sworn to marry since I perceived the first white hair of my chin" (1.2.247–49), Mistress Quickly is also *"old* Mistress Quickly" (2.2.151, my emphasis), and Doll speaks a sad truth for the audience as well as the characters:

> Come, I'll be friends with thee, Jack. Thou art going to the wars, and whether I shall ever see thee again or no, there is nobody cares.
>
> (2.4.66–69)

Third, Falstaff's calculating relation with Hal has become far more evident, or at least Falstaff acknowledges this calculation to himself and the audience in soliloquy far more bluntly:

> I will devise matter enough out of this Shallow to keep Prince Harry in continual laughter the wearing out of six fashions, which is four terms, or two actions, and he shall laugh without intervallums. O, it is much that a lie with a slight oath and a jest with a sad brow will do with a fellow that never had the ache in his shoulders.
>
> (5.1.79–86)

A "lie with a slight oath and a jest with a sad brow" are indeed Falstaff's staple techniques of ingratiation. Being granted this glimpse of the manipulator inside the jest-maker troubles rather than endears, and the sentence concludes with Falstaff's acknowledging that it hurts him to laugh, just as the jokes and laughter are also becoming more painful for the audience. To be sure, Hal's exploitation of Falstaff and Francis and Hotspur and many others made him unattractive in *Part 1*, and similar traits persist in *Part 2*. But Hal never concealed his calculation from the audience, and there are many characters—including Warwick in *Part 2*, 4.3.73–84, virtually quoting Hal's own self-justification (*Part 1*, 1.2.202–24)—who agree with Hal's claim that he acts and speaks not out of self-interest, as Falstaff manifestly does, but out of a desire to heal the social rifts that his father's usurpation opened.

Political transgression—the overthrow and murder of Richard II—historically condemned England, Scotland, and Wales to what Edward Hall named "The unquiete tyme of Kyng Henry the fourthe,"[7] a reign filled with social and political insubordination, overambitious aristocrats, hopes—including Henry's own hope of a holy crusade—deferred and then denied. "Hope deferred maketh the heart sick," the biblical proverb begins, and Shakespeare's characters regularly analogize Henry IV's illegitimate rule with a metaphorical national sickness. The archbishop of York, one of Henry's rebellious enemies, imagines the common people as a dog returning to its vomit:

> The commonwealth is sick of their own choice.
> Their over-greedy love hath surfeited.
> . . . .
> And being now trimmed in thine own desires,
> Thou, beastly feeder, art so full of him [Henry IV]
> That thou provok'st thyself to cast him up.
>   (1.3.91–100)

Justifying rebellion at Gaultree, the archbishop later avers:

>   we are all diseased
> And with our surfeiting and wanton hours
> Have brought ourselves into a burning fever,
> And we must bleed for it; of which disease
> Our late King Richard, being infected, died.
>   (4.1.57–61)[8]

When Henry IV learns of the multiple defeats of his many enemies, the happy news has a paradoxical effect:

> And wherefore should these good news make me
>   sick?
> Will Fortune never come with both hands full,
> But write her fair words still in foulest letters?
> . . . .

I should rejoice now at this happy news,
And now my sight fails, and my brain is giddy.
O, me! Come near me, now I am much ill.

$$(4.3.110-20)^9$$

Rebellious nation, sick king; a sickened nation, a usurping monarch.

Yet the illness is other or more than metaphorical. Illness comes to seem the very consequence of time's passage: the coming of old age, the likelihood of increasing physical weakness, the certainty of death. Falstaff's first words concern pathology:

FALSTAFF   Sirrah, you giant, what says the doctor to my water [i.e., urine]?
PAGE   He said, sir, the water itself was a good healthy water, but, for the party that ow[n]ed it, he might have more diseases than he knew for.

$$(1.2.1-5)$$

Similarly, Henry IV regards "the revolution of the times"—that is, the very passage of time, the revolving of the heavens and earth—as so inevitably degenerative that "The happiest youth," somehow granted a vision of "his [future] progress," "Would shut the book [of fate] and sit him down and die" (3.1.46, 54–56).

Many of the play's many old characters, however, do not sit down and die, however enfeebled of body, mind, and spirit they may seem or be. The first of the three fine scenes (3.2, 5.1, 5.3) at Justice Shallow's Gloucestershire house begins with a sharp illustration of Poins's observation, "Is it not strange that desire should so many years outlive performance?" (2.4.265–66). Here Poins remarks on what he regards as Falstaff's senile sexual desire, but the first Gloucestershire scene argues that other desires persist, too. As Shallow overwhelms Justice Silence with reminiscences of decades before and mournfully contemplates death, he also asks pointed economic questions that seem to anticipate future livestock transactions:

SHALLOW　. . . Death, as the Psalmist saith, is certain to all. All shall die. How a good yoke of bullocks at Stamford Fair?
SILENCE　By my troth, cousin, I was not there.
SHALLOW　Death is certain. Is old Dooble of your town living yet?
SILENCE　Dead, sir.
SHALLOW　Jesu, Jesu, dead! He drew a good bow, and dead? He shot a fine shoot. John o' Gaunt loved him well, and betted much money on his head. Dead! He would have clapped i' th' clout at twelve score, and carried you a forehand shaft a fourteen and fourteen and a half, that it would have done a man's heart good to see. How a score of ewes, now?
SILENCE　Thereafter as they be, a score of good ewes may be worth ten pounds.

(3.2.40–55)

Death is certain to all, unquestionably; Justice Shallow, however, has a lively interest in the present and future values of bullocks and ewes. The scene continues with the cruel humor of Falstaff's press-ganging soldiers for the wars and then Falstaff's promising that he will return to fleece his surprisingly (and for Falstaff, unpleasantly enviable) rich and successful old acquaintance.

Last among the Gloucestershire scenes is a brief late-night drinking party. It displays the most genuine merriment in the play, largely because while Silence says little sober, he sings quite a lot, drunk. Pistol interrupts this country demi-idyll with news of Henry IV's death, Hal's accession, and, or so Falstaff assumes, *his* consequent rise as royal councillor and victor at last over his old antagonist, the Lord Chief Justice:

> Boot, boot, Master Shallow. I know the young king is sick for me. Let us take any man's horses. The laws of England are at my commandment. Blessed are they that have been my friends, and woe to my Lord Chief Justice!
>
> (5.3.137–41)

Falstaff forgets his own experience and his own views here. That experience came seven acts before (if we regard *Henry IV, Parts 1* and *2* as a ten-act play) when Falstaff thought he was playing Hal, addressing Hal playing Henry IV:

> No, my good lord, banish Peto, banish Bardolph, banish Poins, but for sweet Jack Falstaff, kind Jack Falstaff, true Jack Falstaff, valiant Jack Falstaff, and therefore more valiant being as he is old Jack Falstaff, banish not him thy Harry's company, banish not him thy Harry's company. Banish plump Jack, and banish all the world.
>
> (*Part 1*, 2.4.491–98)

Hal's celebrated, and true, reply is not by a pretend Henry IV, but by a real Hal, sooner or later to be Henry V: "I do, I will." Falstaff's increasingly pathetic attempts at ingratiation, combined with his physical isolation from Hal in *Part 2*, suggest he has not forgotten Hal's words nor has he failed to realize their implication. Whether or not we imagine an emotional life for Falstaff that would lead him to repress this strong warning, he

sneeringly concludes the second Gloucestershire scene
with reflections he might better have taken to heart:

> It is a wonderful thing to see the semblable coher-
> ence of his [Justice Shallow's] men's spirits and his.
> They, by observing of him, do bear themselves like
> foolish justices; he, by conversing with them, is
> turned into a justice-like servingman. Their spirits
> are so married in conjunction with the participa-
> tion of society that they flock together in consent
> like so many wild geese. . . . It is certain that either
> wise bearing or ignorant carriage is caught, as men
> take diseases, one of another. Therefore let men
> take heed of their company.
>
> (5.1.65–79)

Falstaff here gives a neatly cynical rendition of his own
technique and his own predicament: he should take as
careful note of his company as Hal does of *his*. Diseases,
whether individual or national, are indeed caught "one
of another."

When Falstaff and Prince Hal meet for the second
time in *Henry IV, Part 2,* Hal has a changed office (he is
now Henry V) and is therefore a changed person.[10]
Prince has become king. Falstaff—who earlier ran
through all the variations of his name and title only to
find they amounted, redundantly, to no more than "Sir
John Falstaff, knight" (2.2.116–17)—has not changed
and is therefore unknown to and unknowable by the
prince-turned-icon, the prince who has become or will
become the "mirror of all Christian kings" (*Henry V*, 2.
Chorus.6).

Prince Hal was always going to become Henry V.
History and the chroniclers Shakespeare read teach us
so. Shakespeare's audiences also knew that historical

fact. The anticipated moment was always going to be fulfilled. And Prince Hal/King Henry V was always going to banish "plump Jack" and all Falstaff's "world," if we believe Hal's long-ago assertion (*Part 1*, 2.4). Even so the merriment of Eastcheap, the remembered gaiety of Justice Shallow's youth in London (*Part 2*, 3.2), the timeless time of agèd Justice Silence's drunken song, "the merry year, / When flesh is cheap and females dear, / And lusty lads roam here and there . . ." (5.3.18–20)—all these must have an end, because as Shallow's already-quoted saying affirms, "Death . . . is certain to all. All shall die."

The extraordinary power of *Henry IV, Part 2* as a play about history does not arise from its dramatizing of historical events; they are few in the play, and Shakespeare omits many he might have included. Rather, the play's power comes from the way it shows how time passes and how with time's passing all that the audience values—friendship and love, physical strength and sexual prowess, ideals of state and duty, parental care and children's love—all these and more must also pass. *Henry IV, Part 2* is a great play about history because it shows how little history cares about all we care about.

"Hope deferred maketh the heart sick: but when the desire cometh, it is a tree of life" (Proverbs 13.12) is a profoundly hopeful hope. That hope is not what we feel at the conclusion of Shakespeare's *Henry IV, Part 2*. To repeat, and the repetition also acknowledges the passage(s) of history and time: "whether I shall ever see thee again or no, there is nobody cares." So says Doll Tearsheet. Her king-to-be, Prince Hal, says much the same: "thus we play the fools with the time, and the spirits of the wise sit in the clouds and mock us" (*Part 2*, 2.2.141–42). Three centuries later, John Arden's character Annie speaks a modern version of Shakespeare's truth: "That's what I call life—it all turns up in the expected order, but not when you expect it."

---

1. An excellent treatment of Shakespeare's histories as a group, taking up among other points this issue, is Phyllis Rackin, *Stages of History* (Ithaca: Cornell University Press, 1990); relevant earlier studies include E. M. W. Tillyard, *Shakespeare's History Plays* (London: Chatto and Windus, 1944), and H. A. Kelly, *Divine Providence in the England of Shakespeare's Histories* (Cambridge, Mass.: Harvard University Press, 1970).

2. John Arden, *Serjeant Musgrave's Dance: An Unhistorical Parable* (New York: Grove Press, 1960), p. 42.

3. See A. R. Braunmuller, "Early Shakespearian Tragedy and Its Contemporary Context: Cause and Emotion in *Titus Andronicus, Richard III,* and *The Rape of Lucrece,*" in *Shakespearian Tragedy,* ed. M. Bradbury and D. J. Palmer, Stratford-upon-Avon Studies 20 (London: Edward Arnold, 1984), pp. 96–128.

4. Raphael Holinshed et al., *The . . . Third Volume of Chronicles* (1587), p. 540, column b.

5. See G. K. Hunter, *"Henry IV* and the Elizabethan Two-part Play" (1954), rpt. in his *Dramatic Identities and Cultural Tradition* (Liverpool: University of Liverpool Press, 1978), pp. 303–18; Harold Jenkins, *The Structural Problem in Shakespeare's "Henry the Fourth"* (London: Methuen, 1956); Sherman H. Hawkins, *"Henry IV*: The Structural Problem Revisited," *Shakespeare Quarterly* 33 (1982): 278–301.

6. "There is, throughout Part II, a musty atmosphere as of stale air in closed rooms, of moral and physical debility" (Sigurd Burckhardt, *Shakespearean Meanings* [Princeton: Princeton University Press, 1968], p. 152); Burckhardt's study of "Shakespeare's Prince Hal Trilo-

gy" (pp. 144–205) is a superb exposition of *Part 2*'s atmosphere of failure, weakness, and aging.

7. Edward Hall, *Union of the . . . famelies of Lancastre & Yorke* (1548), folio 9v (signature Blv).

8. This passage appears in the Folio edition (1623) but not in the play's earliest printing, a quarto (1600).

9. Henry here speaks an inverse of (which also proves an identity with) Northumberland's reaction to news of Hotspur's defeat and death at Shrewsbury: "In poison there is physic, and these news, / Having been well, that would have made me sick, / Being sick, have in some measure made me well" (1.1.150–52).

10. For this distinction and its implications, see Philip Edwards, *Person and Office in Shakespeare's Plays* (London: Oxford University Press, 1970).

Further Reading

Henry IV, Part 2

Abbreviations: *R2=Richard II; 1H4=Henry IV, Part 1; 2H4=Henry IV, Part 2; H5=Henry V*

Anonymous. *The Famous Victories of Henry the Fifth.* In *Narrative and Dramatic Sources of Shakespeare,* ed. Geoffrey Bullough, vol. 4, pp. 299–343. 1962. Rpt., London: Routledge and Kegan Paul; New York: Columbia University Press, 1975.

One of the primary sources for Shakespeare's second Henriad (*1H4, 2H4,* and *H5*), this short play is a freewheeling popular treatment of the Prince Hal story from which Shakespeare borrowed in creating his own crown-stealing episode and rejection of Falstaff sequence in *2H4.* Shakespeare altered the image of a hooligan prince by omitting passages (Hal's explicit wish for his father's death so that he might wear the crown), transposing antagonistic encounters (Falstaff replaces Hal in an early confrontation with the Lord Chief Justice), and reporting rather than depicting certain incidents (Hal's striking of the Lord Chief Justice). Shakespeare supplemented *The Famous Victories* with material from the historical chronicles.

Belsey, Catherine. "Making Histories Then and Now: Shakespeare from *Richard II* to *Henry V.*" In *Uses of History: Marxism, Postmodernism, and the Renaissance,* ed. Francis Barker, Peter Hulme, and Margaret Iversen, pp. 24–46. Manchester: Manchester University Press, 1991.

Belsey provides a reading of the second tetralogy (*R2*, *1H4*, *2H4*, *H5*) that reveals "marks of the struggle to fix meaning, and simultaneously of the excess which necessarily renders meaning unstable." The world of Bolingbroke/Henry IV is one in which words are no longer "anchored" in their referents; by extension, then, there is no longer a direct and simple link between king and kingship. Because the law of succession, "the only power on earth that supports the materiality of titles," is broken in *R2* when the king seizes Bolingbroke's title, the latter's reign "becomes in consequence one of bitter uncertainties, of conflicts for meaning which are simultaneously conflicts for power." Belsey takes issue with the subversion/containment model of New Historicism (see Greenblatt below), arguing that subversion is better understood as the equally valued "defining, differentiating other" of power and not as its justification and reaffirmation.

Berger, Harry, Jr. "What Did the King Know and When Did He Know It: Shakespearean Discourses and Psychoanalysis." *South Atlantic Quarterly* 88 (1989): 811–62.
Berger argues that "speakers should be treated as the effects rather than the causes of their language and our interpretation." To illustrate his theory, Berger focuses on the speeches of Henry IV and finds "behind" what the character says an interplay of "the pressure of the sinner's discourse and the counterpressure of the victim/revenger's discourse"; Henry's language is "torn apart" by the tension between the ethical desire for atonement and the political need for self-justification. Until his final exit, the king vacillates between these two conflicting discourses, always struggling with "the desire for moral legitimacy [and] with despair at the futility of the desire." By focusing not on "what critics think of Harry" but on "what Harry thinks of Harry,"

Berger, while not a "Harry-lover," avoids becoming a "Harry-hater."

Bevington, David, ed. *Henry the Fourth Parts I and II: Critical Essays.* New York: Garland Publishing, 1986.

Designed to collect "the best" that has been written about the *Henry IV* plays, this anthology includes examples of neoclassical criticism, the character criticism of the Romantic and Victorian periods, and several schools of critical thought associated with the twentieth century (e.g., the historical, New Criticism, myth criticism, psychoanalytic criticism, speech-act theory, and performance criticism). The 31 items, spanning the years 1744 to 1983, include Maurice Morgann's "An Essay on the Dramatic Character of Sir John Falstaff," A. C. Bradley's "The Rejection of Falstaff," John Dover Wilson's "The Falstaff Myth" (from *The Fortunes of Falstaff*), E. M. W. Tillyard's *"Henry IV"* (from *Shakespeare's History Plays*), W. H. Auden's "The Prince's Dog" (from *The Dyer's Hand and Other Essays*), C. L. Barber's "Rule and Misrule in *Henry IV*" (from *Shakespeare's Festive Comedy*), G. K. Hunter's "Shakespeare's Politics and the Rejection of Falstaff," Jonas A. Barish's "The Turning Away of Prince Hal," Sigurd Burckhardt's " 'Swoll'n with Some Other Grief': Shakespeare's Prince Hal Trilogy" (from *Shakespearean Meanings*), and Ronald R. Macdonald's "Uneasy Lies: Language and History in Shakespeare's Lancastrian Tetralogy."

Greenblatt, Stephen. "Invisible Bullets: Renaissance Authority and Its Subversion." In *Shakespearean Negotiations: The Circulation of Social Energy in Renaissance England*, pp. 21–65, esp. pp. 47–56. Berkeley: University of California Press, 1988.

In this influential and frequently reprinted example of New Historicism, Greenblatt finds parallels between the English incursions into the New World and Hal's transformation from madcap to monarch. Both the English colonizers, in their attempts to subdue the native inhabitants of the Americas, and Hal, in his efforts to control the domestic underworld associated with the taverns of Eastcheap, paradoxically encourage opposition in order to reaffirm their authority over those confined to the margins of society (the Indians in the former; the vagabonds, thieves, and prostitutes in the latter). If audiences are frustrated at the harshness of Hal's rejection of Falstaff—the final betrayal in a series of "squalid betrayals"—that frustration validates "a carefully plotted official strategy whereby subversive perceptions are at once produced and contained." While the *Henry IV* plays may support a Machiavellian hypothesis about "princely power" originating in force and fraud, Greenblatt questions whether the position of the theater within the state allows drama to raise an alternative voice.

Hodgdon, Barbara. *Henry IV, Part Two.* Shakespeare in Performance Series. Manchester: Manchester University Press, 1993.

In an introductory overview of the play's theatrical afterlife from the seventeenth century to the present, Hodgdon pays special attention to the "Falstaff problem" (i.e., whose play is it—Falstaff's or Hal's—and how is Falstaff's rejection handled?) and urges sensitivity to "intersections" between theatrical events and their cultural contexts. "Tracing how a Falstaff accommodates to or . . . is accommodated with a production is crucial to the history of how [*2H4*] has been appropriated to serve various visions of 'England.'" Hodgdon devotes separate chapters to five twentieth-century productions: Michael Redgrave's 1951 revival at the Shakespeare Memorial Theatre, Terry Hands's 1975 staging at the Royal Shakespeare Theatre, David Giles's 1979 BBC version, Trevor Nunn's 1982 production for the RSC at London's Barbican Centre, and Michael Bogdanov's 1986–89 revival for the English Shakespeare Company. The chapters on the BBC and Bogdanov productions also include observations on Orson Welles's 1966 film *Chimes at Midnight.*

Howard, Jean. "Forming the Commonwealth: Including, Excluding, and Criminalizing Women in Heywood's *Edward IV* and Shakespeare's *Henry IV.*" In *Privileging Gender in Early Modern England,* ed. Jean R. Brink, pp. 109–21. Sixteenth Century Essays and Studies 23. Kirksville, Mo.: Sixteenth Century Journal Publishers, 1993.

Howard uses *Edward IV* and *2H4* to explore how the English history play served to forge and reforge "the links between polis [the state] and patriarchy" amid the changes in gender and class relations precipitated by the increasing urbanization and commercialism of the late sixteenth and early seventeenth centuries. In *2H4* Shakespeare employs "the figure of the whore and the discourse of prostitution to handle cultural anxieties about the leveling implications of social change attendant on the emergence of a 'nation' from a factionalized feudal state." In contrast to *Part 1,* the lawlessness of the tavern world in *Part 2* is no longer general but specifically sexual, and more visibly linked with a female challenge to the socially stratified and hierarchically gendered commonwealth. When Doll Tearsheet is carted off at the end, "what is partly being acted out is the violent reimposition of patriarchal control over female sexuality."

Machiavelli, Niccolò. *The Prince* (1513), ed. and trans. Robert M. Adams. 2nd ed. New York: W. W. Norton, 1992.

In this famous political treatise, Machiavelli draws on his experience as a member of the Florentine government in order to present his conception of the kind of strong leader and tactics required to impose political order for the good of the unified Italy he envisions. Because Machiavelli separates politics from ethics and is more concerned with ends than with means, his name has become identified with all that is cynical and even diabolical in state affairs. In Shakespeare's England, this exaggeratedly negative reputation gave rise to the conventional villain known as the Machiavel. In the scholarship on *2H4*, critics have argued for an affinity between Machiavelli's political tenets and the strategies and policies of Henry, Prince Hal, Falstaff, Northumberland, and Prince John. The phrase "White Machiavel" has been adopted by those who find in Hal a more temperate, attractive development of Machiavellian pragmatism.

McAlindon, Tom. "Pilgrims of Grace: *Henry IV* Historicized." *Shakespeare Survey* 48 (1995): 69–84.

Critical of both the history-of-ideas approach of E. M. W. Tillyard and the "new historicist/cultural materialist" interpretive frameworks constructed by Stephen Greenblatt and Graham Holderness, McAlindon focuses on topical allusions. The *H4* plays' rebellions and the insistent concern with the twinned themes of grace and rebuke suggest a major historical analogy with the Northern Rebellions of 1569–70 and, even more notably, the 1536 rebellion known as the Pilgrimage of Grace, a protest movement that had assumed "archetypal status" in the popular consciousness of Shakespeare's audience. In *Part 2*, the spirit of rebuke is intensified as evidenced by Northumberland's entrapment in his disgraceful past, Prince John's treachery at Gaultree,

Henry's final encounter with his son, and Hal's rejection of Falstaff. The fact that Henry dies in the Jerusalem Chamber signals that "he has, through his son, found grace."

Rackin, Phyllis. "Foreign Country: The Place of Women and Sexuality in Shakespeare's Historical World." In *Enclosure Acts: Sexuality, Property, and Culture in Early Modern England*, ed. Richard Burt and John Michael Archer, pp. 68–95. Ithaca: Cornell University Press, 1994.

Rackin examines early modern texts to show how Renaissance distinctions separating men from women were "grounded" not in biology and psychology but in the "ordered" and "privileged" discourses of theology and history. In Shakespeare's history plays, women— "aliens in the masculine domain of English historiography"—are marginalized through a process of "geographic and generic containment." In *2H4*, this containment takes the form of two marginal spaces clearly marked as "feminized" and "theatrical": the lowlife tavern world of Eastcheap (the female unruliness of which mirrors the disorder of the "disreputable feminized world" of the Elizabethan playhouse) and the epilogue.

Traub, Valerie. "Prince Hal's Falstaff: Positioning Psychoanalysis and the Female Reproductive Body." *Shakespeare Quarterly* 40 (1989): 456–74.

In a feminist "reading of drama through psychoanalysis and psychoanalysis through drama," Traub argues that Shakespeare's plays and modern psychoanalytic theory are linked by a "cultural estimation of the female reproductive body as a Bakhtinian 'grotesque body.'" In the *H4* plays, this "grotesque body" is figured in the character of Falstaff, whose swollen belly is repeatedly feminized—see, for example, his iteration of "womb" (*2H4*, 4.2.22). Falstaff thus represents not the surrogate father of traditional psychoanalytic criticism but "a projected fantasy of the pre-oedipal *maternal*" whose rejection is required if Hal is to assert control and develop into the male subject of *H5*.

Watson, Robert N. "Kinship and Kingship: Ambition in Shakespeare's Major Histories." In *Shakespeare and the Hazards of Ambition*, pp. 14–82, esp. pp. 47–75. Cambridge, Mass.: Harvard University Press, 1984.

Using Freud's Oedipal model to explore the theme of ambition in Shakespeare's plays, Watson argues that the "ambitious refashioning of one's identity constitutes an Oedipal crime." Hal is "the Oedipal son who typically rises against the tyrannical father who was formerly a rebel himself"; in *Part 2*, where his filial identity remains "badly in doubt," Hal ultimately manages to break free of "the long, deadly chain-reaction of patricides." Allowing the private and public implications of rebellion to coalesce in Hal, Shakespeare grounds the story of English usurpation "in a study of the political history of all societies and in the psychological history of all young men." The crown-stealing episode, "the starkest explication of Hal's apparent Oedipal destructiveness," shows how fruitful Shakespeare found the psycho-symbolic situation for exploring the hazards of ambition.

Willson, Robert F., Jr. "Recontextualizing Shakespeare on Film: *My Own Private Idaho, Men of Respect, Prospero's Books*." *Shakespeare Bulletin* 10.3 (1992): 34–37.

Willson examines Gus Van Sant's 1991 *My Own Private Idaho*, a film adaptation of *1H4* and *2H4*, as a representative example of directorial readings that "displace" Shakespeare's characters, themes, imagery, and other patterns "from their traditional nexuses to new and unexpected locations on the cultural landscape." The result is "fresh Shakespeare." In the street life of the contemporary Pacific Northwest, Keanu Reeves plays an updated Prince Hal as the rebel son of Portland's wealthy, dying mayor. The son immerses himself in the city's drug- and sex-ridden subculture where he keeps company with prostitutes, thieves, and junkies. Chief among his companions are "Bob Pigeon," a translated Falstaff, and a narcoleptic prostitute (River Phoenix) who, as a refigured Poins, is searching for his lost mother. The film's conclusion relies on the audience's "awareness of Shakespearean and film/popular culture conventions to elicit sympathy for outcast Poins and Falstaff and not mainstream Hal."

Young, David P., ed. *Twentieth Century Interpretations of Henry IV, Part Two: A Collection of Critical Essays.* Englewood Cliffs, N.J.: Prentice-Hall, 1968.

This collection of important earlier twentieth-century criticism reprints the following commentaries: L. C. Knights's "Time's Subjects: The Sonnets and *King Henry IV, Part II*," Clifford Leech's "The Unity of *2 Henry IV*," C. L. Barber's "The Trial of Carnival in *Part Two*" (from *Shakespeare's Festive Comedy*), Robert B. Pierce's "The Generations in *2 Henry IV*," Harold E. Toliver's "Falstaff, the Prince, and the History Play," and Derek Traversi's "The Final Scenes of *2 Henry IV*" (from *Shakespeare from Richard II to Henry V*). Also included are excerpts from A. C. Bradley's "The Rejection of Falstaff," J. Dover Wilson's "King Henry's Speech" (from *The Fortunes of Falstaff*), E. M. W. Tillyard's *Shakespeare's History Plays*, Harold Jenkins's *The Structural Problem in the Henry IV*

Plays, A. P. Rossiter's "Ambivalence: The Dialectic of the Histories," R. J. Dorius's "A Little More Than a Little," and A. R. Humphreys's observations on the play's style (from the critical introduction to his Arden edition).

Shakespeare's Language

Abbott, E. A. *A Shakespearian Grammar.* New York: Haskell House, 1972.

This compact reference book, first published in 1870, helps with many difficulties in Shakespeare's language. It systematically accounts for a host of differences between Shakespeare's usage and sentence structure and our own.

Blake, Norman. *Shakespeare's Language: An Introduction.* New York: St. Martin's Press, 1983.

This general introduction to Elizabethan English discusses various aspects of the language of Shakespeare and his contemporaries, offering possible meanings for hundreds of ambiguous constructions.

Dobson, E. J. *English Pronunciation, 1500–1700.* 2 vols. Oxford: Clarendon Press, 1968.

This long and technical work includes chapters on spelling (and its reformation), phonetics, stressed vowels, and consonants in early modern English.

Houston, John. *Shakespearean Sentences: A Study in Style and Syntax.* Baton Rouge: Louisiana State University Press, 1988.

Houston studies Shakespeare's stylistic choices, considering matters such as sentence length and the relative positions of subject, verb, and direct object. Examining plays throughout the canon in a roughly chronological, developmental order, he analyzes how sentence structure is used in setting tone, in characterization, and for other dramatic purposes.

Onions, C. T. *A Shakespeare Glossary*. Oxford: Clarendon Press, 1986.

This revised edition updates Onions's standard, selective glossary of words and phrases in Shakespeare's plays that are now obsolete, archaic, or obscure.

Robinson, Randal. *Unlocking Shakespeare's Language: Help for the Teacher and Student*. Urbana, Ill.: National Council of Teachers of English and the ERIC Clearinghouse on Reading and Communication Skills, 1989.

Specifically designed for the high school and undergraduate college teacher and student, Robinson's book addresses the problems that most often hinder present-day readers of Shakespeare. Through work with his own students, Robinson found that many readers today are particularly puzzled by such stylistic devices as subject-verb inversion, interrupted structures, and compression. He shows how our own colloquial language contains comparable structures, and thus helps students recognize such structures when they find them in Shakespeare's plays. This book supplies worksheets—with examples from major plays—to illuminate and remedy such problems as unusual sequences of words and the separation of related parts of sentences.

Williams, Gordon. *A Dictionary of Sexual Language and Imagery in Shakespearean and Stuart Literature*. 3 vols. London: Athlone Press, 1994.

Williams provides a comprehensive list of the words to which Shakespeare, his contemporaries, and later Stuart writers gave sexual meanings. He supports his identification of these meanings by extensive quotations.

Shakespeare's Life

Baldwin, T. W. *William Shakspere's Petty School.* Urbana: University of Illinois Press, 1943.

Baldwin here investigates the theory and practice of the petty school, the first level of education in Elizabethan England. He focuses on that educational system primarily as it is reflected in Shakespeare's art.

Baldwin, T. W. *William Shakspere's Small Latine and Lesse Greeke.* 2 vols. Urbana: University of Illinois Press, 1944.

Baldwin attacks the view that Shakespeare was an uneducated genius—a view that had been dominant among Shakespeareans since the eighteenth century. Instead, Baldwin shows, the educational system of Shakespeare's time would have given the playwright a strong background in the classics, and there is much in the plays that shows how Shakespeare benefited from such an education.

Beier, A. L., and Roger Finlay, eds. *London 1500–1700: The Making of the Metropolis.* New York: Longman, 1986.

Focusing on the economic and social history of early modern London, these collected essays probe aspects of metropolitan life, including "Population and Disease," "Commerce and Manufacture," and "Society and Change."

Bentley, G. E. *Shakespeare's Life: A Biographical Handbook.* New Haven: Yale University Press, 1961.

This "just-the-facts" account presents the surviving documents of Shakespeare's life against an Elizabethan background.

Chambers, E. K. *William Shakespeare: A Study of Facts and Problems*. 2 vols. Oxford: Clarendon Press, 1930.

Analyzing in great detail the scant historical data, Chambers's complex, scholarly study considers the nature of the texts in which Shakespeare's work is preserved.

Cressy, David. *Education in Tudor and Stuart England* London: Edward Arnold, 1975.

This volume collects sixteenth-, seventeenth-, and early-eighteenth-century documents detailing aspects of formal education in England, such as the curriculum, the control and organization of education, and the education of women.

De Grazia, Margreta. *Shakespeare Verbatim: The Reproduction of Authenticity and the 1790 Apparatus*. Oxford: Clarendon Press, 1991.

De Grazia traces and discusses the development of such editorial criteria as authenticity, historical periodization, factual biography, chronological development, and close reading, locating as the point of origin Edmond Malone's 1790 edition of Shakespeare's works. There are interesting chapters on the First Folio and on the "legendary" versus the "documented" Shakespeare.

Dutton, Richard. *William Shakespeare: A Literary Life*. New York: St. Martin's Press, 1989.

Not a biography in the traditional sense, Dutton's very readable work nevertheless "follows the contours of Shakespeare's life" as he examines Shakespeare's career as playwright and poet, with consideration of his patrons, theatrical associations, and audience.

Fraser, Russell. *Young Shakespeare*. New York: Columbia University Press, 1988.

Fraser focuses on Shakespeare's first thirty years, paying attention simultaneously to his life and art.

Schoenbaum, S. *William Shakespeare: A Compact Documentary Life*. New York: Oxford University Press, 1977.

This standard biography economically presents the essential documents from Shakespeare's time in an accessible narrative account of the playwright's life.

Shakespeare's Theater

Bentley, G. E. *The Profession of Player in Shakespeare's Time, 1590–1642*. Princeton: Princeton University Press, 1984.

Bentley readably sets forth a wealth of evidence about performance in Shakespeare's time, with special attention to the relations between player and company, and the business of casting, managing, and touring.

Berry, Herbert. *Shakespeare's Playhouses*. New York: AMS Press, 1987.

Berry's six essays collected here discuss (with illustrations) varying aspects of the four playhouses in which Shakespeare had a financial stake: the Theatre in Shoreditch, the Blackfriars, and the first and second Globe.

Cook, Ann Jennalie. *The Privileged Playgoers of Shakespeare's London*. Princeton: Princeton University Press, 1981.

Cook's work argues, on the basis of sociological, economic, and documentary evidence, that Shakespeare's audience—and the audience for English Renaissance drama generally—consisted mainly of the "privileged."

Greg, W. W. *Dramatic Documents from the Elizabethan Playhouses.* 2 vols. Oxford: Clarendon Press, 1931.

Greg itemizes and briefly describes many of the play manuscripts that survive from the period 1590 to around 1660, including, among other things, players' parts. His second volume offers facsimiles of selected manuscripts.

Gurr, Andrew. *Playgoing in Shakespeare's London.* Cambridge: Cambridge University Press, 1987.

Gurr charts how the theatrical enterprise developed from its modest beginnings in the late 1560s to become a thriving institution in the 1600s. He argues that there were important changes over the period 1567–1644 in the playhouses, the audience, and the plays.

Harbage, Alfred. *Shakespeare's Audience.* New York: Columbia University Press, 1941.

Harbage investigates the fragmentary surviving evidence to interpret the size, composition, and behavior of Shakespeare's audience.

Hattaway, Michael. *Elizabethan Popular Theatre: Plays in Performance.* London: Routledge & Kegan Paul, 1982.

Beginning with a study of the popular drama of the late Elizabethan age—a description of the stages, performance conditions, and acting of the period—this volume concludes with an analysis of five well-known plays of the 1590s, one of them (*Titus Andronicus*) by Shakespeare.

Shapiro, Michael. *Children of the Revels: The Boy Companies of Shakespeare's Time and Their Plays.* New York: Columbia University Press, 1977.

Shapiro chronicles the history of the amateur and quasi-professional child companies that flourished in

London at the end of Elizabeth's reign and the beginning of James's.

The Publication of Shakespeare's Plays

Blayney, Peter. *The First Folio of Shakespeare*. Hanover, Md.: Folger, 1991.

Blayney's accessible account of the printing and later life of the First Folio—an amply illustrated catalog to a 1991 Folger Shakespeare Library exhibition—analyzes the mechanical production of the First Folio, describing how the Folio was made, by whom and for whom, how much it cost, and its ups and downs (or, rather, downs and ups) since its printing in 1623.

Hinman, Charlton. *The Norton Facsimile: The First Folio of Shakespeare*. 2nd ed. New York: W. W. Norton, 1996.

This facsimile presents a photographic reproduction of an "ideal" copy of the First Folio of Shakespeare; Hinman attempts to represent each page in its most fully corrected state. The second edition includes an important new introduction by Peter Blayney.

Hinman, Charlton. *The Printing and Proof-Reading of the First Folio of Shakespeare*. 2 vols. Oxford: Clarendon Press, 1963.

In the most arduous study of a single book ever undertaken, Hinman attempts to reconstruct how the Shakespeare First Folio of 1623 was set into type and run off the press, sheet by sheet. He also provides almost all the known variations in readings from copy to copy.

Key to Famous Lines
and Phrases

I am not only witty in myself, but the cause that wit is in other men. [*Falstaff*—1.2.9–11]

Your Lordship, though not clean past your youth, have yet some smack of an ague in you, some relish of the saltness of time . . . [*Falstaff*—1.2.98–101]

But it was always yet the trick of our English nation, if they have a good thing, to make it too common. . . . I were better to be eaten to death with a rust than to be scoured to nothing with perpetual motion.
[*Falstaff*—1.2.219–26]

I can get no remedy against this consumption of the purse. Borrowing only lingers and lingers it out, but the disease is incurable. [*Falstaff*—1.2.242–44]

He hath eaten me out of house and home.
[*Hostess*—2.1.76]

Away, you mouldy rogue, away! I am meat for your master. [*Doll*—2.4.126–27]

. . . O sleep, O gentle sleep,
Nature's soft nurse, how have I frighted thee. . . .
Uneasy lies the head that wears a crown.
[*King*—3.1.5–31]

We have heard the chimes at midnight . . .
[*Falstaff*—3.2.221–22]

A man can die but once. We owe God a death . . . and let it go which way it will, he that dies this year is quit for the next.   [*Feeble*—3.2.242–47]

I do remember him at Clement's Inn, like a man made after supper of a cheese paring. When he was naked, he was, for all the world, like a forked radish with a head fantastically carved upon it with a knife.

                    [*Falstaff*—3.2.318–23]

Thy wish was father, Harry, to that thought.

                    [*King*—4.3.245]